Digital Photography Pocket Primer

Richard Romano

Requests for permission or further information should be addressed to:
Permissions Department
Windsor Professional Information, LLC
11835 Carmel Mountain Road, Suite 1304
San Diego, CA 92128

This and other books in this Pocket Primer series are available at special quantity discounts for use as premiums and sales promotions, or for use in corporate training programs. For more information, please contact:
Special Sales
Windsor Professional Information, LLC
11835 Carmel Mountain Road, Suite 1304
San Diego, CA 92128
858-487-2945   Fax: 858-487-3279
e-mail: windsorpub@earthlink.net

Library of Congress Cataloging-in-Publication Data
On file with the Library of Congress
ISBN 1-893190-07-2

Printed in the United States of America
First edition   A B C D E

Credits:
Copy Editing: Shaun Doole and Phyllis DeBlanche
Production Management: LUX Design, San Diego
Cover Design: Douglas Hyldelund

Introduction

Remember the good old days, the days when "prepress" meant something tangible? Remember? Pages were literally pasted up by hand on thick boards, and photos were shot with a process camera and stripped in with the film that was shot for the text and line art. Everything smelled of chemicals. Rubber cement was fun to play with.

Well, those days are probably gone forever, although we can look back on them with something akin to nostalgia (or nausea, as the case may be). We've watched over the past 20 or so years how more and more of what was at one time called "prepress" has been "digitized" and moved into the computer. QuarkXPress or InDesign pages on monitors have replaced paste-up boards and X-Acto knives. Flatbed scanners have replaced process cameras for getting images to a form where they can be merged on a page with text and art.

And even scanners are being replaced with...digital cameras. Given the title of this book, you figured we were going to get around to digital cameras at some point.

There has been for some years a dubious flirtation in the graphic arts with digital photography. It's taken a while for the technology to reach a point where digital cameras are viable, in terms of image quality as well as cost effectiveness, and are able to play an important role in the graphic arts.

And that time is now.

Graphic artists, publishers, content creators, and designers of all stripes (and even polka dots) are using digital cameras in their workflows, and many have been doing so for years. Digital cameras are replacing scanners in many workflows, as publishers and other content creators bypass film and prints entirely and acquire images in digital form right at the outset. Which only makes sense. The continuing evolution (or perhaps it's devolution) of prepress is a tendency toward the elimination of steps. And using a digital camera eliminates some of those steps. In some ways, you can't get more digital than a digital camera, unless you could beam images directly from your brain to a platesetter.

How is that a help? Well, that very subject is what this book is about. In the next 220-plus pages, we'll look at all the myriad issues involved in selecting, evaluating, buying, and using digital cameras, both at the low end and the high end. We'll look at how you can get a digitally captured image from the camera to the computer—and what you can do with the images from there. And we'll look at some of the applications for digital photography.

I should point out at the outset that this is not really a book on photography. I am not a photographer per se, so I could never hope to guide you through that complex topic.

Instead, this book will focus on the digital side of photography. There are many who see these as two different things—that "digital photography" is not "real photography." That's not true. Digital photography is, at the present time, just as valid as conventional photography, and new developments in hardware and software are bridging the gap faster and faster. If you want to learn photography, the same considerations you'll deal with there—focal lengths, f-stops, exposure, aperture, etc.—will all apply in the digital realm as well.

Digital photography is a new approach, and questions abound. What do I look for in a digital camera? What can I do with the images? How do I get them out of the camera? How many pixels do I *really* need? Do I really need a PC to use a digital camera? How can I print digital images without having them look crappy? Are there are high-end uses for digital photography? Should I incorporate a digital camera into a graphic arts workflow?

And so on.

We'll attempt to answer these questions, and many more. We'll begin in the next chapter with an overview of digital photography, a little history, and a look at where we stand as of this writing. Things change very quickly in this industry. In fact, just between the first draft of this book and the draft that is being sent to the publisher, whole new "baseline" specs for digital cameras have come out, as have a slew of new models and features. That may sound like this book will be woefully out of date, but there are certain basic things that will not change, or not change much, so although we will be looking at some specific models that may be a little behind the leading edge, the issues with which we will be concerning ourselves will continue well into the future.

So, in Chapter 1, we will start with a look at what digital photography is, *why* digital photography is, what some of the issues are, and how the market has evolved.

In Chapter 2, we'll look at some of the technical considerations: area arrays versus linear arrays. Color depth. How many dots you need to worry about. And we'll cover some basic photographic issues, as well. All the things you'll need to know to read a camera's spec sheet.

In Chapter 3, we'll dissect a digital camera and point out its major organs. We'll look at the external controls and go through the internal menus. We'll look at the various types of cameras, what the differences are, and what the applications for each might be.

In Chapter 4, we'll do some informal photo shoots with a couple of digital cameras, and you'll be able to see how you get the things to work, and work well. We'll look at outdoor applications as well as indoor "product photography." We don't have a high-powered photo studio, so much of this will of necessity be quick and dirty, but you'll see that you can get decent results even under somewhat adverse conditions.

In Chapter 5, we'll look at how you can get a image out of the camera—and there are more ways of doing this than you might think. We'll look at direct connectivity, the burgeoning cottage industry of "digital film," and even ways of obtaining images without bothering with a computer at all.

In Chapter 6, we'll look at working with images. We'll bring digital camera captures into Photoshop and see what our image-editing options are. We'll also look at how large a image needs to be to yield good-quality output. We'll also take you step-by-step through a sample, real-world digital camera/imaging workflow.

In Chapter 7, we'll look at the applications for digital photography. In other words, all this is not mere blue-skying; real people are doing real things with digital cameras. We'll find out who they are and what they're up to.

In Chapter 8, we'll look at the upper end of digital photography—namely, the digital photography studio and high-end digital camera backs. We'll look at how one might set up a high-end studio, as well as why you might want to become a client of one.

And finally, in Chapter 9, we'll take a peak at the horizon and see what is in the cards for the digital photography market. Technology changes, and new ways of capturing images digitally are appearing. What are some of them? Will they catch on? I'm not sanguine about predicting the future, but there are a few things we can look at with some degree of certainty that they'll come to pass.

A lot of the progress in the digital camera realm has been targeted primarily toward consumers. Camera makers, not surprisingly, see the consumer as the holy grail of digital photography, and they are eagerly awaiting that day when the consumer market takes off.

But at the same time, the graphic arts and related industries are in large part driving the digital camera market at the moment, and it is in those fields that a lot of the applications have developed. Therefore, we will be looking at how digital photography is well suited for graphic arts, content creation, and Web imaging workflows.

Digital photography is an exciting topic, especially in the realm of the graphic arts and publishing. Digital cameras can serve a variety of workflow needs. One just needs to know where to begin.

Acknowledgments

First of all, I must thank the staff of *Micro Publishing News* and Cygnus Publishing for all their help, inspiration, and encouragement—especially editorial director David Griffith, whose amazingly sharp eye and probing questions keep me honest; publisher Ken Spears; art director Wendy Quintanilla; associate publisher Ken Nicholas; contributing editor Alison Blasko; and group publisher Bill Lewis. Executive editor Joe LiPetri has also been a great source of material and a very good sounding board. Print On Demand executive editor Noel Jeffrey has also been a good friend, and a source of material as well.

A very special thank you to founding publisher Jim Cavuoto, without whose faith and support I probably would not have written this book. And of course, an extra special thanks to my father, Frank Romano, without whom I also would not be writing this book—but for very different reasons.

And last but not least, a thank you to Ken Aniolek, for unflagging friendship and support.

Richard Romano
Torrance, California
January 2000

Contents

1

Introduction to Digital Photography

The first question one is inclined to ask is "What is digital photography?" But let's face it, this isn't a very interesting question, especially since you plunked down money for a book on the subject and you probably have some idea.

In a nutshell, digital photography is capturing images so that they are already in digital form by the time they come out of the camera. We are just beginning to see some good commercial applications of the technology.

The Advantages of Digital Photography

A good question to ask, rather than "What is digital photography?" would be "*Why* is digital photography?" If you listen to the skeptics, they say that the process is expensive. It's not as good as film. It's a pain in the butt. And so on.

These are not falsehoods. Digital photography can be expensive. A good, reasonably high-quality digital camera will cost you more than $400 or $500. If you don't have one already, you'll need a PC of some kind. Or at the very least you'll need a printer, probably a color printer. Although you can get a good, high-quality inkjet printer for probably under $200, that may or may not be expensive for you. Plus there's removable storage, disk space, and all the other peripherals that are needed.

It is not my intention to dissuade you from investing in digital photography. I just think you should be aware of what you're getting yourself into.

So, Why Digital Photography?

Digital photography is increasing in quality quite rapidly, and, in line with Moore's Law, price is coming down as well. Digital "workflows" are creeping into consumer life. Color desktop scanners, once strictly the province of design shops or desktop publishing firms, are now bundled with many consumer-oriented PC systems. The general public has become hooked on the World Wide Web; even people who have no professional reason to do so are developing their own Web sites for their friends and family to check out.

I use the word "workflow" because in the industry in which I spend most of my days—prepress and publishing—that is the latest buzzword. "Workflow" and "solution" are two words that really don't mean anything, but which product managers and public relations people bandy about when they have no concrete way of describing what it is that they do.

But I digress. It hardly seems appropriate to use the word "workflow" to refer to people's non-work lives. How about "playflow"?

A Brief History of Digital Photography

Paradoxically, the camera that first triggered an interest in digital photography was not really a digital camera at all. It was an electronic camera, meaning that it didn't use film, but it was not truly digital. It was the Sony Mavica, introduced in 1981. It was called a "still video" camera and was essentially a video camera, such as you would take on holiday to film your family cavorting about the Grand Canyon or wherever, only it could capture single frames. This analog still video system wrote images to a 2-inch floppy disk. These images were analogous to the video signal that would be recorded to videotape.

Although similar, still video photography provided a better means of capturing an image than freeze-framing a videotape, especially as the cameras were able to synchronize with a flash just as a traditional film camera is.

Two years later, in 1983, the Electronic Still Camera Standardization Committee (ESCSC) devised the standard for still video analog devices, which was compliant with the National Television Standards Committee (NTSC) format that is the North American standard for television and videotape signals. The original still video standard involved 360 lines of resolution, which meant that, like the lines that comprise a television image, each still frame comprised 360 lines. Eventually, a new standard emerged that boosted the resolution to 500 lines.

The medium on which images were recorded was a floppy disk, but this is more a colloquial descriptive term rather than a strictly technical one. It is tempting to think of these floppies as akin to the disks used to store computer data, but they were very different. The capacity of a video floppy disk ranged from 740 KB to 1 MB.

A pioneer in the still video camera arena was Canon, which developed a line of electronic cameras that were identical to its line of 35mm film cameras. A major difference had to do with the focal length of the lenses, which could be up to four times as long for an electronic camera as for a conventional film camera. This tended to make photographers uneasy, as it was hard to find short focal-length lenses. As you might expect, various government agencies were keen on these cameras, as the long focal lengths made them well suited for surveillance applications.

Early electronic cameras included Canon's RC-470 and the Canon Xapshot. Sony introduced the ProMavica 5000, which featured two charge-coupled devices, or CCDs (we'll look at what a CCD is in the next chapter). Minolta also introduced the Maxxum, which was essentially a conventional camera with an electronic still video back. The concept of the "digital back" attached to a conventional view camera is still very much with us, especially at the high end of the digital photography market.

Many camera manufacturers such as Casio, Konica, Olympus, Pentax, Sanyo, Vivitar, and others came out with electronic still video cameras. Many of these were used for broadcasting (especially since they already conformed to the NTSC standard), and biomedical, scientific, and publishing became niche markets for the devices. In the late 1980s, as PC and Macintosh desktop systems began to proliferate, software (and software and hardware kits) began to appear that made it relatively simple to convert the still video images to digital form.

Analog versus Digital

The basic difference between an analog and a digital signal is that, as you probably know, an analog signal is a wave that varies in intensity (or amplitude). A good example is sound. A loud sound comprises a wave of high amplitude. Waves also have frequency and wavelength, which also control how, say, a sound is heard. But the important thing to remember about an analog signal is that it is continuous.

A digital signal, on the contrary, is not continuous. It is called "digital" because it can only be represented by one of two digits, a 0 or a 1. On or off. Yes or no. Thus, a digital sound comprises a long series of 0s and 1s that are grouped together to approximate a sound wave. As you can imagine, the more 0s and 1s (or "bits"; *bit* is an abbreviation for "binary digit," or essentially, a 0 or 1) that are involved, the more approximately continuous the digital signal can be. In modern parlance, this is translated as "the more data exists, the better the quality."

An analog signal is converted to a digital signal by a device called an analog-to-digital (A/D) converter. What this device does is "sample" the analog signal, or convert the amplitude of the wave into discrete values. The sampling rate, or how many times per second or unit of length a bit is assigned, determines the quality of the digital signal—in other words, how well it replicates the original analog signal. Again, the more data that is captured, the better the fidelity.

The same principle applies to digital imaging technology—i.e., scanners and digital cameras. A device samples an image in much the same way as a sound is sampled. The sampling rate in imaging is often referred to as "resolution."

The first digital cameras featured the same CCDs as the electronic still video cameras, but with a new wrinkle: an A/D converter that recorded three signals: one for red data, one for green data, and one for blue data. (We'll look at this in more depth in the next chapter.) So, in a digital camera, the image information is converted to digital data right inside the camera and stored in RAM or ROM.

One early digital still camera was a joint development between Fuji and Toshiba, but eventually—in Darwinian fashion—each manufacturer's version evolved in directions that soon became incompatible. The Toshiba Model MC200 Digital Still Camera System featured a ⅔-inch, 400,000-pixel CCD and used 8-megabit memory cards to store up to twelve images. The Fuji DS-100 Digital Electronic Camera featured a ½-inch, 390,000-pixel CCD and used 8-megabit DRAM cards to store up to twenty-one images.

Models proliferated soon after. At 1990's Photokina—an international photo show held every two years in Cologne, Germany—Chinon, Kodak, Konica, Minolta, Olympus, and Ricoh debuted prototypes of new digital cameras.

It was in the early 1990s that Kodak Professional debuted its new Digital Camera System (DCS), a product line that continues to this day. The DCS line combined digital imaging technology with a professional conventional camera body and optics. The DCS model was based on a Nikon F3 camera, and all the aperture, metering, shutter speed, and focus settings operated exactly as they did in the film world. But since the imaging area of the DCS was only half that of a conventional 35mm film frame, the focal lengths of the lenses were doubled, so that a conventional 50mm lens became a 100mm lens when attached to the DCS.

The DCS could take color and black-and-white images by means of a 1,280 × 1,024-pixel CCD.

The DCS 100 cost $20,000 at the time, and later models from Fuji were comparable in price. But they were very good products.

Enter Apple

In 1994, digital imaging began to come of age. In the graphic arts, a slew of flatbed scanners were bringing reasonably high-quality and low-cost color scanning onto the desktop. At the same time,

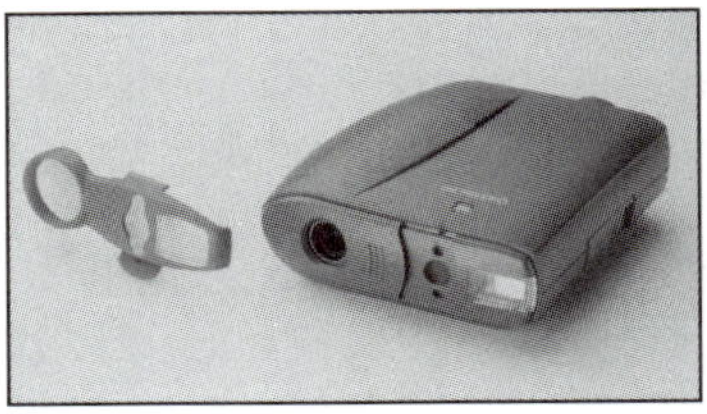

The QuickTake 150, a follow-up to the successful QuickTake 100, also had a maximum image size of 640 × 480 pixels. It also featured a snap-on "macro lens" system that let users take pictures of subjects from 10 to 14 inches away.

the first true consumer-level digital camera appeared. It was a collaborative venture between Apple and Kodak, and was called the QuickTake 100. In a surprising move for Apple (you would think), it was compatible with both Mac and Windows systems. The QuickTake 100 had two modes—high-res, which was VGA resolution (640 × 480 pixels), and low-res, or 320 × 240 pixels. It had a fixed focus lens and an auto flash (with a range of 4–9 feet). It didn't use any sort of memory card; it stored up to thirty-two low-res and eight high-res images internally, and images could be imported to a computer by means of a serial connection. All images were 24 bits deep.

The QuickTake was touted as being useful for small images to be used in print, but those who were involved in multimedia development (this was before the advent of the Web, and CD-ROMs were still big juju at this time) found it a boon, and it was looked to longingly as a way of avoiding having to shoot film and get the prints scanned. But it had a street price of about $700 or so, a bit on the pricey side.

But it was my first contact with a digital camera, and at the time, I thought it was extremely cool.

Around the same time, Sony introduced its DKC-5000 "Cat's Eye," which boasted a 440,000-pixel CCD (actually, it had three of them—red, green, and blue) and was touted as a studio camera. Also at this time, the AP News Camera 2000 incorporated technologies from Kodak's DCS 100 and 200 and was targeted at photojournalists. At the high end, there were also studio cameras and camera backs from Leaf and Dicomed.

Attendees at the Fall Comdex show in 1994 were treated to a host of competitors to the QuickTake 100. The Logitech Fotoman Pixtura had a high resolution of 768 × 512 pixels, and Chinon announced its

ESC-3X, which boasted a 3× zoom lens and a macro mode. Both models had list prices of just under $1,000.

If 1994 sowed the seeds of the future of digital photography, then 1995 was the first harvest, as more models appeared than ever. Kodak, Canon, Casio, Logitech, Chinon, and AT&T introduced new models that ran the gamut of high-end models to the low-end consumer models. By year's end, there was a Kodak DS-40, a Casio Digital Camera, and even the new Apple QuickTake 150. And high-end digital studio cameras were well ensconced in digital photography studios.

Fall Comdex in 1995 kicked off some lines we've been seeing ever since, and marked the first dramatic drop in the price of entry-level cameras. Epson's PhotoPC still only had a maximum image size of 640 × 480, but had a list price of $599, with a predicted street price of under $500. Fuji's DS-220 featured a dual telephoto/wide-angle lens and NTSC video output for real-time image previewing. Minolta's RD-176 had a resolution of 1,528 × 1,146 pixels and used PC cards for image storage. And the "Byte Best of Comdex" was Ricoh's RDC-1, which could capture digital video, digital still images, and audio, and used a 24-MB PC card. It started selling in spring 1996 for $1,800.

In the digital film world, 1995 saw the establishment of the CompactFlash Association by Kodak and Polaroid. The CompactFlash card itself had been introduced by SanDisk in October 1994, and the goal of the CompactFlash Association was (and continues to be) to standardize the card's technical specifications, a boon to those seeking to manufacture the technology. A flash memory card the size of a matchbook, the CompactFlash card was based on the older and larger PC cards, but its smaller size made it ideal for smaller digital cameras, especially those that sought a home in a photographer's pocket. The CompactFlash started appearing in cameras in 1997. (We'll look at CompactFlash in more detail in Chapter 5.)

The good news for graphic arts pros was that 1996 was the year that digital cameras invaded the prepress workflow. The low-end cameras, though cheap, were still too low in quality to have a great deal of usability, but for many with the budget, the midrange cameras were well suited to getting images in digital form right out of the gate.

Notably, the Associated Press used digital cameras in January 1996. At Super Bowl XXX, 20 AP photographers equipped with 1,280 × 1,024-pixel, $15,000 AP News Camera 2000s shot thousands of pictures of the game, and AP photo editors selected some 130 of the best and sent them over the AP network to newspapers across the

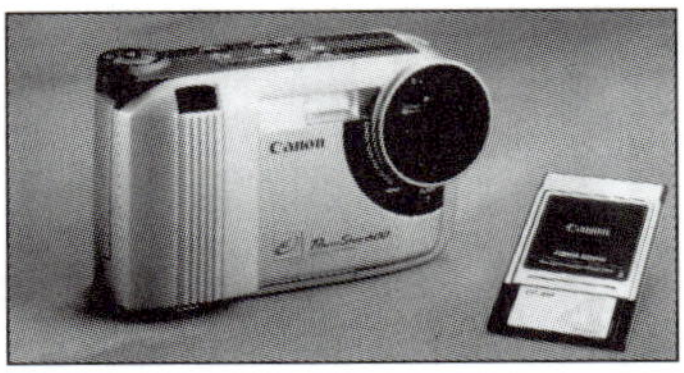

Canon's PowerShot 600 appeared in mid-1996 and featured a 1-MB internal memory, as well as the ability to record to 4-MB SanDisk flash memory cards, which could hold up to seventy-two images.

country. For perhaps the first time, digital photography appeared on front pages of newspapers.

At Photokina in 1996, excitement at the low end of the digital camera spectrum began to increase. Fuji and Minolta's new digital

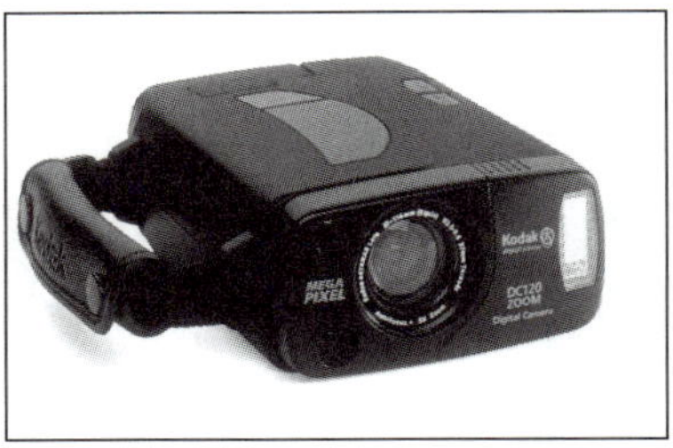

Kodak's DC120 Zoom Digital Camera appeared in mid-1997 and boasted a 1,280 × 960-pixel resolution, a 3× zoom lens, and Flashpix file support.

cameras used as storage media the new SmartMedia, originally developed by Toshiba. Described as "anemic" at the time, the SmartMedia card is still with us.

Now We're Talking

The turning point in the point-and-shoot digital camera world came in mid- to late 1997 when the first megapixel cameras debuted. "Megapixel" is a neologism that refers to a CCD array that comprises (and/or can capture) 1 million pixels or more. Thus, a camera that has a CCD having 1,310,720 pixels would be called a 1.3-megapixel (Mp) camera.

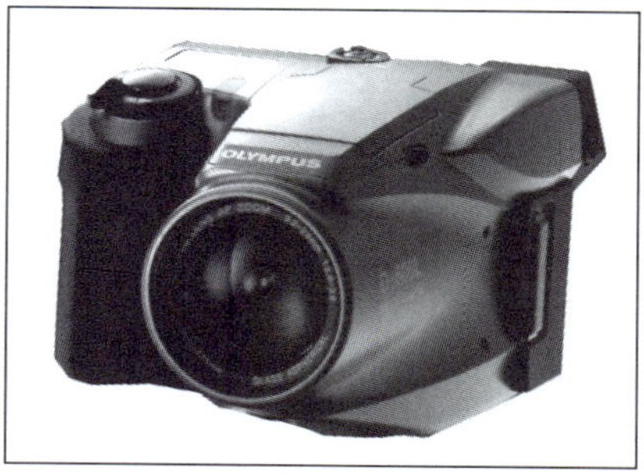

The Olympus D-600L was the first megapixel digital camera that combined high image resolution (1,280 × 1,024 pixels), advanced photographic features, and reasonably low price ($1,299).

Not that there weren't high- and higher-resolution cameras all along, but megapixel resolution came with a steep ($2,000–$10,000) price tag. The first camera to combine price with performance was the Olympus D-600L. The D-600L was a 1.4-Mp camera that could capture 1,280 × 1,024-pixel images. And the list price of the D-600L was $1,299. A complete departure from the earlier line of very Instamatic-like digital cameras, the D-600L had many features usually found in much higher-quality cameras. It had a 3× zoom lens, an f-2.8 aperture, 100 ISO equivalency, and a through-the-lens (TTL) viewfinder. The D-600L also boasted the sort of optics usually found only in cameras costing more than twice as much.

The D-600L (and its release companion, the 800,000-pixel D-500L)

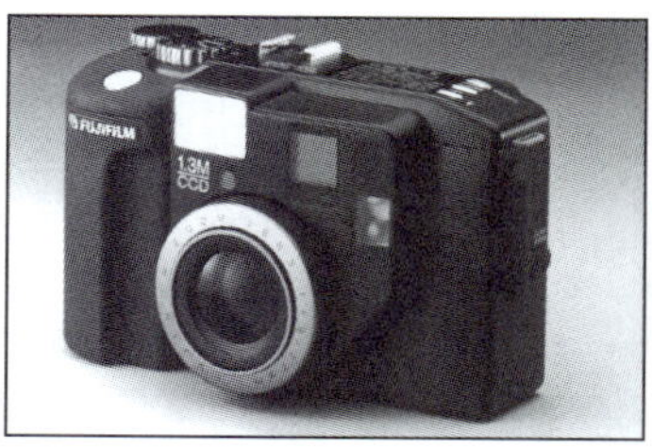

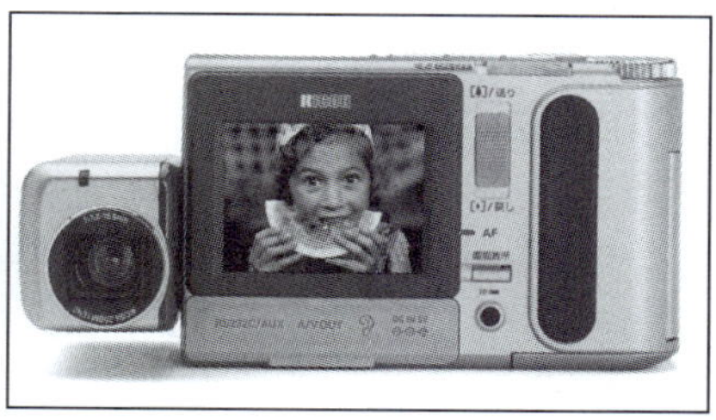

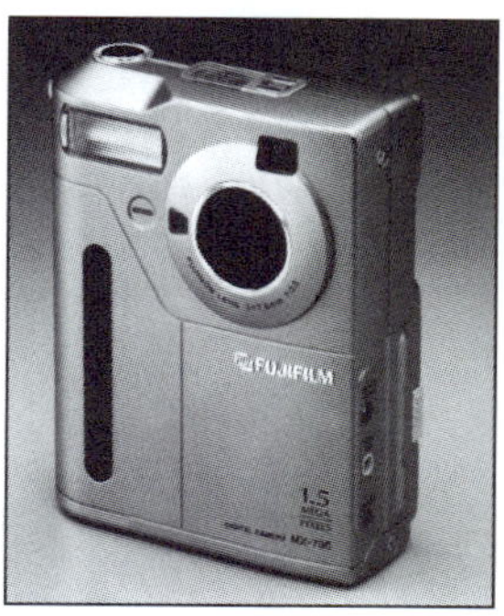

Fuji's DS-300 (above left) appeared in late 1997, boasted a 1,280 × 1,000-pixel resolution, and carried a price tag of $2,500. This is probably mixing apples with oranges, but Fuji's MX-700 (left), which appeared in early 1998, took 1,280 × 1,024-pixel images, cost $799, and was one of the biggest-selling digital cameras ever. Meanwhile, Ricoh's RDC-4300 (above right) was a 1.3-Mp camera that was also billed as a "multimedia device," as it could record sound and combine that sound with still images to create presentations inside or outside the camera.

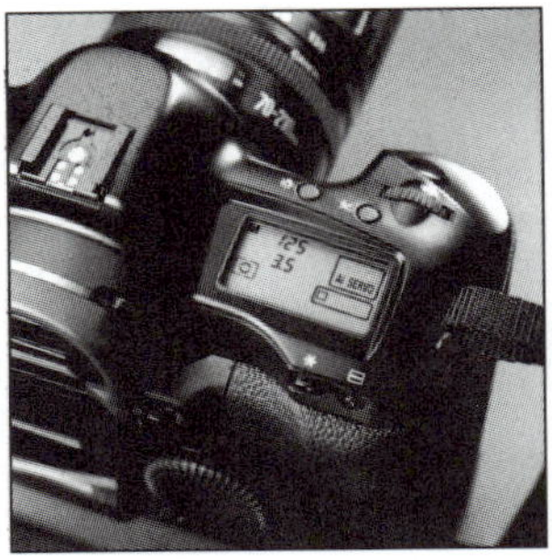

Meanwhile, in the world of the professional DCS cameras, Kodak had consulted with professional photojournalists and commercial photographers to create the DCS 520, which offered a burst rate of 3.5 frames per second and provided support for a 6-MB file with 1,736 × 1,160 resolution. It listed for $14,995.

also had four-mode flash and a back-panel LCD and used a SmartMedia card as its media of choice. Announced simultaneously, Olympus' P-300U dye-sublimation photoprinter allowed images to be printed directly from the Olympus cameras.

The Market Explodes

But nothing is ever invented—or marketed—in a vacuum, and many new megapixel models began appearing in early to mid-1998. These included the Kodak DC210, the Polaroid PDC-2000, and later the Fuji MX-700, with its 1,280 × 1,024 CCD, became one of the best-selling digital cameras ever.

Nikon's Coolpix 900 and 950 became hot sellers as well, and Epson introduced its first megapixel camera, the PhotoPC 700. The slightly later PhotoPC 750Z added a 3× zoom.

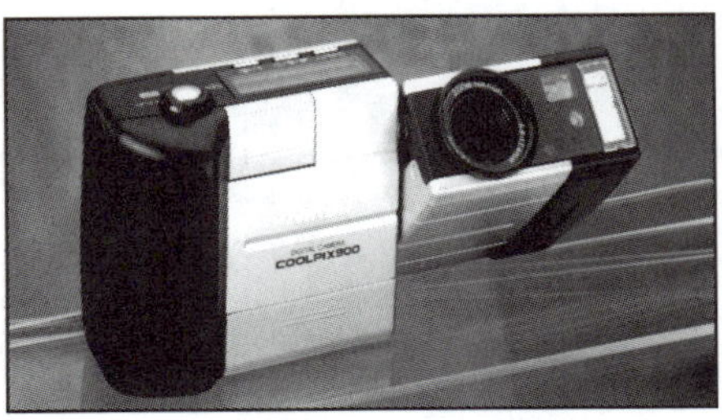

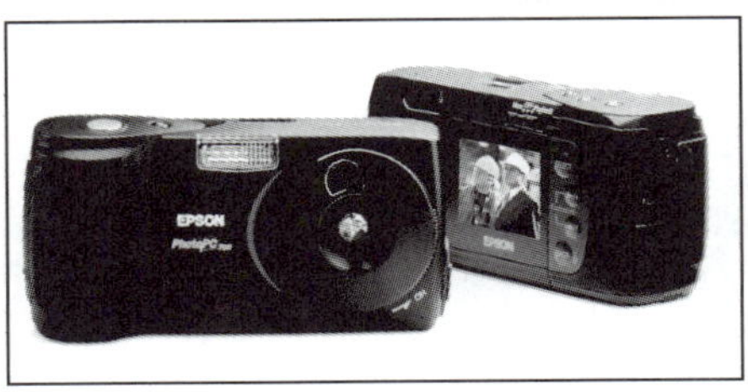

With a list price of $699, Nikon's 1,280 × 960-pixel Coolpix 900 (above left) was a hot seller in mid-1998. Meanwhile, Epson debuted its first megapixel camera in 1998, the 1,280 × 960-pixel PhotoPC 700 (left). New models in both the Coolpix and the PhotoPC series are still appearing regularly.

Most of 1998 was spent refining camera designs and standardizing features. Where once a color LCD for image playback or live previewing was a luxury item, now it's de rigueur. Not every camera has an optical zoom, but most now do.

Consumer interest in digital cameras also began increasing in earnest in 1998 and continued into 1999. And graphic arts pros began to realize that they could solve many of their imaging

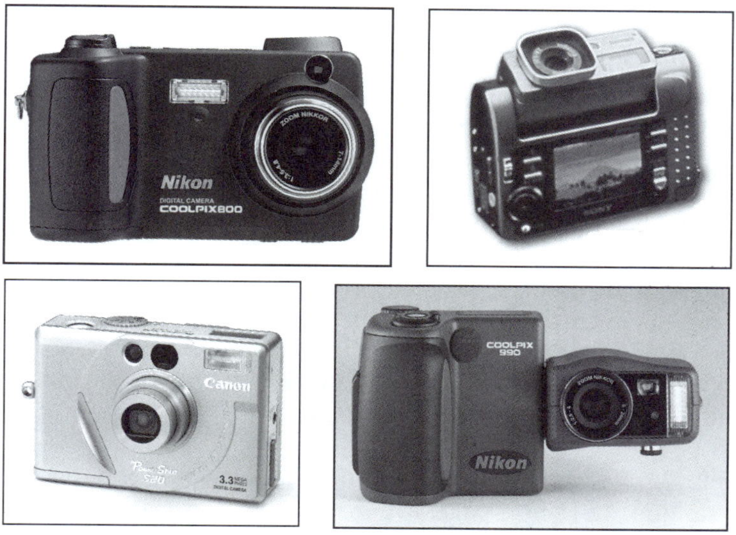

Two successive generations of digital cameras. Top row, left to right: the 2.X-Mp Nikon Coolpix 800 and Sony Cyber-shot. Bottom row, left to right: The 3.X-Mp Canon PowerShot S20 and Nikon Coolpix 990.

needs with under-$1,000 cameras rather than far more expensive models.

Another milestone was reached in May 1999, when manufacturers began releasing the 2.X-Mp cameras. Finally, in February 2000, at the Photo Marketing Association show, the 3.X-Mp cameras debuted.

Megapixels Galore

That's where we stand now. We've got megapixels galore. The next steps in "megapixellage" may be a case of diminishing returns, but the advantage to this prolonged flurry of activity is that the new models tend to debut at around $1,000, which results in a sort of trickle-down effect with regard to lower-Mp models, which can now be had pretty inexpensively.

But manufacturers are still introducing low-Mp models even as they are introducing higher-Mp models. Why? By introducing cheaper models, they can whet the public appetite, letting them get their feet wet in digital photography without a great deal of initial expense. Whether that makes sense is debatable, but it exists.

So, Yet Once Again, Why Digital?

As we have seen, albeit in an abbreviated manner, the development of digital photography has paralleled a number of other trends with regard to technology, both in graphic arts and in the consumer world. In graphic arts, since as early as the late 1980s and more profoundly beginning in the early to mid-1990s, we've seen the trend toward the elimination of prepress. Remember when you set type with phototypesetters, pasted up boards, shot film, and then made plates that were then hung on the press? And if you used color images, you sent out your prints or transparencies for color separations that were done photographically. These were then combined with your black type film on the plates.

Well, we've watched many of those processes wither and die. Type is set directly from a page-layout program, and color and black-and-white images are incorporated in the same document as the text. Even in Open Press Interface workflows, you have low-res "proxies" in your page layout, but eventually the "real" file is linked. At one time, the lot was sent out to film, and plates were then made. Well, computer-to-plate (CTP) workflows are eliminating the need for film. Page layout files are sent directly to a CTP system, and plates are burned directly from the file. (That file can also be in Portable Document Format, too, by the way.) No film.

And direct digital printing systems are even doing away with the need for plates! One more step, and we'll do without the need for actual printing, I suppose. (Some call that the Web, but I remain dubious about that.)

So what we've seen is the development of technology that is as direct as possible. Even as middle managers proliferate in corporate life, in the graphic arts we are increasingly cutting out the middleman.

So it's no surprise that digital photography is playing a part in this. Dealing with color (and even black-and-white) images has always been a case of too many middlemen. Think about how things used to be done. You shot pictures on film. You made prints from the film. The prints were then shot *back into film* for platemaking. Did that make any sense? Actually, it did, but with 20-20 hindsight it seems a bit odd.

And once electronic publishing began, we shot film, developed the film and made prints or transparencies, which then needed to be scanned so they could be put on a page. The photo CD was a stopgap solution, but it was a temporary one until desktop flatbed scanners and digital cameras reached the point where most digital imaging could be done in-house.

Digital photography lets us be digital from the beginning of the process. And by developing these devices in such a way that image and color quality can be maintained at the outset, we introduce few variables and margins of error into the process.

And we can save time and effort in file transport as well. We can shoot our images and e-mail them (or WamNet them) immediately to where we need them to go. And in minutes (depending on the speed of your connection, of course). No more overnighting prints and slides. Whether we want to encourage the sorts of deadlines we're starting to see is another issue unto itself. But the point is that working digitally makes life easier in many ways.

Shoot First and Ask Questions Later

In a sense, we've all been waiting for the period we're at now, when we can shoot digitally and keep everything digital from the get-go. Especially as repurposing imagery for the Web becomes more and more of a concern, we have the ability to shoot our pictures first and ask questions later.

On the consumer level, more and more of human life is moving into cyberspace. Not that everyone wants to remain there for long periods of time; I think most people think of the Internet as "a nice place to visit, but I wouldn't want to live there." Kind of like Los Angeles, really. But even in the consumer space, digital imaging has a role. As we become more separated from friends and family, we can use the Internet to keep in touch. Not that this should replace the telephone; I love it when software manufacturers tout the ability of their Internet software to "facilitate real-time on-line chats with other people." Uh, guys, that was invented more than 100 years ago and was called the telephone.

Be that as it may, shooting our holiday, vacation, family get-together pictures digitally and e-mailing them to friends and relatives is a good way to keep in touch across the miles. (We'll look at this in more detail in Chapter 7.)

Onward

We've come a long way, baby, and we still have a ways to go. But we've reached the point where digital photography can solve many dilemmas and problems we've had in our workflows. From here, we'll look a bit more closely at the technological underpinnings of today's digital cameras. You saw some of the issues involved in our little stroll down random-access memory lane. Now let's look at those issues a bit more closely, the goal being to be able to read a specification sheet for a digital camera, so that you know what you're getting yourself into before you buy. In fact, we've even invented our own digital camera, whose spec sheet we'll look at in close detail.

2

What's a Pixel? And Other Technological Questions

In the previous chapter, you probably picked up some of the technological issues involved in digital photography and digital cameras. Some of these issues will be covered in this chapter; others in succeeding chapters.

Don't be scared—even if you're technophobic (and if so, why are you reading a book on digital photography?), you'll find that the material we are about to cover really isn't much harder to fathom than the technological issues involved in conventional photography. In fact, many of the same issues come into play—questions about optics, focal length, depth of field, and all that good stuff. But instead of dealing with latent images in silver halide substrates and the chemistry needed to reveal those images, we'll be looking at CCDs, linear arrays, and movements of electrons.

The CCD

The most basic technological issues we need to be concerned with here involve the building block of the digital camera, the CCD. The CCD—which stands for *charge-coupled device*—is the heart or, more precisely, the eyes of a digital camera. If you think of a traditional film camera, you know that on the inside of the camera, opposite the lens, is the film. When the shutter opens, light is focused through the lens onto the film, and an image is recorded.

The same basic principle is involved in digital photography. But instead of the plastic and silver halide-based film, in its place is a CCD. A CCD is basically a small, light-sensitive photocell or semiconductor chip that comprises many photodiodes. This chip is able to convert the light that is falling on it into electric charges, the strength (voltage) of which is equivalent to the amount of light hitting it. This voltage is then translated into digital data so that it can be understood by the computer processor inside the camera, and by any other computer that may attempt to retrieve the images captured.

A CCD has as its most fundamental unit of image capture the *pixel*. As you may have guessed, you haven't heard the last of this term, and at this point I dare say you haven't heard the first of it either. We'll look at pixels in greater depth (so to speak) in a bit, but in terms of a CCD, a pixel is the smallest element that can capture a portion of an image. In digital camera specification sheets, you often see the sensor described in terms of how many pixels it contains. As you can imagine, the more pixels a CCD has, the better the image quality, or at least the greater the resolution (another term you haven't heard the last of). To put it another way, the more pixels a CCD has, the more data it can capture.

There are basically two types of CCDs: linear arrays and area arrays. A *linear array*, as you would expect, has all its pixels arranged in a straight line. This line of pixels advances forward and captures data one row at a time. You've no doubt seen the imaging mechanism inside a photocopier or scanner; you know how a line of lights passes slowly over the original. That's essentially how a linear array works.

So when you read specification sheets that involve linear arrays, the horizontal resolution number refers to how many pixels the CCD has in its linear array (i.e., 600 per inch). The vertical resolution number refers to how many times per inch the array "snaps" a shot (i.e., 1,200). Thus when you see a resolution of 600 × 1,200, and you know the camera or scanner has a linear array, well, then you know that the array has 600 actual pixels per inch, and it stops 1,200 times per inch as it moves along the original.

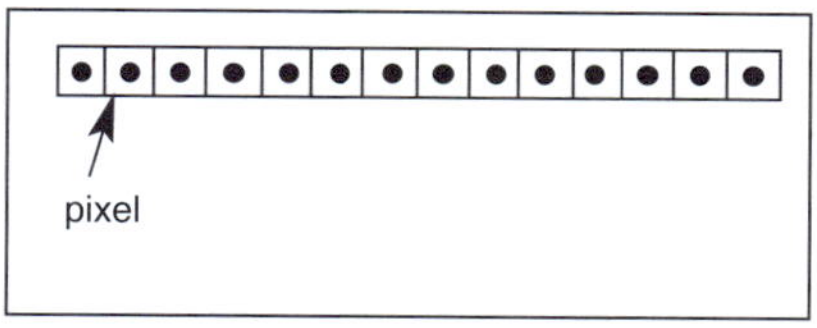

Basic structure of a linear array (left), compared with the basic structure of an area array (below left).

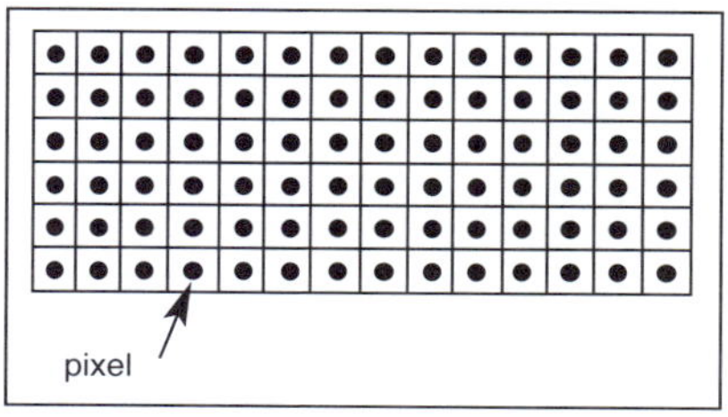

An area array, on the other hand, is a two-dimensional linear array, if that makes any sense. Essentially, an area array is a rectangle comprising several rows of pixels. This array doesn't usually move but rather captures an entire scene in one fell swoop. As you would expect, area arrays are quicker, but they also capture lower-quality images.

When you read spec sheets and you know that the camera or scanner features an area array, the resolution given refers to how many pixels are in a horizontal row and how many are in a vertical column. Thus, an area array CCD having a resolution of 640 × 480 has 640 pixels in a horizontal row and 480 pixels in a vertical column. If you do the multiplication, you come up with 307,200 pixels in a 640 × 480 array. Spec sheets for digital cameras often give the total number of pixels in the array.

Pixels

Okay, so we think we know what a pixel is. But as you can imagine, that's only part of the story. A "pixel" is a relative thing. It's probably best thought of in terms of what it abbreviates: a *picture element*. (There was a dubious flirtation some years ago with the alternative term *pel*, but fortunately that fell into disuse. Not that "pixel" is a word to inspire the poets, but the last thing we need is more than one word to describe the same thing.)

If you look at your computer monitor, you can probably see the most fundamental element of the screen, each pixel. Depending upon the platform you're using, you've probably got somewhere between 72 and 90 pixels per inch. Macintosh monitors are constrained to 72; Windows system monitors can go a skosh higher. This means that in every horizontal inch of screen, there are 72 pixels, or picture elements.

If you examine your black-and-white laser printer output, you may need a loupe to determine that your laser printer can output up to 600, maybe even 1,200, pixels per inch. Each of the small dots you can see, which together compose each printed character, is a pixel.

If you run down to your local service bureau and have a sheet of negative film output on an imagesetter, you will definitely need a loupe to see that the imagesetter can output about 2,500 pixels per inch, often more.

We'll leave it at that, but you can see that a pixel can change in size depending upon the output device.

Resolving Resolution

Let us pause here for a moment to dwell on the term *pixels per inch,* often abbreviated *PPI.* This is an equivalent term to *dots per inch,* which is abbreviated *DPI.* Pixels output by a printer are sometimes referred to as spots rather than dots—but let's not go there. Pixels, dots, spots, schmots, whatever. Dots per inch (DPI) is the most common iteration, so from here on in we're going to stick with it.

To recap, then: A pixel is the smallest element that comprises an image.

When we talk about digital cameras as hardware, we refer to the CCD in terms of the number of pixels it contains. As we saw, a CCD having a 640 × 480-pixel array has a total of 307,200 pixels; it's thus a 307,200-pixel array. This becomes important when talking about larger arrays. For example, two years or so ago, a new breed of digital cameras came out that had area arrays of around 1,280 × 960 pixels. This works out to 1,228,800 pixels. These were often referred to as 1.2 million-pixel cameras, or 1.2-megapixel cameras. A *megapixel,* thus, is an array of 1 million or more pixels. As of this writing, the current "high end of the low-end" models are 3.X-megapixel cameras. As we'll see in the next chapter, there are many higher-end cameras with much larger linear and area arrays.

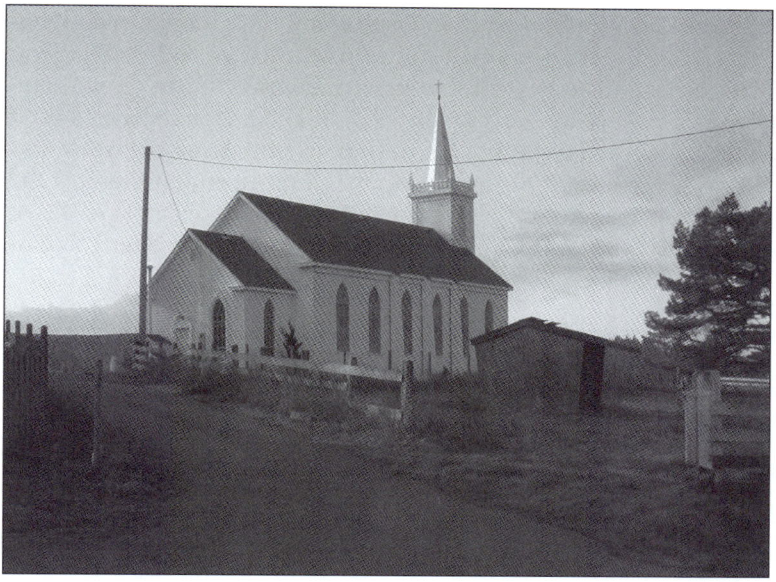

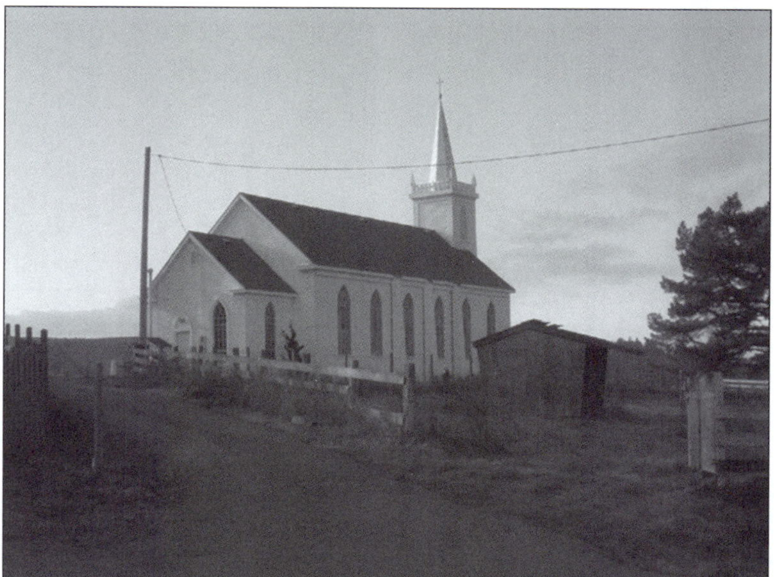

The number of pixels you capture directly affects image quality. The top image was captured with 1,600 × 1,200 pixels and looks reasonably good at 300 DPI. The bottom image was captured with only 640 × 480 pixels (VGA) and looks pretty awful at 300 DPI, at least at this size.

Here's some alphabet soup to keep you warm. As you may recall from your monitor-buying days, a resolution of 640 × 480 pixels was referred to as VGA. You often come across this in digital camera specs, especially at the low end. Whenever someone doesn't want to openly admit that a resolution is only a measly 640 × 480, they refer to it as "VGA," which takes the curse off it a bit. At the next level, a resolution of 1,024 × 768 pixels is referred to as XGA. We're currently up to 1,600 × 1,200 pixels, which is referred to as UXGA.

We'll be looking a bit more closely at what resolution and the number of pixels mean in terms of print output in Chapter 6, when we actually work with images.

Color Depth

Another specification you often come across in digital camera technical literature is color depth, sometimes referred to as "pixel depth." This is usually a number such as 24, 36, or 42.

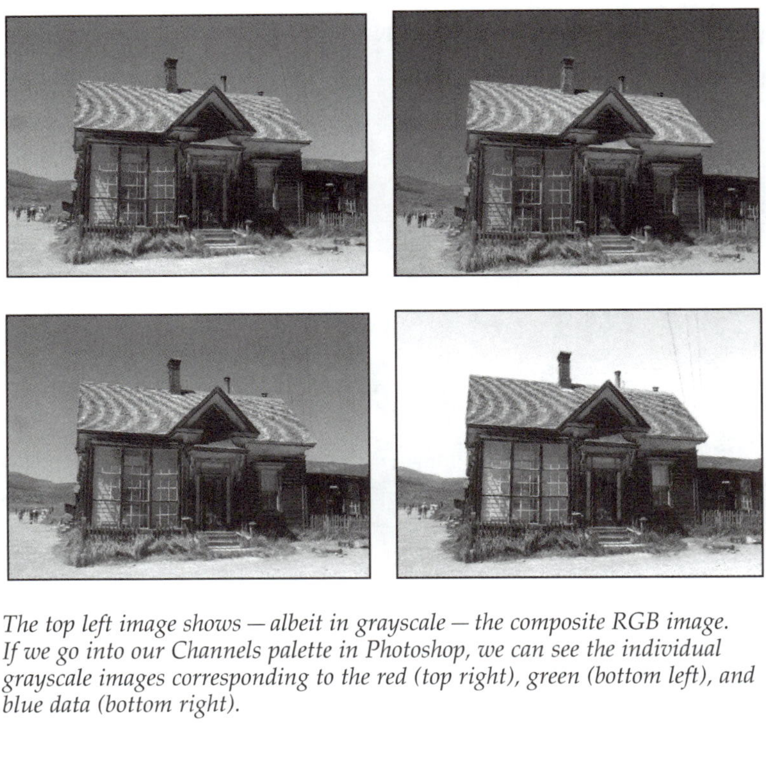

The top left image shows — albeit in grayscale — the composite RGB image. If we go into our Channels palette in Photoshop, we can see the individual grayscale images corresponding to the red (top right), green (bottom left), and blue data (bottom right).

This number refers to the number of bits needed to describe each pixel. Hoo boy. Let's take this bit by bit, as it were.

A particular pixel, whether displayed on a computer monitor or printed by some type of output device, requires some number of bits to describe it. A *bit*, as you may recall, is an abbreviation of the term "binary digit" and refers to digital data, which can only be 0 or 1, on or off, yes or no.

Let's think in terms of black and white. A monitor with a depth of 1 bit per pixel can only describe two colors. The single bit can either be 0 (white) or 1 (black). The next level is grayscale. At 8 bits per pixel, you can have up to 256 different shades of gray ($2^8 = 256$). For example, a pure white pixel can be represented by 00000000, and a pure black pixel by 11111111. All the intermediates—such as, say, 10011110—are shades of gray.

When thinking in terms of color images, we need to remember that a monitor, scanner, or digital camera operates in the RGB (red, green, and blue) color space. Red, green, and blue are the additive color primaries and are the three basic colors that nature uses in various combinations to construct all the colors of the spectrum. (We need not get into color theory here, but it's quite interesting, if you care to delve into the literature.) In this color space, each of the three primary colors is represented by shades of gray.

Okay, I see you sent up a flag on that last statement. Let's back up. When, say, a digital camera or a scanner captures an image, it's essentially capturing three different images. There are the elements of the CCD that have special dyes that let those pixels capture only the red image data. Other elements have dyes that let those pixels capture only green image data. And of course, pixels that have dyes that let them capture only blue image data. Each of these three "passes" is represented as a grayscale image. (Go into Adobe Photoshop and look at the various channels for a good look at how this works.) That is, one grayscale image represents all the various levels of red, another grayscale image represents all the various levels of green, and a third grayscale image represents all the various shades of blue.

Now, we saw that an 8-bit grayscale image can represent 256

shades of gray. This means that if each color that is captured by a digital camera is represented by an 8-bit grayscale image, then that means the red channel includes 256 shades of red, the green channel includes 256 shades of green, and the blue channel includes 256 shades of blue. Together, this means that each color pixel is described by 24 bits of data (8 bits times the three primary colors). This works out to each pixel being able to represent one of 2^{24}, or 16,777,216, different colors.

But 24-bit color was your daddy's color depth. Today's scanners and digital cameras have 36-bit (12 bits per pixel per color) or even 42-bit (14 colors per pixel per color) color. In 42-bit color, this means that each pixel can represent one of 2^{42}, or 440 *trillion* different colors. That's a lotta do-re-mi.

Up the Downsample

We've looked at resolution and pixels and all that good stuff. One aspect of digital imaging—and this goes for scanners as well as digital cameras—about which you need to be wary is the concept of *upsampling*. First of all, the term *sampling* itself refers to the frequency with which an image is digitized. (By the way, it also refers to the digitization of audio as well, so when you see "samples" or "sampling" in conjunction with music, you know that some portion of it has been digitized from other sources.)

If you read the technical descriptions of scanners in places like MacWarehouse or PC Zone catalogs, you've seen the term *optical resolution* followed by some other number. That other number is higher than the optical resolution, right? The reason for that is that scanners and some digital cameras often artificially boost the resolution of captured images with what is known as software interpolation. This is sort of the equivalent of a silicone breast implant or penile implant. And like the cosmetic equivalents, interpolation has varying degrees of effectiveness.

What interpolation—or upsampling—does is mathematically insert pixels in those images that have already been captured. Basically, the software takes a small portion of an image and calculates the average color in that region and sticks that color pixel in there. It then does that with all the other little areas of the image. (It does it a bit more scientifically than I've just described it.) The goal is to

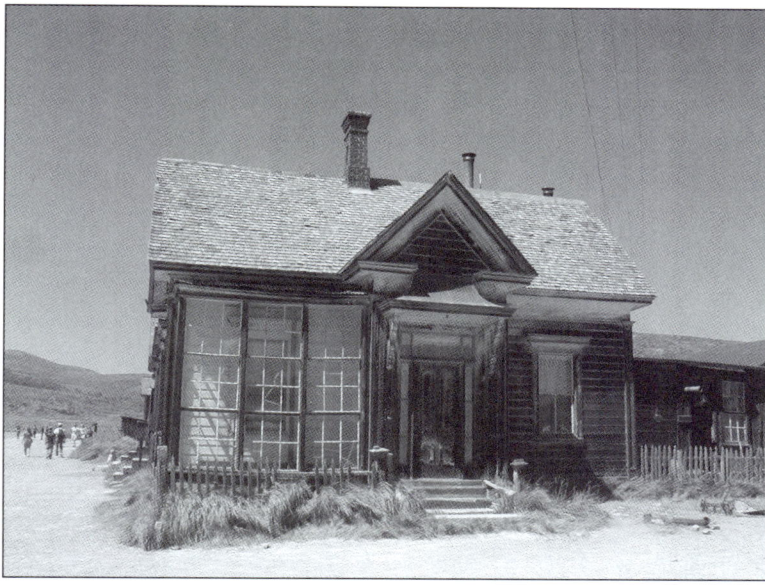

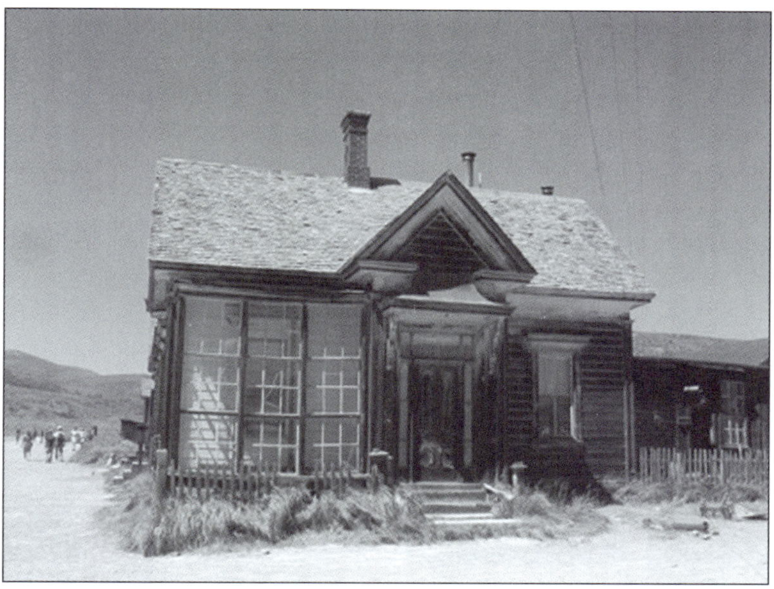

The image on top is an actual 266-DPI, 1.8-MB image. The image on the bottom is a 72-DPI, 300-KB image upsampled to an equivalent resolution and file size in Photoshop using bicubic interpolation. Not overly wretched, but you're better off capturing the data optically.

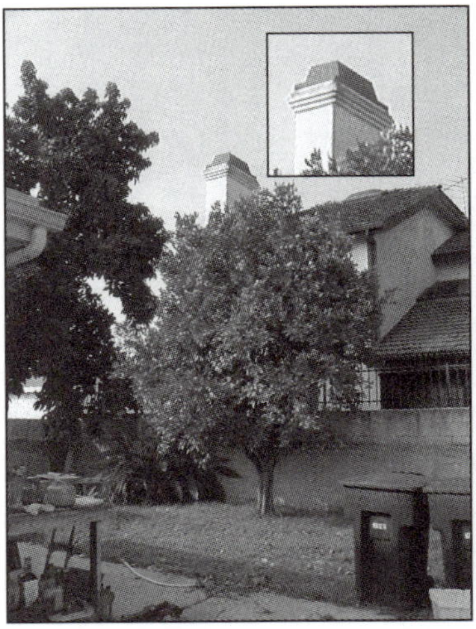

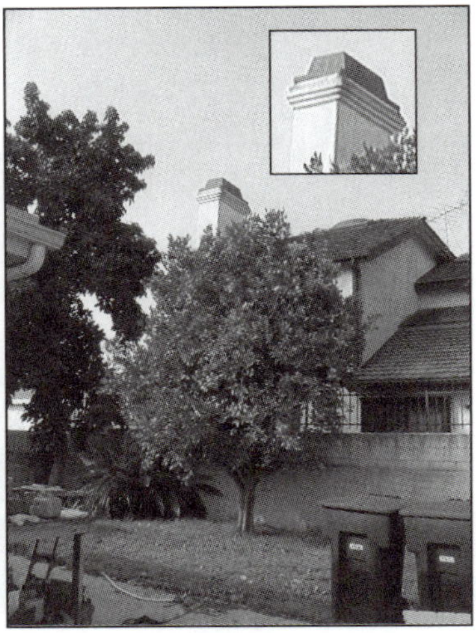

Above: Epson's digital cameras feature a software upsampling system called HyPict. The PhotoPC 750Z captures 1,280 × 960-pixel images that have file sizes of 3.52 MB (left). With HyPict turned on, the resolution is boosted via software to 1,600 × ,1200 pixels (right), for a file size of 5.5 MB. As you can see, it doesn't do a bad job, although if you look at the inset of the chimney (which is at 100 percent size), you can see a little fuzziness in the straight diagonal lines.

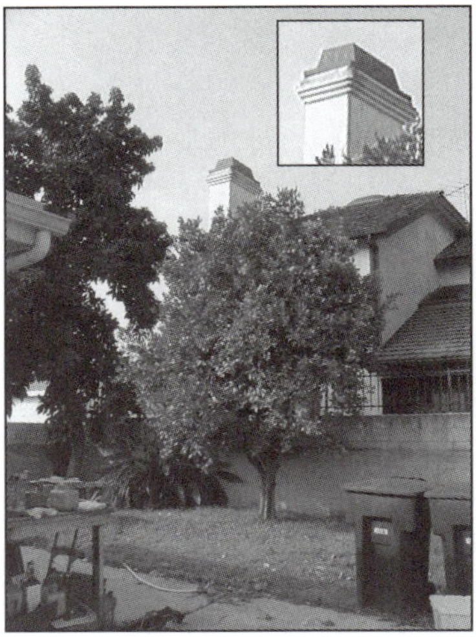

Here, we took the original 1,280 × 960-pixel image and upsampled it in Photoshop to 1,600 × 1,200 pixels. As you can see, the results are pretty comparable to what HyPict can do, and the fuzziness is a tad less egregious here. The upshot is that upsampling is okay if your needs are modest and you need to squeeze just a little bit more resolution out of your images.

put more pixels in the image, and those pixels must be related to the pixels surrounding them.

Upsampling as a technology is getting better, and two systems in place in point-and-shoot digital cameras currently on the market—Agfa's PhotoGenie and Epson's HyPict—work reasonably well. Despite that, it is always best that, if you have stringent resolution needs, you try your best to achieve that resolution optically rather than softwarily.

Alternatively, you can also attempt to upsample an image in a program like Photoshop.

We'll cover what your specific resolution needs are likely to be when we talk about working with captured images in Chapter 6.

File Formats

On the subject of upsampling, we should talk briefly about the idea of compression. Compression is, essentially, a means to make a captured image smaller, usually for reasons of file storage and transport. Just about every digital camera on the market (with the exception of extremely high-end models) makes provisions for some type of image compression, usually some form of JPEG.

Ah, JPEG. Can't live with it, can't live without it. Well, that's not really true. These days, you can live quite comfortably with JPEG. JPEG stands for Joint Photographic Experts Group—the International Standards Organization (ISO) body that defined

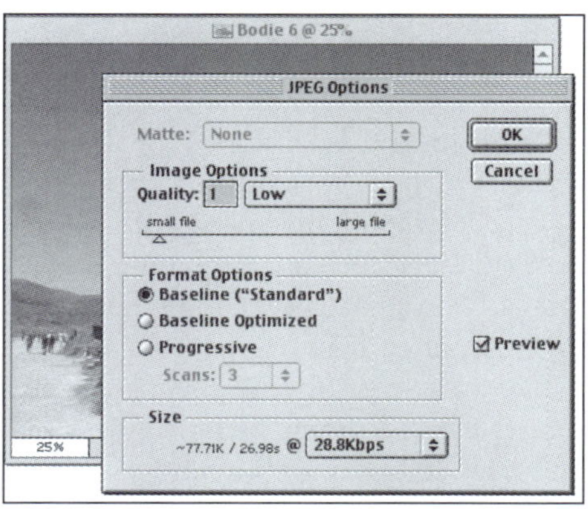

The dialog box in Photoshop that lets you set your JPEG compression when saving. Smaller file sizes yield lower quality, as you would expect.

what JPEG is—and it is two things: a standard file format and an image-compression algorithm. The two sort of go hand in hand.

If you've worked in Photoshop, you know that when you save images in JPEG format, you are given a dialog box that lets you specify the level of JPEG compression.

JPEG is considered a "lossy"—as opposed to "lossless"—compression scheme. But here's the deal on compression schemes: The point of compression is to make an image smaller by throwing away data but embedding an algorithm for the reconstruction of that data. As you would expect, some data is more difficult to describe via an algorithm than others. Thus, when you compress an image heavily, you're going to lose some data. There's no way around that. It's like they say—you don't get something for nothing. Let's face it: If it takes a certain number of megabytes to describe an image, then it takes that number of megabytes to describe the image.

Therefore, the only real question is: Can I live with the results of compression? And I'm afraid I can't answer that for you. The only way to answer that question is to experiment. What we have found, in our testing of the various digital cameras that have appeared over the past few years, is that the JPEG compression they use is not that bad; there is some occasional artifacting or loss of image detail, but we've rarely found it to be a serious problem.

What we are also finding, though, is that as the storage media available for digital cameras get larger (see Chapter 5), the need for compression gets smaller, to the extent that many digital cameras now are starting to offer an uncompressed TIFF mode.

In a TIFF

Yes, I thought you'd ask what TIFF meant. TIFF stands for "Tagged Image File Format." It was developed by Aldus Corporation (which also gave us PageMaker, FreeHand, and many other tools before becoming part of Adobe in 1994) and has become the standard file format for *bitmap* images, continuous-tone images that are captured by a digital camera or scanner. If you ever want to send an image to a friend or relative via e-mail, by all means use the JPEG format , if only to cut a few years off their download time. But if you are ever submitting an image to a service bureau for output, especially if it is a link in a QuarkXPress or InDesign document, by all means make it a TIFF. In professional imaging circles, you can't go wrong with TIFF, especially in cross-platform environments. Even though the Windows version of TIFF is different from the Macintosh version of TIFF, most popular graphics programs have no problems with either one.

There is also a compression algorithm that can be used with TIFF (as users of Photoshop are aware). It is called LZW (for Lempel-Ziv-Welch) compression, and it is deemed to be lossless.

In terms of digital cameras, you occasionally find formats other than JPEG and TIFF. (There is a file format called Flashpix that turns up occasionally but has yet to make any significant inroads.) There are other graphics file formats, which we will cover in Chapter 5, but JPEG and TIFF are the two that cause the least number of problems for imaging pros.

JPEG2K

Imaging amateurs and pros alike may also find of interest the recent announcement of the new JPEG 2000 file format, a major revamping of the admittedly creaky file format. Slated to appear sometime in early 2001, the new version will provide several major enhancements to take JPEG into the new millennium.

The first is that JPEG 2000, like Flashpix, is what is known as a "multi-resolution" file format. This means that a single file comprises several different versions of the same image at different resolutions. This allows only the image data that is strictly needed to be piped in. For example, if you are working with a 600-DPI image file on a monitor, do you really need all the image data? It can strain system resources and is overkill, because the monitor can only display at 72 DPI anyway. Multi-resolution file formats take this into account. (It's not surprising that JPEG 2000 takes a Flashpix-like approach; JPEG 2000 was jointly developed by the Digital Imaging Group, an industry consortium that was also behind Flashpix. For more information on what the Digital Imaging Group is up to, visit www.digitalimaging.org.)

The new JPEG 2000 will also support metadata, which is essentially additional information beyond the image itself. This can involve things like date and time settings, lens, exposure, aperture, and flash settings, copyright info, etc. In other words, the file format thus becomes a kind of database of which the image itself is only a part.

There's a lot more to the new JPEG, but you get the idea.

Photographic Issues

In addition to the purely digital aspects, we should also touch on the more photographic terms you'll likely come across. Most of the cameras you're likely to see at the lower end of the digital camera continuum have automatic modes, which keep you from having to worry unduly about things like aperture, exposure compensation, spot metering, and ISO settings. But for those experienced users who want and/or need more control over how their cameras capture images, many offer manual modes, which add varying degrees of customization to these settings.

Focal Length and Focal Point

Without getting into a great deal of optics here, let's say that light enters a camera through the lens. Seems reasonable enough. The job of the lens is to focus that light on a specific spot—preferably the film or the sensor. This specific spot, where all the light rays entering the lens converge and the image is the sharpest, is called the *focal point*. The distance between the center of the lens and the focal point—when the lens is focused at infinity—is called the *focal length*.

Aperture

The camera's *aperture* is the hole that allows light to pass from the lens to the film or the CCD. The size of this hole can be narrowed or widened. By widening it, you let more light hit the sensor. By narrowing it, you let less light hit the sensor. As you can imagine, by adjusting the aperture, you are affecting the exposure.

The size of the aperture is also called the *f-stop* of the lens. Well, sort of. A specific f-stop is a number—called, cleverly enough, an *f-number*—that refers to the ratio of the focal length of the lens to the diameter of the aperture. So, to use a large example, in a traditional graphic arts process camera, you could very well find a lens with an 8-inch focal length and a 1-inch aperture. Thus, the f-number for this camera setting would be $8 \div 1 = 8$, or f/8. If we were to reduce the aperture to ½ inch, we would get $8 \div \frac{1}{2} = 16$, or f/16.

In theory, any f-number can be produced, but there is a standard set of f-stops that camera makers and lens manufacturers (and photographers) recognize: f/1.4, f/2, f/2.8, f/4, f/5.6, f/8, f/11, f/16, f/22, f/32, and f/64. The greater the f-number, the smaller the diameter of the aperture. Each f-stop also differs by a factor of 2 in the amount of light that is allowed to pass into the camera.

Shutter Speed

The camera's shutter is the actual mechanism that lets light into the camera to hit the film or CCD. How long the shutter remains open determines, naturally, how much light hits the film or CCD. Thus, the *shutter speed* refers to how long the shutter remains open. On higher-end cameras, you can adjust this, as well.

ISO Values

Another photographic term that has made the transition to digital—with some degree of reservation—is the *ISO value*. ISO is short for International Standards Organization and was formerly referred to as ASA (from the American Standards Association). This value refers to film sensitivity, or film speed. Film comes in various levels of sensitivity to light, from what are called "slow" film speeds (ISO 25–64) to "fast" film speeds (greater than ISO 1,600). In general, using fast film lets you shoot under a greater variety of lighting conditions, and fast film is occasionally used in low-light situations. The drawback to fast film is that you tend to get a grainier image.

Like film, CCDs have a range of different sensitivities, which camera manufacturers have tried to make roughly analogous to the corresponding ISO values in the film world. In digital photography, we usually find CCDs that can be adjusted to act as ISO 100, 200, or 400. Higher-end cameras give us a higher range of ISOs.

Putting It All Together

Okay, we've looked at focal lengths, apertures, shutter speeds, and ISO values. So what? Well, all these things control the way the light hits our CCD. After all, what is photography? Looked at strictly in terms of the etymology of the word itself, it means "writing with light." Thus, all these ways of controlling the light that hits our CCD affect how our image comes out.

Photography is a complicated subject, and I haven't even scratched the surface of what a professional photographer could tell you about the interplay of all these factors and settings. But we'll attempt to put it all together very shortly.

How to Read a Spec Sheet

So we've seen what a pixel is, and that a CCD is an array of image-capturing pixels. We've looked at how resolution is a measure of how many pixels make up an image, and how color depth is a measure of how many colors a pixel can describe.

We've also looked at image compression and two popular file formats often used in digital cameras. We've also looked at some of the factors that affect how light hits the CCD.

We've mentioned all of this because the ultimate goal of this chapter is to help you read and understand a digital camera spec sheet. To that end, we present a sample spec sheet on page 31.

Let's go through it line by line, and look at it in the context of our previous discussion.

Image capture device

This is essentially the CCD. This tells you how big the CCD is. In this case, it is 1/1.8 inch, and has 3,340,000 pixels. Thus, this would be considered a 3.34-megapixel camera.

One little trick camera manufacturers occasionally do (though not too much anymore) is interpolate some of its pixels. You want to know how many *optical* pixels there are, not how many interpolated pixels there are.

Color Depth

This tells us that it has a color depth of 24 bits, or 8 bits per pixel × three colors. We've seen what this means—it can generate millions of colors. That's about par for the course with these types of cameras. Anything under 24 bits is unacceptable (generally).

JOE'S IMAGING DIGIPIX 8700

Type of camera:	Digital still camera with built-in flash, 2X optical zoom
Image capture device:	3,340,000-pixel, 1/1.8-inch CCD
Color depth:	24 bits (8 bits × 3 colors)
Resolution:	SHQ: 2,048 × 1,536 (uncompressed TIFF) HQ: 1,024 × 768 (low JPEG compression) FQ: 1,024 × 768 (high JPEG compression) VGA: 640 × 480
Sensitivity:	Equivalent to ISO 100, 200, 400
Lens:	6.5–13mm, f/2.9–f/4.0 zoom (equivalent to 32–64mm in 35mm format)
Shooting modes:	Automatic, manual, flash, self-timer, macro
Focus range (from lens):	Standard: 1.5 feet to ∞ Macro: 0.4 feet to 1.5 feet
Recording media:	CompactFlash (CF)
Shutter speed:	2–1/1,000 sec.
Auto focus:	TTL AF
Flash range:	0.6–10.8 feet
White balance control:	Auto, manual
Exposure compensation:	+/– 2.0 EV in 1/3 EV steps
Optical viewfinder:	Approx. 80% coverage
LCD:	⅛″ a TFT color LCD display
Power sources:	Four AA NiMH batteries, or four AA NiCd batteries AC adapter (optional)

Our sample spec sheet for a fictional digital camera.

Resolution

This can be called different things on different spec sheets, but is what we really need to know. It says that in Super High Quality mode, it has a resolution of 2,048 × 1,536 pixels. If we needed to reproduce images captured with this camera at a resolution of 300 DPI, this means we could go as big as about 5 × 7 inches.

We'll look at this is more detail in Chapter 6, but for those who don't mind math, think of it as 2,048 pixels ÷ 300 pixels per inch = 6.8 inches and 1,536 pixels ÷ 300 pixels per inch = 5.2 inches. Rotating the image 90 degrees clockwise, we get about 5 × 7 inches. If you can get by with a smaller resolution, the image size you can reproduce can be larger.

You'll see that it also tells us that it is an uncompressed TIFF file that the camera produces in this mode. This tells us that we will get an uncompressed file, and we don't have to worry about JPEG artifacting, or blemishes in an image caused by data lost during the compression process. But on the other hand, it also tells us that we are going to be producing large files and may need a higher-capacity memory card for image storage. (The spec for this is coming up, but most cameras will supply you with a card that is at least big enough to hold one image in its highest quality mode.)

But that's in Super High Quality mode. As we can see, this, like most cameras, has more than one mode. We also have a High-Quality mode, which gives us an image size of 1,024 × 768 pixels. Using our formula, a quick "back of the envelope" calculation shows us that could give us a 300-DPI image at about 3.5 × 2.5 inches. That may be okay, but look: This mode uses low JPEG compression. Truth be told, you will probably not see a great deal of artifacting in the image, but the potential is there. On the plus side, you will be able to fit more images on your storage card.

You'll also notice that there is a Fine Quality mode. This is the same resolution as High Quality but with high JPEG compression. Again, you may not see any JPEG artifacting, but there is an even greater potential for it. But again on the plus side, you will be able to fit even more images on your memory card.

Lastly, you'll find low-quality or, euphemistically, VGA mode, 640

× 480 pixels. This is unacceptable for anything but Web imaging. Most cameras give you this option for precisely that reason—you may need an image only for the Web. Why take huge images when you don't need them?

Sensitivity

We've seen that it is a somewhat dodgy proposition to assign ISO numbers to digital cameras. But people do, and we have to live with it. Most digital cameras give you a range (typically from 100 to 400) of ISO equivalencies, as this one does. If you're shooting in rather murky places, you can try setting the camera's ISO equivalency to 400, which essentially turns up the "gain" on the image sensor. It may or may not help alleviate the low-light situation, but you may also get grainier images.

Lens

This spec tells us approximately what f-stops the camera lens can use. It also tells us that we have an optical zoom lens, which is a good thing. For those who are knowledgeable about 35mm cameras, this spec sheet (like most decent spec sheets) tells us what the lens equivalent in the 35mm world is.

Shooting Modes

This camera gives us several options for shooting. The Auto mode means that we can point and shoot. It'll use default settings and *wham!* We can get a image without needing to worry about focus, exposure, etc.

But for those who want control—and sometimes default settings are not all that great—we also have a Manual mode that lets us set a variety of controls (We'll cover these in the next chapter.) We also have a Flash mode, which lets us shoot with the built-in flash. There is also a Macro mode, which lets us shoot objects close up. Macro modes usually work very well for product shooting. The next spec tells us how close we can get to our subjects.

Focus Range (from lens)

In Standard shooting mode, we can get a sharp image of the subject if it is at least 1.5 feet from the lens. It can be as far away as infinity (∞). In Macro (i.e., close-up) mode, you can shoot subjects from 0.4 to 1.5 feet.

Recording Media

This tells us that the camera uses CompactFlash rather than SmartMedia. As we'll see in Chapter 5, both have their pluses and minuses. All I'll say on the subject for now is that CompactFlash at the moment comes in higher capacities than SmartMedia, but that gulf is closing, as is the difference in price. If the choice of removable media is a serious issue to you, be sure to look for this section of the spec sheet.

Shutter Speed

We can adjust our shutter speed, in this case from 2 seconds (for low-light situations) to 1/1,000 second. Some cameras can go as quickly as 1/10,000 second.

Auto Focus

This tells us that it uses a through-the-lens (TTL) auto focusing (AF) system. Usually you can refer back to the focus range spec to see what the auto focus range is.

Flash Range

This tells us what the range of the built-in flash is. If the camera has a "hot shoe" for attaching external flashes, you may want to avail yourself of one if you need greater distance. Most built-in flashes on these types of cameras do not have a very wide range at all.

White Balance Control

Despite its name, white light comes in different colors, which can vary according to the light source you're shooting with. For example, incandescent light (the kind you normally find in standard light bulbs) tends to be yellow-red or somewhat orangey. Fluorescent light tends to be kind of greenish. And natural sunlight will also have different color characteristics. The color of light will naturally affect how your images look. White balance controls on cameras can—either automatically or manually—compensate for the predominant light source. Alternately, if you are doing somewhat artsy types of photography, you can change your white balance to a setting other than what predominates, to add color effects to your images.

Exposure Compensation

Many cameras give you the ability to under- or overexpose an image, an ability called exposure compensation. Many digital photographers have found that digital images tended to be overexposed, and by setting the exposure compensation to slightly underexpose an image, they have gotten better images. Some photographers—in both film and digital—use a technique called *exposure bracketing,* taking a set of images with different exposure settings. This will hopefully result in at least one image with a proper exposure.

Optical Viewfinder

It's comforting to know that this camera has an optical viewfinder; not all digital cameras do. Some models rely on the LCD on the back of the camera to frame images. That's good and bad. On the plus side, it is more comfortable, especially if you wear glasses. It can also be easier to frame images at odd angles, and some camera models have a swiveling lens design that lets you shoot over people's heads when you're in crowd situations. You can hold the camera up high, point the LCD down, and see what it is you're shooting, even if your eyes don't have a direct line of sight to the subject. But on the downside, cameras that rely on the LCD in lieu of an optical viewfinder tear through batteries like crazy. Most digital cameras come with rechargeable batteries, but it can be a pain to have to change them so frequently. And let's face it, we aren't always good about recharging them.

Anyway, back to the optical viewfinder. Some cameras have TTL (through the lens) viewfinders, which means that you're seeing in the viewfinder what the lens is seeing. In most of the Instamatic-like cameras, the viewfinder is separate from the lens view. This results in the problem of parallax, or the difference in what you see through the viewfinder versus what the lens sees. This spec (80 percent coverage) means that in the viewfinder you'll see about 80 percent of what the lens sees. Some optical viewfinders also have what are known as diopter adjustment wheels, which let the focus be adjusted in the viewfinder to compensate for near- or farsightedness on the part of the photographer.

LCD

This tells us that we have a color LCD on the back of the camera. Most digital cameras do; it's scarcely worth buying one that doesn't.

Power Sources
This tells us that the camera uses four AA-size nickel metal hydride (NiMH) or nickel-cadmium (NiCd) batteries, which are usually rechargeable—a great boon, since these cameras drain batteries very rapidly. Most camera manufacturers supply a set of batteries, and some are kind enough to supply a recharger. Only use the types of batteries that are specified by the manufacturer, or you could end up destroying the camera. Also, if you do get a recharger, I implore you never to try to recharge disposable batteries, or you'll have an explosion on your hands, which would be bad juju.

So, we've come to the end of our sample spec sheet. Different manufacturers organize their spec sheets in different ways, and some features are called different things, but what we've covered above tends to be the most pertinent information you'll need to read a spec sheet and decide whether a camera is suited for your purposes.

CMOS Interlude
Before we get to the next chapter, let's digress briefly into the world of CMOS. As you would expect, the CCD hegemony in the digital camera arena has been challenged—though by many accounts unsuccessfully—by what are known as CMOS cameras. CMOS stands for complementary metal-oxide semiconductor, a type of integrated circuit often found in computer processors or memory chips. The CMOS chip was developed by VLSI Vision Ltd. of Edinburgh, Scotland. The chip works with a high-speed digital signal processor from Texas Instruments and has an active-pixel sensor that helps provide "live viewing" that allows users to compose and focus their shots.

The first camera to generate any hoopla about CMOS was the CMOS Pro, developed by Sound Vision. The camera, which came out in mid-1997, could capture 1,000 × 800-pixel—or 2.4-MB—images. The CMOS Pro was targeted primarily toward studio photographers, and the vendor reported that the chipset could handle "hot highlights" better than CCD cameras.

CMOS chips are more typically used for making memory chips, and CMOS advocates tout the inexpensive manufacturing process, as well as the ability to perform on-chip processing, a function that is lacking in CCDs.

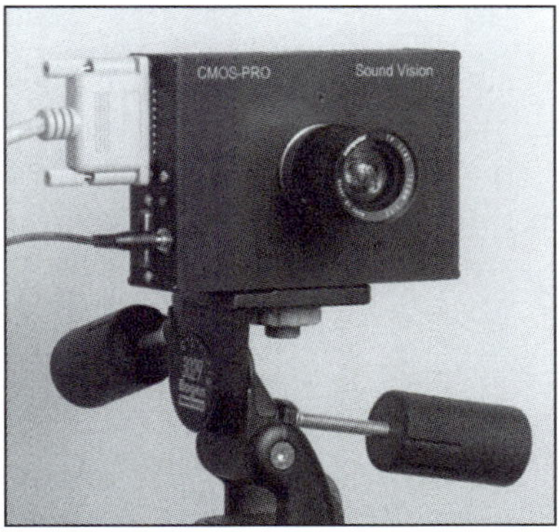

SoundVision's CMOS Pro, which debuted in 1997, could capture 1,000 × 800-pixel images and was targeted primarily toward studio photographers.

That said, the bulk of the cameras on the market, especially those at the market end that we will be covering in the bulk of this book, use CCDs. It is worth the occasional cursory glance at CMOS technology, and it is likely that hot new developments in that area will appear in the not-too-distant future.

As this book was being finalized, Leaf, a division of Scitex that makes high-end professional digital camera backs, announced its C-MOST Sensor. See Chapter 9 for a discussion of this new technology.

Also, Fuji has also announced a new CCD technology called the Super CCD. The first cameras to use this technology debuted at the Photo Marketing Association (PMA) show in February 2000. We'll also look at the new Super CCD in more detail in Chapter 9.

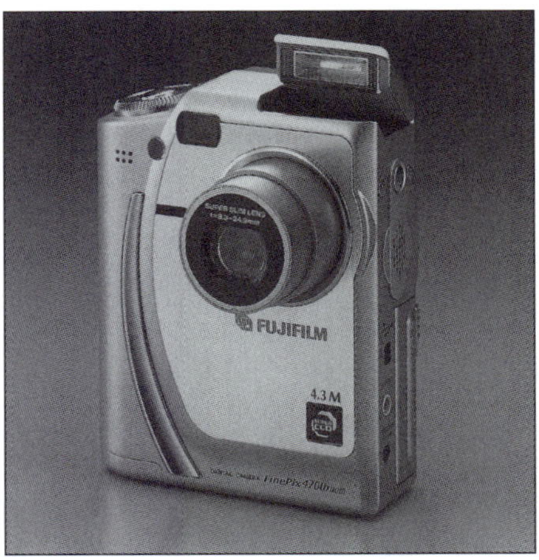

At February 2000's PMA show in Las Vegas, Fujifilm was showing off one of the fruits of its new Super CCD technology, the FinePix 4700. Fuji claims that a 1.9-Mp Super CCD can produce images comparable to 3.X-Mp images taken with a conventional CCD.

Onward

Now that we've looked at the basic technology that underlies digital cameras, in the next chapter we'll look more closely at the cameras themselves. We'll begin with a short overview of the three primary types of cameras, then we'll zoom in a bit closer on a couple of different models and run through all their salient features.

3

Anatomy of a Camera

Now that we've seen the basics of digital camera technology and what the major features are, let's zoom in—as it were—and look at a camera itself.

Choosing the Right Type of Camera

Although strict delineations are dangerous, and there will no doubt be some who would argue with this, we can divide the gamut of digital cameras into essentially three different classes, which correspond to price/performance levels. At the least expensive and, not surprisingly, lowest quality end are the "megapixel point-and-shoots."

Now, before you fire off angry letters to the publisher of this book, let me qualify what I mean by "lowest quality." I don't mean that the pictures are terrible. I'm simply referring to the fact that the image quality of an under-$1,000 camera is going to be nowhere near the quality of a high-end $30,000-plus camera. The bulk of this book is going to focus on this lower end, primarily because this is the largest market segment, both for consumers and for graphic arts pros with less stringent image requirements. The cameras in this class generally have 1.X to 3.X-megapixel CCDs and generally cost under $1,500.

The second class of digital camera is what we often refer to as "mid-range" professional cameras. These tend to cost in the $2,000 to $30,000 range and are essentially high-quality professional camera bodies with 3.X+-megapixel CCDs.

Finally, at the highest end, we have the high-quality camera backs and inserts. These cost in the $25,000-plus range, can capture 8,000 × 8,000-pixel images (often higher), and are used for extremely high-end photographic applications.

Let's look at these classes in a bit more detail.

Megapixel Point-and-Shoots

As we just mentioned, this is the lowest end of the digital camera gamut and is also the end with the greatest quantity of new developments. Although not really taken seriously by serious photographers, these cameras are the digital equivalents of the Instamatic types. Since we'll be looking at these cameras in much more depth later on in this book, we don't need to dwell on them at length here.

This is the fastest-growing class of digital camera, and between the time this book was started and the time it was published, an entire generation of cameras has come and gone. For example, in early 1998, the first 1.X-megapixel cameras appeared. In May 1999, the first 2.X-megapixel cameras debuted, and in January 2000, as this is being written, the first 3.X-megapixel cameras have debuted.

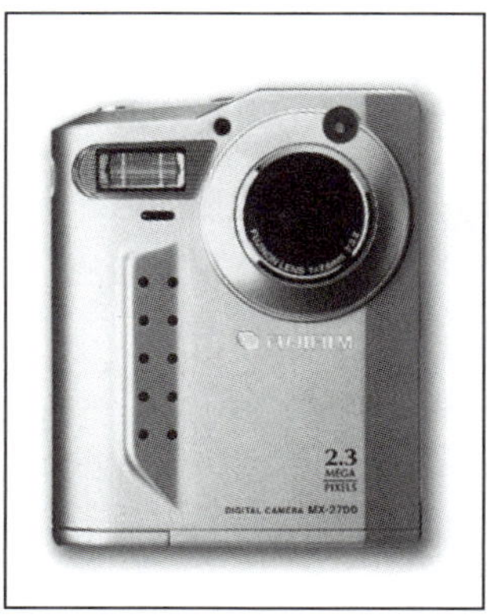

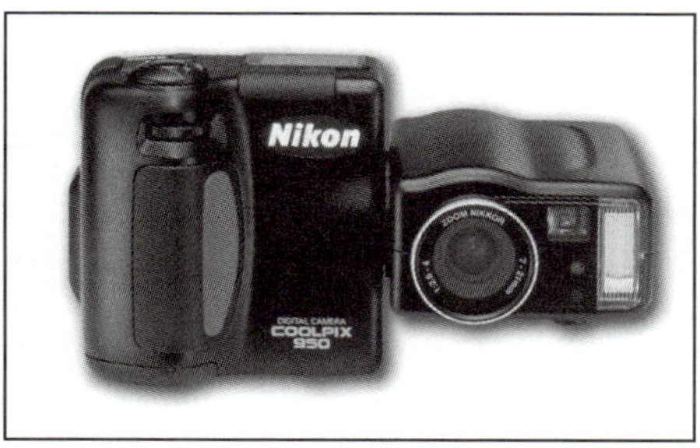

Two early 2.X-megapixel point-and-shoots—the Fuji MX-2700 (left) and Nikon Coolpix 950 (above).

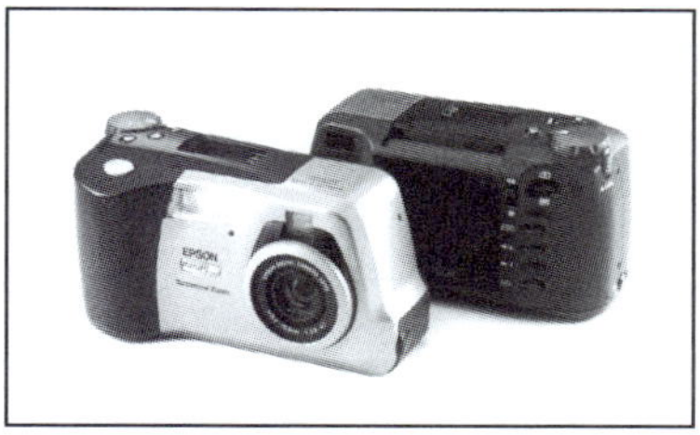

Epson's PhotoPC 750Z, which debuted in late 1998, can capture 1,280 × 960 pixels and print directly to Epson inkjet printers.

The most basic of these cameras can be had for less than $400, but don't expect terrific resolution. Resolutions in this class usually start at 640 × 480 pixels, which is suitable for Web imaging but not good for print. The maximum resolution for this class of cameras is, as of this writing, around 1,700 × 1,300 or so. Other common features of these cameras include built-in flash (which doesn't often have a very large range) and an LCD that lets you review the images you've shot. You can also usually use the LCD in a "live"

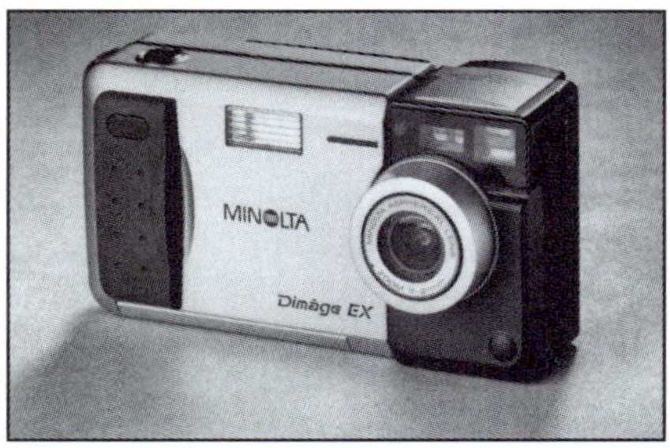

Minolta's late-1998 offering, the Dimâge EX Zoom 1500, boasted a modular body that could purportedly let users swap the CCD with larger CCDs, rather than replace the entire camera.

mode to compose a shot. (Some cameras, such as the higher-end Olympus models, have a through-the-lens viewfinder, which takes the place of the "live viewing" mode on the LCD.) Many of these cameras now have standard optical zoom lenses, and many have what is variously called a "digital zoom" or "digital telephoto." Essentially, what a digital zoom does is enlarge a 640 × 480-pixel section (usually the center) of an image. The effect is an artificial

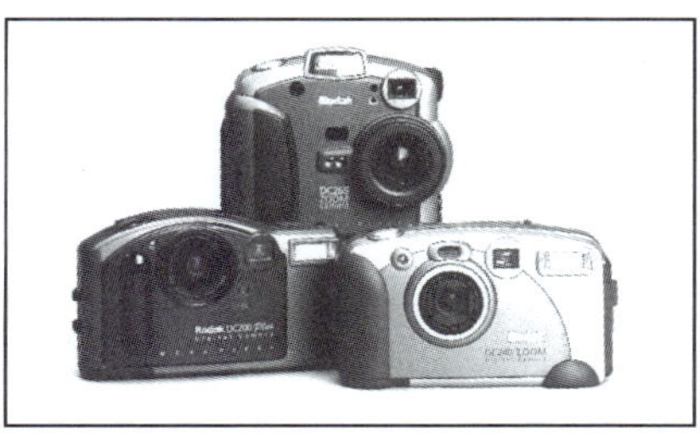

A short stack of Kodak's 1.X-Mp point-and-shoot cameras — the DC200, DC 240, and DC 265 — which debuted in spring 1999.

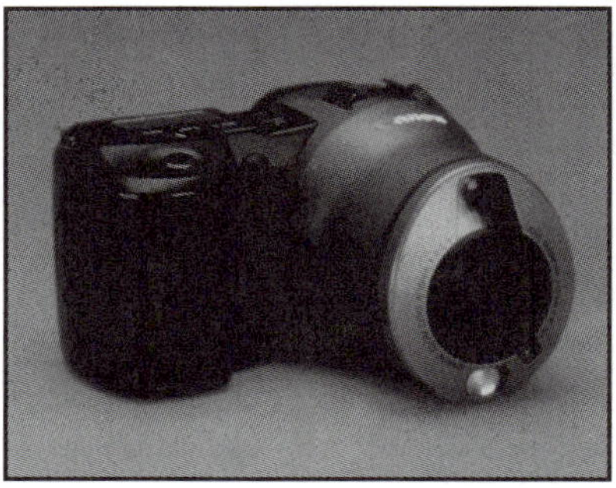

Canon's 1.68-Mp PowerShot Pro70 was targeted at the high end of the "prosumer" market.

zoom, but the low resolution of the enlarged image limits your output options. (See the section on "How Big Can I Go?" in Chapter 6 for more on this issue.)

These cameras also give you some control over camera settings, such as ISO speed (most vendors try to equate digital ISO settings with the corresponding film speed, but that isn't necessarily accurate), white balance, aperture settings, exposure, etc. The customization is good for those who know enough about photography to take advantage of them, but the advantage of these cameras is that they function very well when left in their default settings. As a result, they can accommodate the user as s/he gains more knowledge about the photographic aspect of digital photography.

These cameras also come with a variety of connectivity options for hooking the camera up to a computer. Most initially used ser-

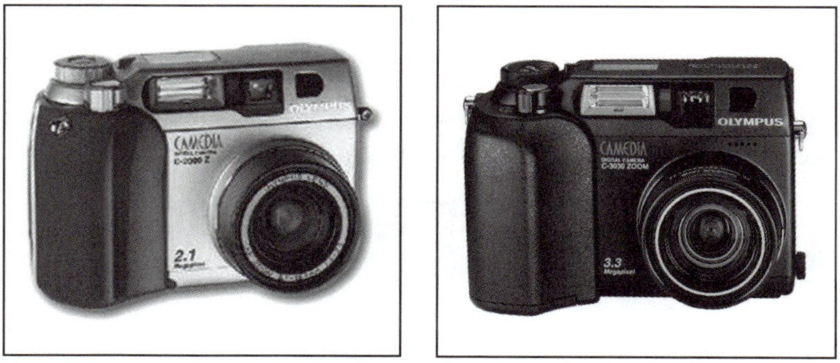

It seems like only yesterday.... In May 1999, Olympus debuted its first 2.X-Mp camera, the C-2000Z (left). In February 2000, it debuted its first 3.X-Mp camera, the C-3030Z (right).

ial or parallel connections, but many are migrating to the new Universal Serial Bus (USB), a high-speed, cross-platform connectivity option. Most also use either SmartMedia or CompactFlash removable storage cards (see Chapter 5, "Getting the Image Out of the Camera").

Most also have some type of application that lets you view thumbnails of the captured images, download images, and even perform some rudimentary image editing. Some also come bundled with third-party software for image editing, typically Adobe PhotoDeluxe, a sort of low-rent Photoshop. Some cameras also come with a TWAIN driver for letting you import images directly into Photoshop.

Many camera bundles also include some type of image-management software that lets you create and organize digital "photo albums." Some even have tools that facilitate direct e-mailing or Web posting of images. Some bundles also include panorama-stitching software, such as Enroute Imaging's QuickStitch or PowerStitch. With this type of software, you can take series of adjacent images and the software will automatically stitch them together to give you a panorama of a much larger scene than you could capture in a single frame.

At any rate, depending on whom the camera is targeted—the consumer, "prosumer," or professional—you'll find corresponding tools, utilities, or games in your camera bundle.

We'll come back to the megapixel point-and-shoots later on in this chapter.

Mid-Range Professional Cameras

Although camera manufacturers are going after the consumer market with the point-and-shoots, some of the larger camera makers like Nikon and Kodak are also targeting serious photographers and photojournalists, and there is a nice range of cameras that are high-end enough for many of their applications. These cameras are distinguished by high-quality camera bodies and optics (usually based on high-quality film cameras) and larger CCDs than you find at the lower end. For example, 6 Mp is not unusual in this class. Most allow the same level of camera-setting customization that

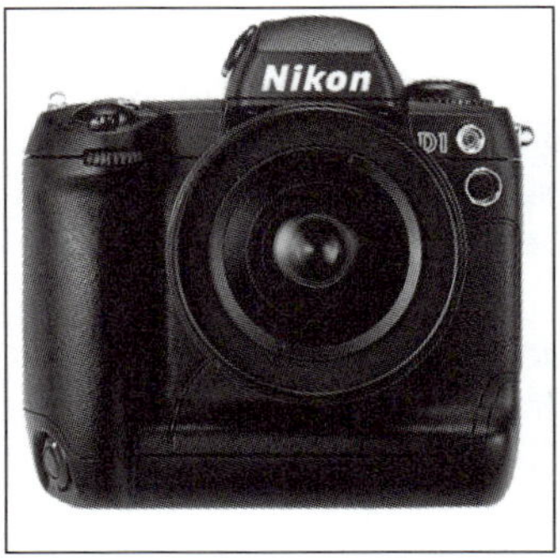

Nikon's D1, priced at $5,800, has a 2.74-Mp CCD, and accepts more than 80 different Nikon F-mount lenses. The D1 also offers ISO equivalencies up to ISO 1600, which makes the D1 well-suited to low-light photography.

high-end film cameras would give you; after all, these are meant for people who know what they're doing. Many also let you view histograms of images that have been captured, which lets you determine very precisely and quantitatively whether or not an image is of good enough quality (often the LCD itself isn't good enough to see how well an image came out). And since the file sizes are very large, they usually use higher-capacity PCMCIA cards as the storage option.

These cameras also feature serial-based camera-to-computer interfaces, although with large file sizes that can take a great deal of time. As a result, most people using these cameras tend to prefer PC card readers, which are more than a bit faster.

These cameras, as you would expect, also let you add different lenses and flashes, just like professional film cameras. So even

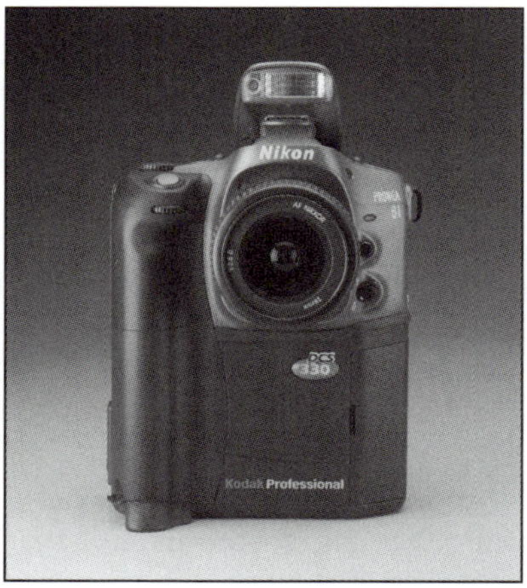

Kodak Professional's DCS series of professional digital cameras includes the DCS 330. Based on Nikon's Pronea 6i SLR camera body, the DCS 330 uses a 3-Mp CCD to capture 9-MB files. It utilizes a different type of CCD than that usually found in digital cameras, which Kodak says increases spectral response. The camera lists for $5,995.

though the CCDs of the lower-end cameras may very well catch up to these, the professional nature of these cameras makes it unlikely that point-and-shoots are going to take their place any time soon. And there's more to a CCD than just its megapixellage; Kodak Professional's DCS 330 uses a different type of CCD (indium tin oxide rather than polysilicon) that, though only a "mere" 3 Mp, captures a greater amount of light than lower-end CCDs of the same number of pixels. Also, the DCS 330 can capture up to 10-bit color per RGB channel.

High-End Scanning Backs and Inserts

At the extreme high end are the professional studio cameras, and the digital camera backs and scanning backs or "inserts." We'll take a somewhat detailed look at these cameras when we look at digital photo studios, but essentially these devices are high-quality and high-resolution CCDs that attach to the backs of view cameras, such as those made by Bronica, Hasselblad, Mamiya, and others. Some scanning backs, such as Better Light Model 6000 (and newer systems), can capture images up to 6,000 × 8,000 pixels—a file size of 137 MB.

These are very expensive systems—think in the tens of thousands of dollars—and are often found in studios.

We'll look at these in a bit more detail in Chapter 8.

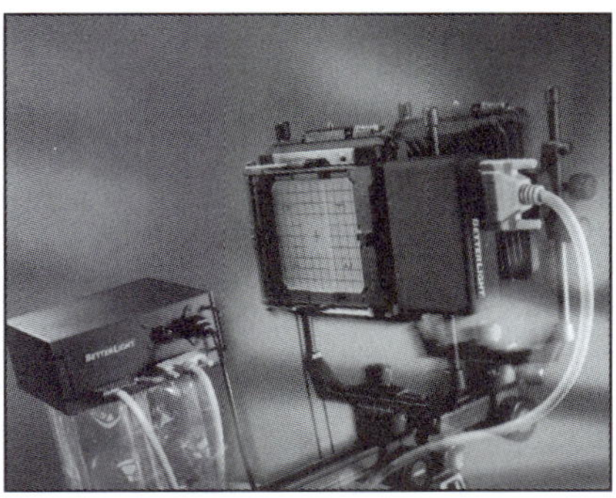

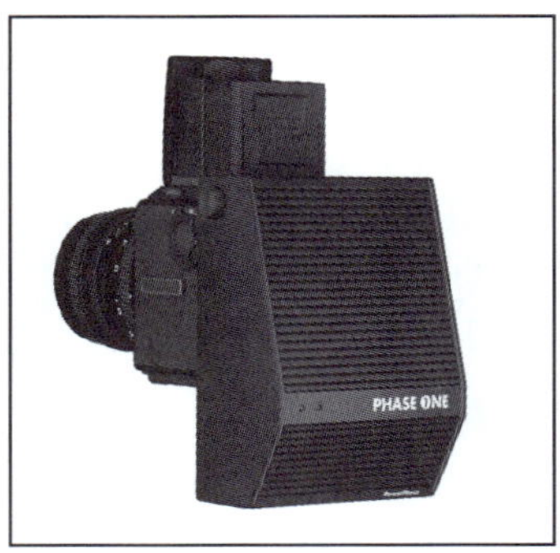

Two examples of high-end scanning systems — the Better Light Model 6000 (left) and the Phase One PowerPhase. The Better Light insert (and newer Better Light models) is compatible with any 4- × 5-inch view camera. The PowerPhase is compatible with a variety of cameras from Hasselblad, Bronica, and others.

Understanding External Camera Controls

Back to the megapixel point-and-shoots: Let's now look at the external controls that one finds on these types of digital cameras. The model we are looking at in this chapter—and the camera we've been using for much of this book—is the Olympus C-2500L, a 2.5-Mp camera. This is a bit higher-end than most of the cameras you find in this class, but it's one of my favorite models, and a good example to use here, as many of its features are also found on less expensive models.

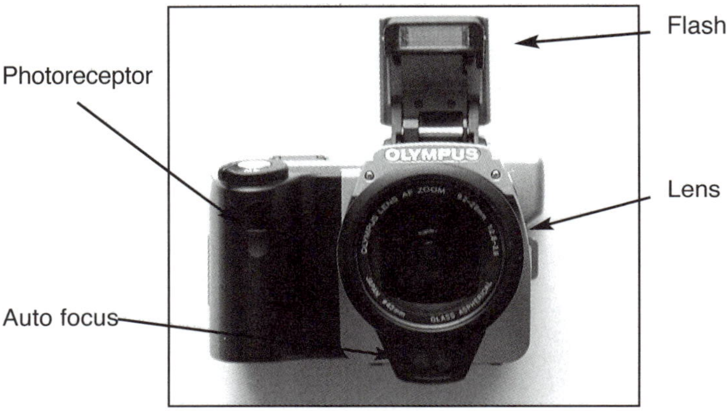

Lens

Starting at the front, the most obvious part is the lens. This particular camera has a 3× optical zoom, corresponding to a 9.2mm–2.8mm lens on a traditional film camera. Higher-end cameras in this class let you add additional lenses, and this one indeed does. An adapter or step-up ring can be screwed over the lens, and a 1.45× teleconverter lens, or an 0.8× wide-angle lens, can be added. As you would expect, this gives your digital camera added functionality if you want to become a serious hobbyist or use this camera in a professional situation.

Auto Focus

Directly beneath the lens is the auto-focus illuminator, which compensates for low brightness when using the auto-focus feature. On this camera, this feature also doubles as the self-timer signal.

Photoreceptor

There is also a photoreceptor on the front of the camera that receives the remote signal from the self-timer remote control, much like the receptor on your TV set or VCR that receives the signal from the remote.

Flash
This camera has a pop-up flash, which is released by pressing the flash pop-up button on the side of the camera. Most cameras in this class have the more traditional Instamatic-type flash that is always visible.

Turning the camera counterclockwise, we see the right side of the camera.

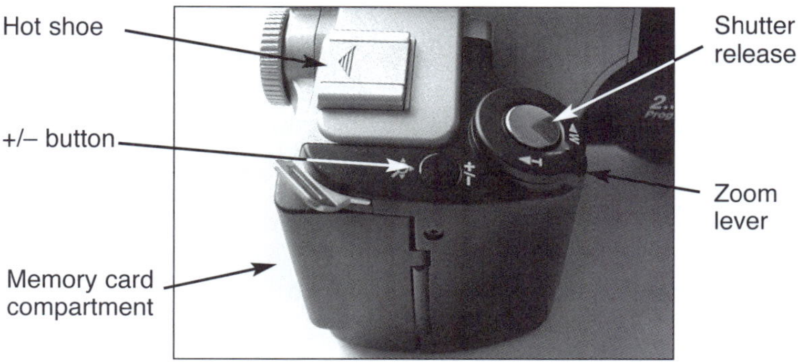

Shutter Release/Zoom Lever
The shutter release button is where you would expect it to be. Holding it down partway sets the auto focus, and pushing it down all the way snaps the shot. Holding it down lets you take a "burst" of images.

Swaddling the shutter release is the zoom lever. Pushing it counterclockwise zooms out; pushing it clockwise zooms in on the subject. Different cameras use different letters or icons to indicate which way you're zooming. In the case of this camera, it uses a "T" to designate telephoto (zoom in) and a "W" to indicate wide-angle (zoom out).

+/– Button
This button has different functions, depending upon what mode you're in. When in shooting mode, it lets you set your exposure

compensation. In playback mode, it lets you scroll through your captured images.

Hot Shoe

Some cameras have what is called a hot shoe to let you add an external flash, which may be more powerful than the meager built-in one. This also makes the camera more useful in professional applications.

Memory Card Compartment

Cameras that use flash memory cards naturally need to have a slot for them. This camera, rather unusually, has slots for both SmartMedia and CompactFlash.

Sometimes this compartment is located on the bottom of the camera, but it is usually protected by a hinged flap. This camera also has a flashing light that tells you when the camera is reading or writing to the card.

It is important that you never open the compartment or try to remove a card while the camera is writing or reading, as data or the card can be damaged. That should be obvious, but people do it anyway.

Turning to the back of the camera, where a good portion of the action is:

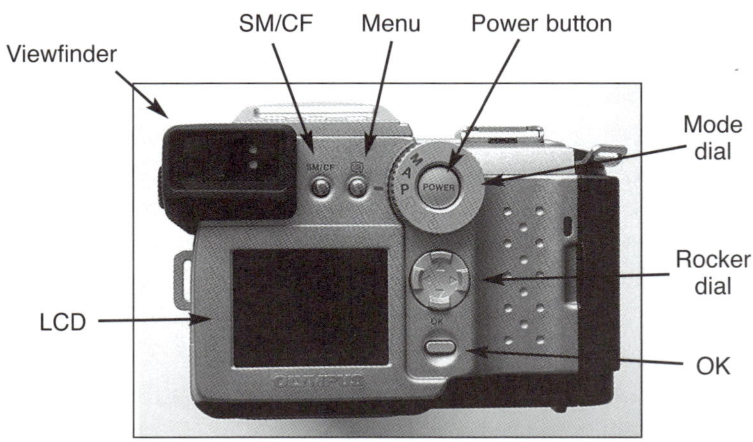

Power Button/Mode Dial

Fairly prominent is the power button, which, as you would expect, turns the camera on and off. In earlier Olympus models, the power button was where you would expect the shutter release button to be, which caused some problems. Olympus has since rethought the design. Different cameras handle power on and off in different ways. Some don't have a button, per se; they have a single dial that turns from off to record to play.

Speaking of mode dials, this one has six modes. "M" is the manual mode, which is the mode you would select when you want to set your own exposure and shutter speed, rather than let the camera do it automatically. "A" is the aperture mode, which lets you set your own aperture, but the camera determines its own shutter speed. "P" is the program mode, which is the fully automatic mode. Aperture and shutter speed are set automatically.

There is also playback mode, which activates the LCD and lets you review your captured images. There is a printer mode, which lets you print directly to a connected printer, such as the P-330U printer from Olympus. (Manufacturers prefer that you print to their own printers.) Lastly, we have a computer mode, which is the mode you use when connected serially, parallelly, or USBly to a computer.

Rocker Dial

Most cameras use what are known as rocker dials or jog dials. These can be confusing, especially as they move in four directions, and their functions vary depending on which mode you're in. In this case, it lets you set your aperture and/or shutter speed while in shooting modes, or maneuver around menus, or scroll through images if you're in playback mode.

OK

And there is an OK button that is essentially an "enter" button. These are sometimes called "select" buttons on other cameras and are the button you press when you want to select something in a menu.

Menu

This button lets you activate the on-screen menus on the LCD. The menus, which we'll get to, let you select various camera settings, playback options, record modes, etc. Again, depending on which mode you're in, you may get a different set of menus. It varies by camera and by how much control a camera gives you over various camera settings. Cameras that don't give you many options obviously don't need many menus.

SM/CF

Most cameras don't have this button, because most cameras don't use two different memory cards. But on this camera, this button toggles between the SmartMedia and the CompactFlash card.

LCD

The big black square is the LCD, which is where you review your captured images and set your menu settings. It's inconceivable that a digital camera wouldn't have an LCD; after all, the primary benefit of digital is that you can see your images as soon as you've taken them and discard them if they are not very good. Some cameras also have a live preview mode, which lets you use the LCD to frame and compose shots, rather than using the optical viewfinder. However, that is because many cameras do not have through-the-lens (TTL) viewfinders. As you may recall from the last chapter, viewfinders that are not TTL can suffer from the problem of parallax, causing that what-you-see-may-not-be-what-you-get result. Using the live preview feature on the LCD alleviates this problem but also eats up battery life. In this case of this camera, the viewfinder *is* TTL, so there is no real need for a live preview via the LCD.

Viewfinder

As you would expect, this is the thing you look through to take a picture. There is a little wheel on the side that lets you make diopter adjustments, useful if you wear glasses and need to sharpen or blur the image as seen through the viewfinder. This doesn't affect the captured image, just how it is viewed in the viewfinder.

Viewfinders often have one or two lamps that mean various things. Usually, a green light that does not blink means that the camera is happy, and you are clear to take a picture. If the green light is blinking, there could be a problem, such as the focus not being locked (in the case of this camera). This camera also has an orange lamp, which lets you know if either a flash is required or the flash is not ready. Other cameras have red lights that provide various warnings, usually about low light or flash unavailability.

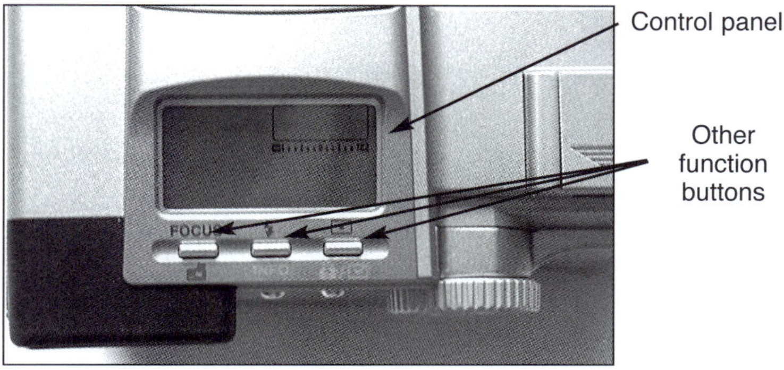

Control Panel

Depending on your camera, you may have a simple or complex control panel. Some can seem like a fever dream at first, but as you get used to it, you'll become a pro at figuring out what each little icon and number means. Here you'll usually find a battery level indicator, your quality mode (SHQ, HQ, etc.), the number of images you have left, whether you are in macro mode or some other specialty mode, whether the flash is on and if it is in manual or auto mode, whether spot metering is on, your aperture, your ISO equivalent speed, and any errors, such as memory card problems.

Other Function Buttons

You have to feel for the designers and engineers of digital cameras. Users want more controls and commands, but they don't want a camera studded with a thick layer of buttons. As a result, different buttons have to do different things, depending upon your mode. In this case, we have three buttons that have six functions. The leftmost lets us, while shooting, enter the macro mode or take shots of close-up objects. Macro mode is usually good for images as close as 1 foot. This camera, as well as some others, has a super macro mode, which lets you get closer to your subjects.

In playback mode, this button erases an image.

The center button, while shooting, lets you turn the flash off and on.

When playing back, this button displays information about the image you are viewing, such as aperture, ISO, exposure compensation, etc., which can be useful to know (especially when writing a book on how to use a digital camera and you lose track of what images were shot with what settings).

The rightmost button, while shooting, lets you use spot metering, which helps get the right exposure with dark subjects. While playing back, this button lets you write-protect an image, meaning that it can't be accidentally erased.

Okay, I think we're nearly done. One more counterclockwise turn, and we're on the left side of the camera.

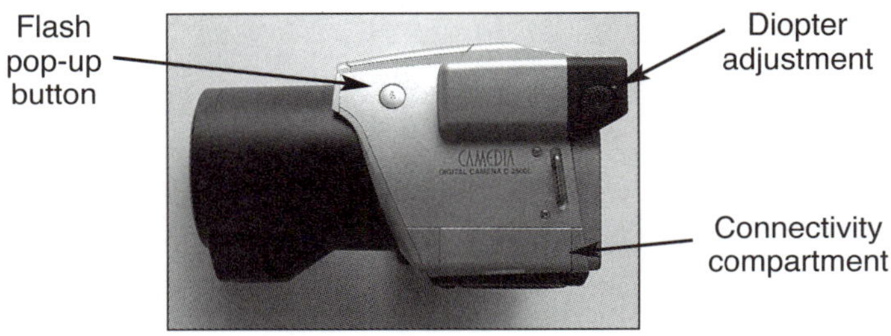

Connectivity Compartment

Most cameras have a compartment with various input/output jacks, the exact configurations of which can vary. This one has a computer connectivity jack. This is a ⅛-inch jack. The cord (supplied) can then be connected to a PC's parallel port or a Mac's serial port. Some cameras are increasingly offering USB connectivity. There is also a place to plug in the AC cord (sometimes supplied, sometimes optional), which lets you save on batteries if you're shooting or playing back within close proximity to an

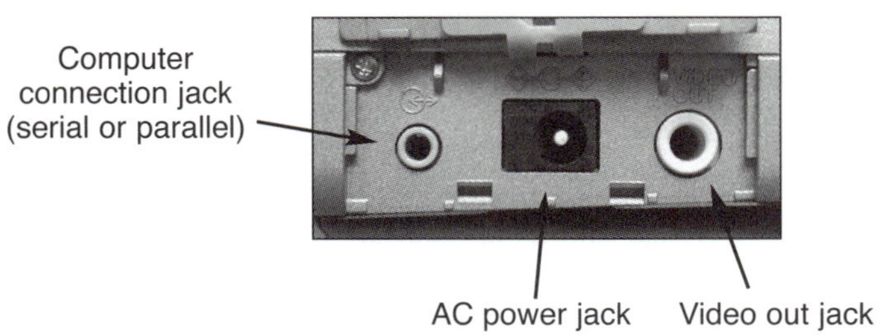

electrical outlet. And most cameras also have a video-out port, which lets you connect to a VCR or TV and view your images on television.

The bottom of the camera also has a battery compartment as well as a socket for attaching the camera to a tripod.

For Comparison's Sake

To show you how camera designs can vary, let's look briefly at a lower-end digital camera, the PhotoPC 750Z from Epson. We won't go through each control in detail, but you can get an idea of how models differ from each other.

On the front of the camera:

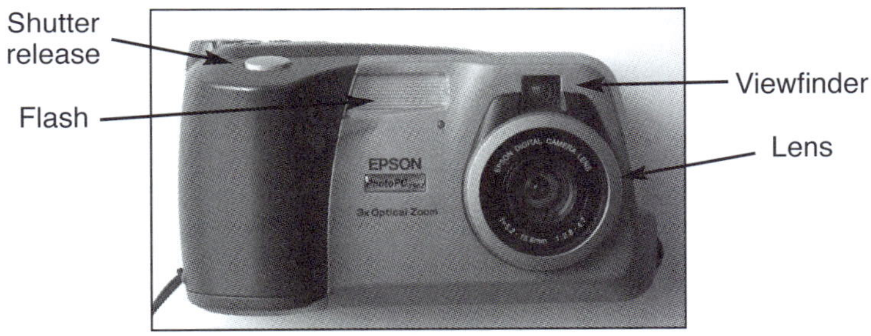

We've got lens, viewfinder, and flash on the front. Very Instamaticky. Simple shutter button at the top left.

On the top:

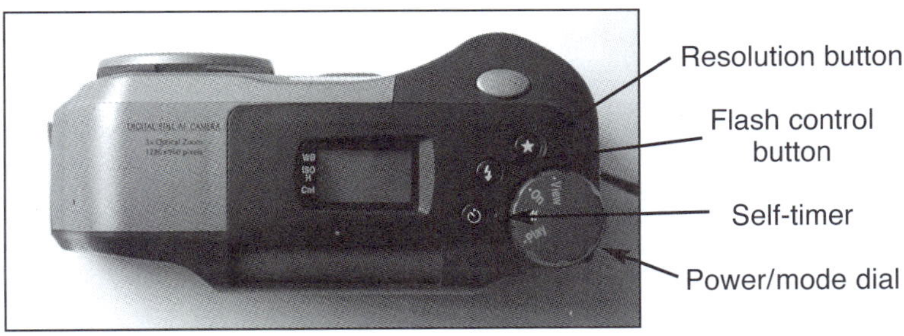

We've got the power/mode dial. The On mode lets you shoot without the LCD, and View is the live preview via the LCD mode. Play is, as you would expect, the playback mode. The star button lets you set your resolution; the flash button turns the flash off and on; and the self-timer button lets you set the self-timer.

On the back:

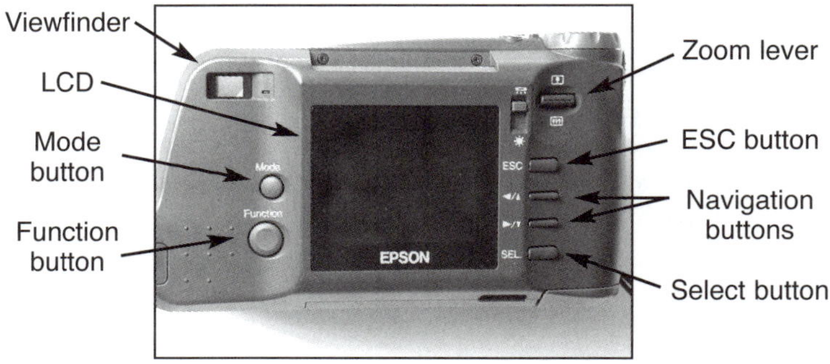

We've got, at the top right, the zoom lever; up is telephoto, down is wide-angle. This camera also has a 3× optical zoom (5.2–15.6mm). The buttons on the back correspond to various menu modes and the navigation thereof. The ESC button gets you out of a menu, and the SEL button is essentially an OK or enter button.

Understanding Internal Menus and Controls

Now that we've explored the exterior, let's turn the camera on and have a look at some of the typical menu settings and see what they all mean.

We're once again going to use the Olympus C-2500L as our example, but many of these features will be common to most digital cameras, although this model is a bit more involved. We'll look again at the Epson PhotoPC 750Z for a comparison and a contrast.

When in any of the shooting modes, hitting the menu button on the back of the camera brings up four different screens that are scrolled through using the rocker dial.

Hitting the up or down arrow moves the cursor up or down, and hitting the left or right arrow moves the cursor left or right. Seems fairly straightforward.

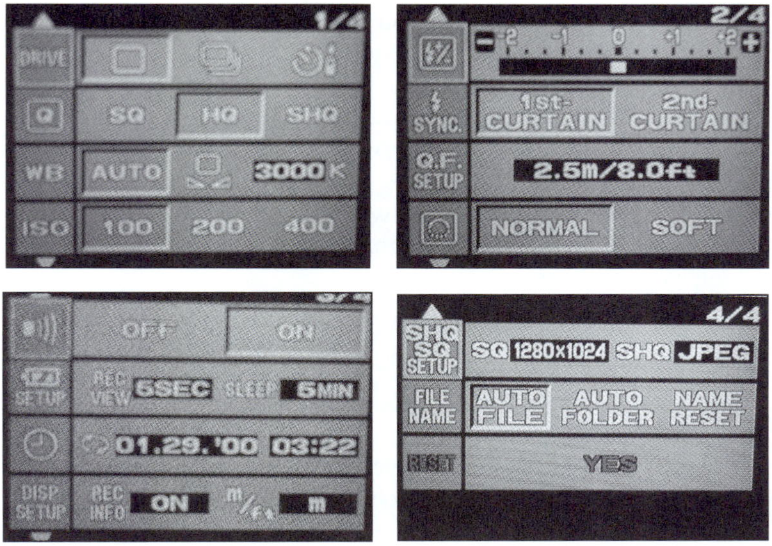

So, beginning with the first line of the first menu screen:

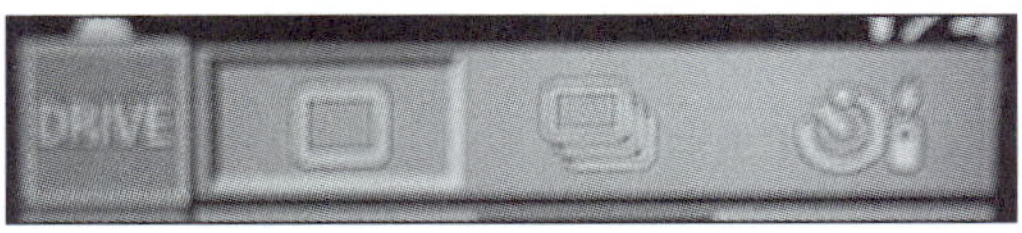

The first menu line refers to whether you want to take only one image when the shutter release is depressed, or whether you want to shoot in "burst" mode. In burst mode, you can take up to five images in rapid succession. Alternately, you can use the self-timer and set it in this menu field. Many cameras have a burst mode of varying power. It is often expressed as some number of images or frames per second. The number you can take is also a function of how much memory card space you have available and what resolution setting you're in.

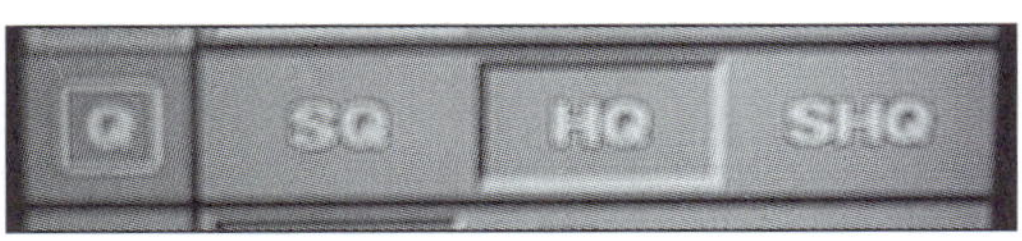

The second menu line is where you enter your quality setting. Just about every camera has this kind of setting, although many have it as a hardware button on the exterior of the camera.

Our choices are SQ (standard quality), HQ (high quality), and SHQ (super high quality). In almost all cameras, high quality is not the highest quality. There is always just one more quality—an "11," if you will. It's kind of like when you order a pizza and there is no small; small is actually medium. You can drive yourself crazy trying to make sense of it.

The third menu line is where you set your white balance. You can always use auto, if you want. Alternately, you can set it using a reference. By selecting the second icon, you then snap a shot of a white piece of paper, which the camera will then use as a white reference. You use this mode when you don't like the way colors are coming out.

Alternately, you can set your white balance based on color temperature. Lowering color temperature makes colors look "cool." For example, a red sky at sunset may end up looking like blue sky. Conversely, raising color temperature makes colors look "warmer." That same red sky will have the accent on the red. Color temperature is measured in degrees Kelvin (K); 5,000 K is the standard color temperature. Many cameras let you set it lower or higher. Playing with white balance settings can give you a good sense of how color temperature affects image quality.

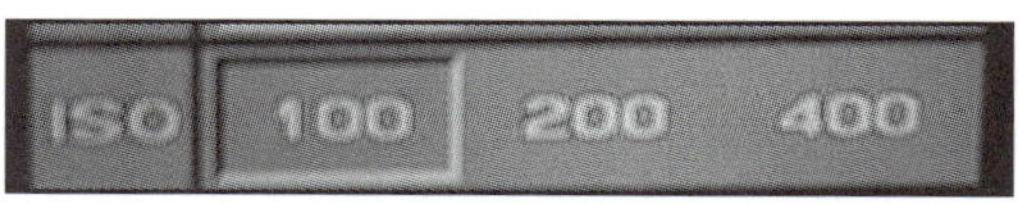

The fourth menu line is where you set your "film speed" or the ISO equivalency. In low-light situations, using the ISO 400 setting may yield a better image, at least in terms of lighting, although you may end up with a somewhat grainier image.

The second menu screen mostly involves your flash settings.

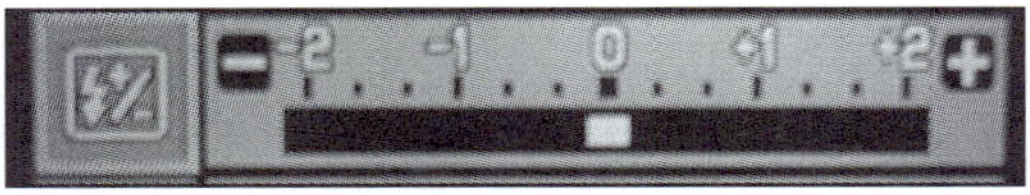

The first line is where you set your flash control, or your exposure compensation, or how much or how little flash is used. Moving the cursor in the "–" direction dims the flash in ⅓ EV increments; moving in the "+" direction brightens the flash in the same increments.

By the way, this is the second piece of the exposure compensation puzzle that relates only to the flash. The other, more typical means of exposure compensation is achieved via the +/– button on the top of the camera.

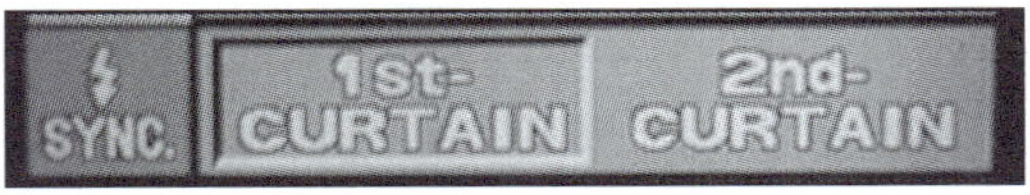

The second line of this menu screen refers to flash synchronization. First curtain and second curtain refer to the beginning or end of a slow shutter release, respectively. Each has a different effect, and they are used to create special effects. We'll cover them in the next chapter, albeit briefly.

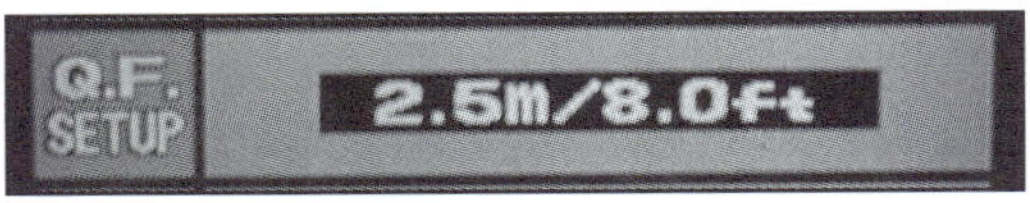

The third line in this screen is where you specify your focal distance for quick-focus picture taking. This lets you specify how far away an object is, allowing you to focus on it more easily.

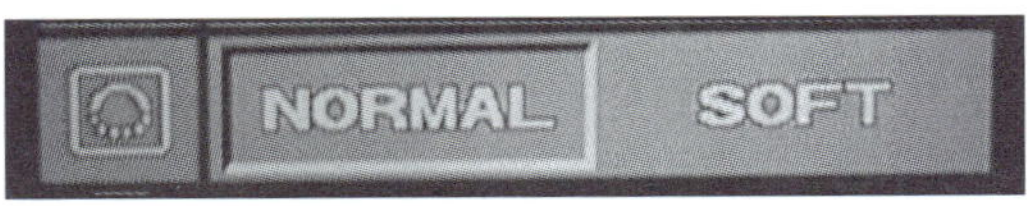

The fourth line lets you set your sharpness, if you want a sharp image or more of a soft focus. Normal is the default, and for a reason.

The next menu screen, like that for many digital cameras, lets you set various "housekeeping"-related functions.

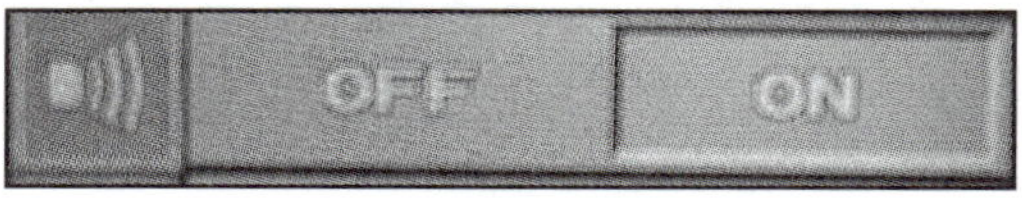

For example, the first line lets you determine whether you want the camera to beep when it snaps a picture. This may seem like a silly point to dwell on, but when the flash is turned off, some cameras are so quiet that you don't really know that a picture has been snapped. Thus, the beep lets you know that you (and your subject) can move.

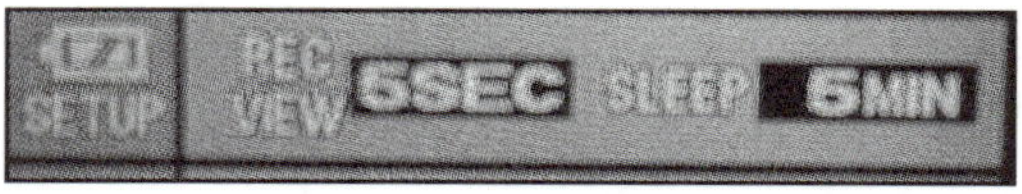

One convenient battery-saving feature of many digital cameras is a sleep mode. What this means is that if you're out on a shoot, such as, say, a tour of Hearst Castle, you don't have to keep turning the camera on and off to save battery life. You can set how long the camera is to remain inactive before it goes to sleep.

Remember, though, that setting it at less than a minute can be a pain (you'll need to keep waking it up just about every time you want to take a picture) but too long can be ineffective at saving battery life. I've always found about 5 minutes to be effective. And in this menu line, you can also set how long the just-snapped picture remains on the display.

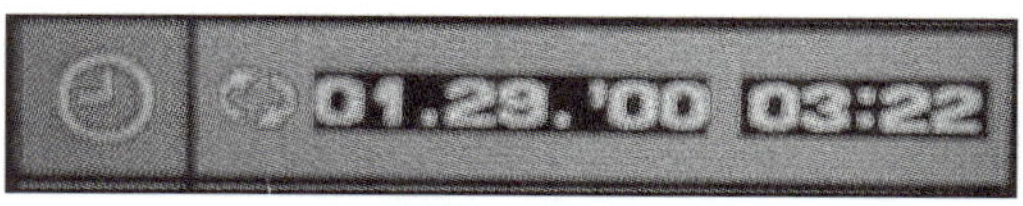

Some cameras don't let you *not* set the date and time, but it can be convenient to know when a picture (or set of pictures) was shot.

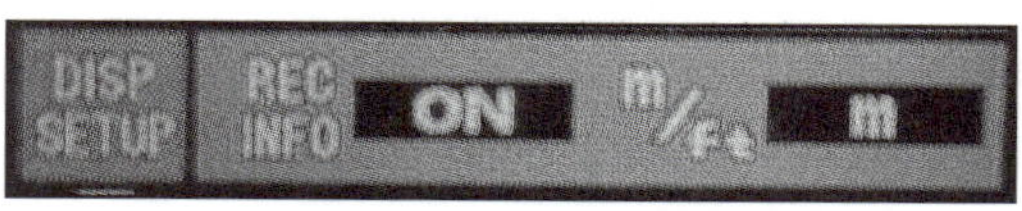

Here, you can set whether you want information about your settings (exposure, shutter speed, etc.) to display on the monitor. You can also decide what units you want your manual focusing to use—meters or feet.

Finally, the last menu screen lets you determine how you want to save the image:

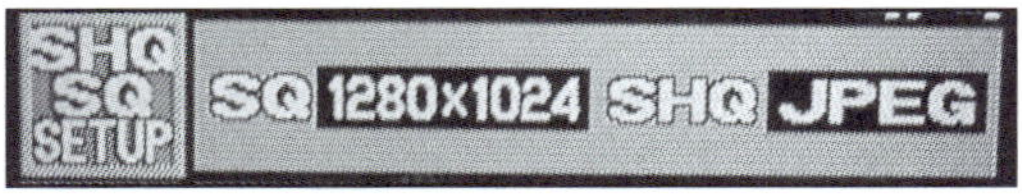

The top row lets us toggle among a variety of resolutions and file formats (well, actually only TIFF and JPEG).

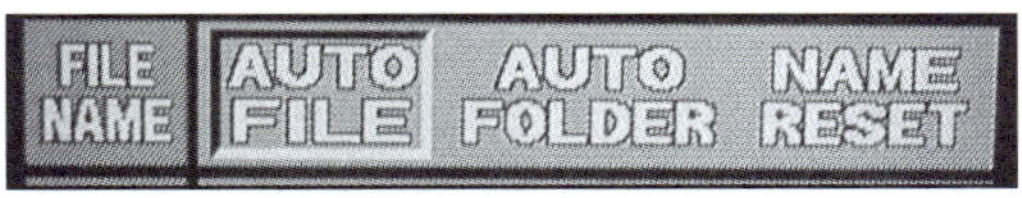

Some cameras let you specify how files and the folders they're in are named and organized. Or you can leave it up to the camera to decide.

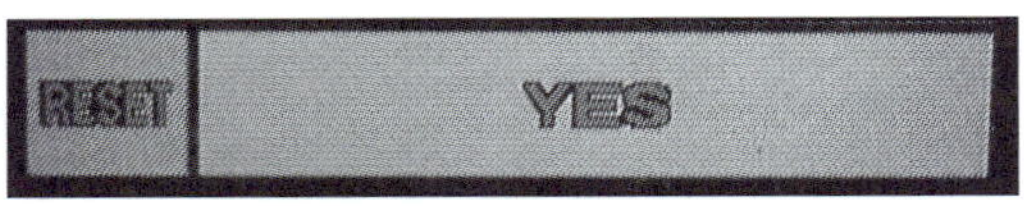

Finally, you can just have the camera reset the whole kit and caboodle.

In playback mode, you don't have a great deal to choose from.

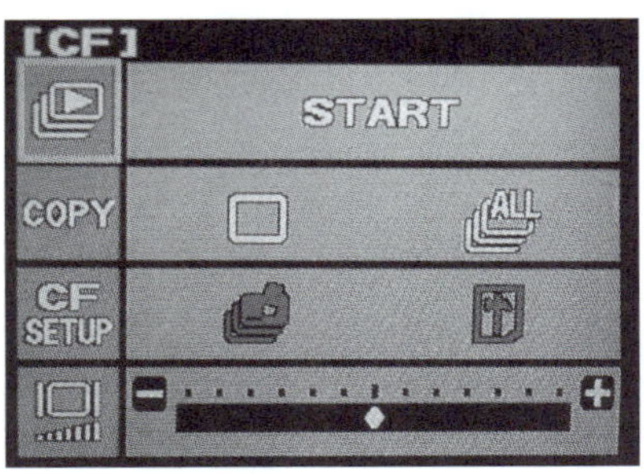

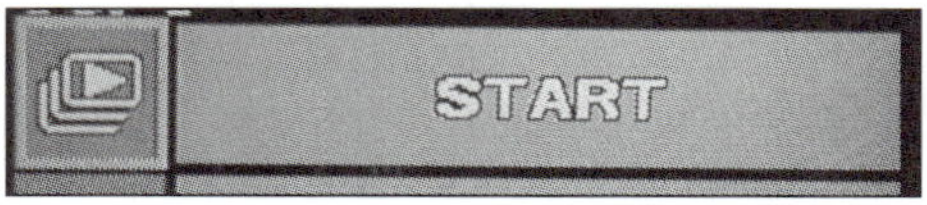

The first line lets you start an auto-segue, or a kind of slide show whereby the camera automatically scrolls from one image to the next.

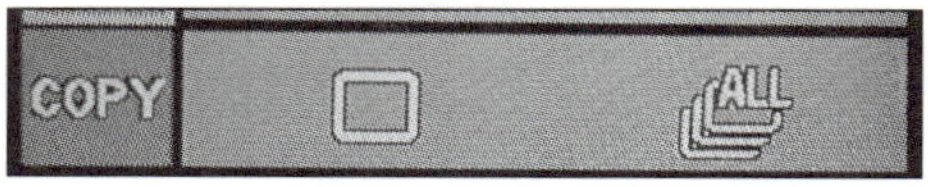

This camera, by virtue of the fact that it has both CompactFlash and SmartMedia, can let you back up your images. This command lets you determine if you want to copy one image at a time or en masse. It's an unusual feature in single-card cameras.

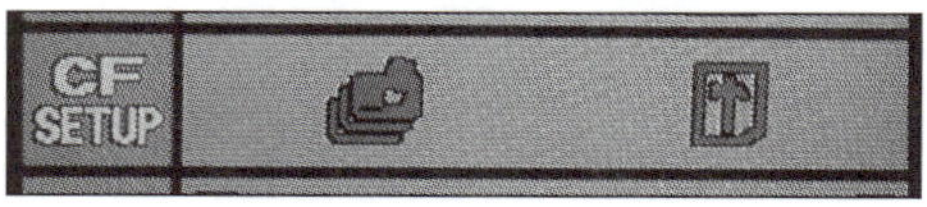

Most cameras, though, let you erase images one by one or reformat an entire card. This model lets you erase single images from a button on the top of the camera.

The icon on the left will simply erase all the images. The one on the right will reformat the card, which may need to be done if using a third-party card that has been formatted by a computer or other camera, etc.

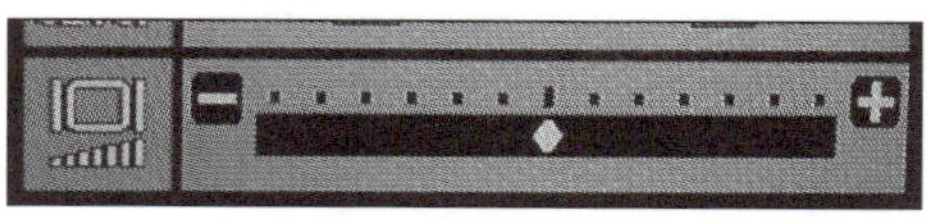

And finally, you can set the brightness of the LCD display, which you may want to do while reviewing your images on a PC, so you can determine from looking at the LCD whether images are too over- or underexposed. With wildly inaccurate LCDs, it can be hard to tell.

Again, for Comparison's Sake

Let's just zip through a few of the menus on the Epson PhotoPC 750Z and see what options Epson gives us.

We turn the power dial into the view mode, and immediately the following message comes up.

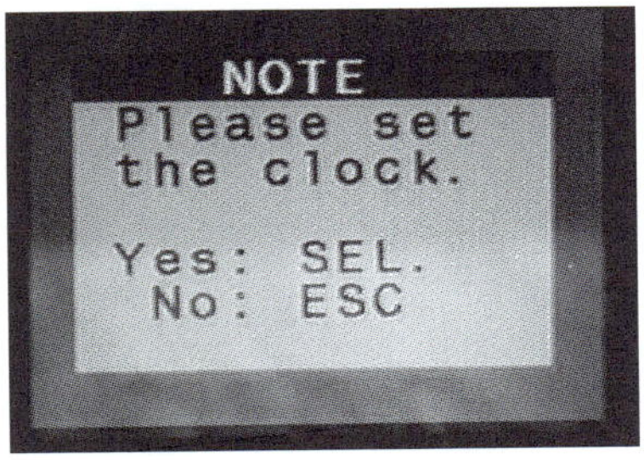

Nag, nag, nag. Fine, we set the clock and the date, and then we hit the SEL button. This lets us make our various camera settings. You'll note that our options aren't as extensive as on the Olympus, but then this camera is about $1,000 less than the Olympus.

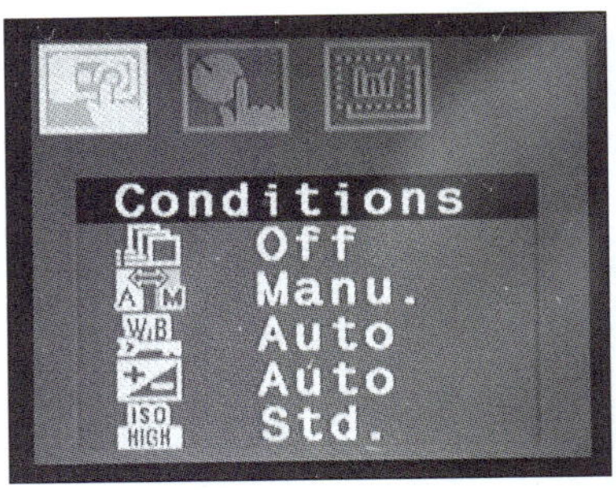

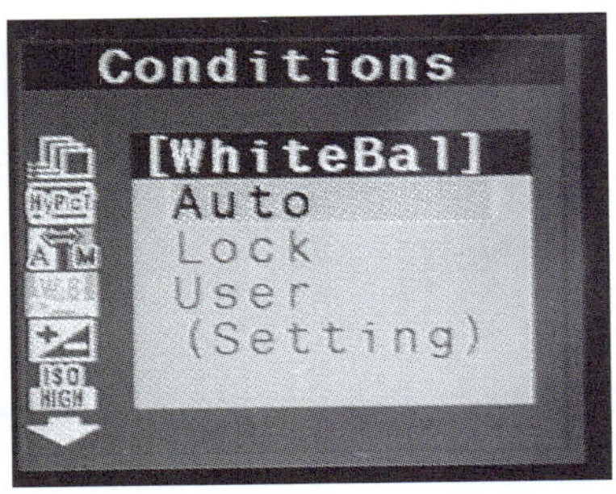

By setting the camera to manual (Manu.), we can "ungray-out" the manual settings (left). The first thing we can set is the white balance (right).

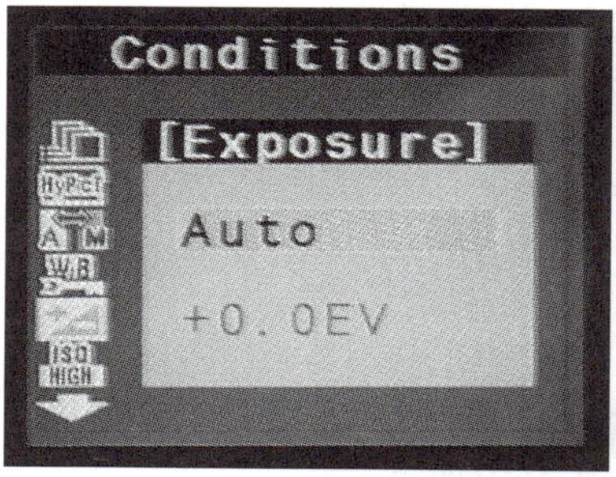

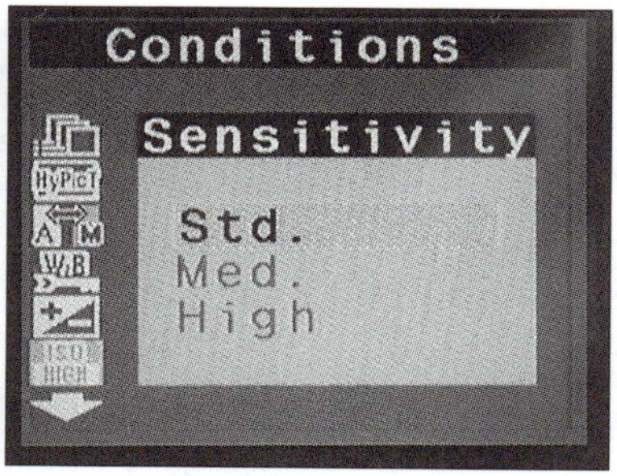

We've also got options to set the exposure compensation (left), much like we saw with the Olympus. We can also set the sensitivity, or ISO equivalency. Here, rather than confuse matters, Epson uses standard, medium, and high (right), roughly corresponding to ISO 100, 200, and 400 respectively.

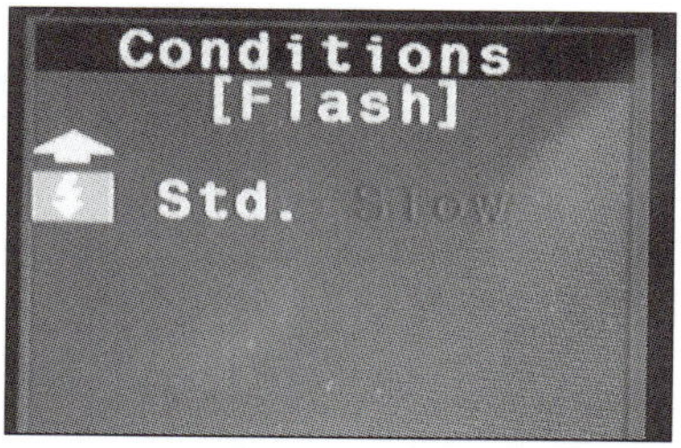

We can also set the flash to fire slowly, if we desire.

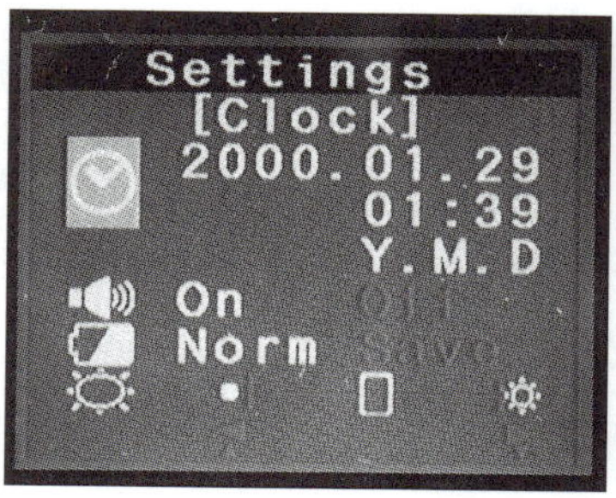

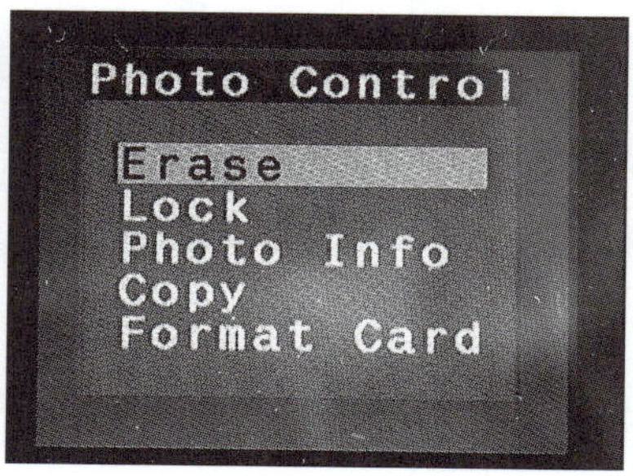

In playback mode, we hit SEL and get a number of options and different screens. Most notably, we get our time and date settings (now that the camera is happy that we set them), as well as our battery status, whether we have the sound turned on, and other housekeeping tasks. We can also erase images, lock an image or the card, copy images, and format the card. Other menus allow us to print to an Epson inkjet printer, see all the menu displays in Japanese rather than English, and other such things.

We can see how these two cameras differ from each other in their functionality. But we shouldn't conclude that the Epson is a "cheap" camera. It's actually one of the best digital cameras with which we've experimented. It's just not targeted toward the high-end, professional or "prosumer" that may salivate over the Olympus.

The following are the things you need to bear in mind when looking for a digital camera.

Accessories

No good digital camera comes without accessories. Listed here are some of the typical sorts of gear that you usually find in the box with a point-and-shoot megapixel camera.

Batteries

A great boon to digital camera users are reusable, rechargeable batteries, typically nickel-metal hydride (NiMH) or nickel-cadmium (Ni-Cd). You also usually get a recharger in the box.

The rechargers are small plastic trays that hold all four batteries and have a pop-out electrical plug on the back, which just pops into an outlet. A set of red lights tells you when your batteries are done charging (it usually takes a few hours to recharge batteries from completely dead to completely alive).

As of late, camera manufacturers have been including a battery charger that has a detachable AC cord. This is useful for use on power strips and surge protectors and other electrical setups where it is unwieldy to plug in the whole recharger. It is a bit less elegant, though, and the cord can be cumbersome.

Strap

Most cameras come with some sort of strap to help keep you from dropping the camera. The lower-end models have a basic type of

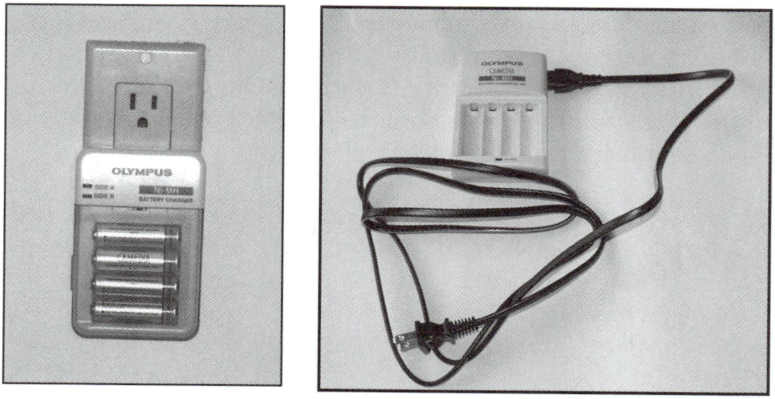

Typical battery rechargers come in one of two configurations, a direct-to-outlet version and a version that uses a detachable AC cord. Chacun à son goût.

cord that wraps around your wrist, while the higher-end models have a neck strap that lets you wear the camera around your neck.

Lens Cap

Most cameras feature a lens cap, the design of which varies from model to model. Some are simple press-on-and-hope-they-stay affairs, while others have plastic latches that fasten them securely to the lens. An even cooler design are the cameras that have a built-in lens cap, an iris-like arrangement that opens when the camera is powered on. This prevents you from ever losing the lens cap.

AC Cords

Given how quickly digital cameras can go through batteries, it is fortunate that some models come with AC cords (some have optional AC cords that are sold separately). Although AC cords are not practical when out shooting in the field, an AC cord can help save battery life if you are shooting in a stationary location indoors or if you are tethered to your computer for downloading.

Lenses and Lens Adapters

We'll look at this in a tad more detail in the next chapter, but some cameras let you add additional lenses, usually by screwing on a lens adapter. At the lower end, you're pretty limited, but as you go higher up the food chain, you can attach a greater variety of lenses.

Flashes
The built-in flashes that come with most digital cameras do not have a great range, and some models (even some lower-end models) have a hot shoe for attaching an external flash. Be sure to check the documentation for the specs of the flashes you can attach.

Cords
The cameras also usually come with the cords needed to connect them to a computer, be it USB, serial, parallel, or other.

Memory Cards
We'll look at memory cards in more detail in Chapter 5, but most cameras come with some type of memory card, usually SmartMedia or CompactFlash.

Carrying Cases
Some models even come with carrying cases of the type that strap to your belt in a Batman kind of way.

Onward
Now that we've looked at all the different types of cameras, and looked in detail at a couple of different models, let's take them out into the field (or into the studio) and take some pictures. In the next chapter, we'll look at how you go about getting images into the camera. Mind you, this won't be a high-powered photo shoot with a ton of lights and other related gear. Rather, this is going to be rather informal—the type of shooting that is often done with these types of cameras.

4

Getting the Image into the Camera

Okay, we've talked enough about the technology underlying all of this. Let's now get out of the office and into the field—or into another office, as the case may be. In this chapter, we're going to take a digital camera on two separate photo shoots—one indoors and one outdoors—to show you how these cameras work and what you can do with them. In later chapters, we'll also be working with some of the images we capture on these shoots, so you'll be able to get a good sense of how to work with digital images from capture to output.

Our Informal Photo Shoot

We'll be using a couple of different point-and-shoot cameras on our shoots, primarily to give you some sense of how models can differ. Our primary camera will be our old friend the Olympus C-2500L, a 2.5-Mp camera that, as of January 2000, lists for $1,499. I chose this model because it is one of the best digital point-and-shoots I've seen, and it offers a great deal of customizable camera settings, as we saw in the last chapter. Granted, we won't be taking advantage of all the features it has, but you'll be able to see what kind of results can be achieve by someone with only a scant amount of photographic skill.

We will also be using an Epson PhotoPC 750Z, a 1.X-Mp digital camera that came out in early 1999. It is at the lower end of the digital camera market at the moment (it can be had for about $599), but we liked it a great deal when it came out, and looking at the differences between two successive generations of cameras is educational. You may even find that a 1.X-Mp camera will suit your needs more economically than a 2.X-Mp—or even the new 3.X-Mp cameras that are hitting the market as this book goes to press.

We took the Olympus camera to a recent event held in Redondo Beach—a beach city just south of Los Angeles. From the images, you'd never know it was a California beach city—it looks like the Northeast. That is primarily because pop songs are often wrong; it does in fact rain in Southern California, which worked out well for this experiment. I had hoped for a sunny day, but it was winter here, and it can get very cloudy and rainy.

At any rate, our event was a political rally at a Redondo Beach high school. We had the Olympus camera and used default settings for the most part (we'll get to what those were in a moment).

We will also spend a great deal of time doing some informal "product shots." This is one of the most common applications for digital photography, and in fact it was the advent of digital studio cameras in the mid-1990s that helped the catalog publishing industry take off in a big way. We'll be using our friend the Olympus again, as well as the Epson—for comparison's sake. We also have an Olympus C-2020Z—a lower-end model than the C-2500L—a scant amount, also for comparison's sake.

Caveat Lector

Reader beware: You'll notice that I use the word "informal" to refer to these photo shoots. This is because, as I mentioned at the outset of this book, I am not a professional photographer. My experiments with digital cameras over the past five years or so have made me more of a hobbyist than anything, but I primarily write about the cameras in the context of "quick-and-dirty" imaging for the graphic arts. I don't have an elaborate photo studio, nor do I have special lighting equipment or a vast arsenal of lenses and flashes. Basically, we'll be using the cameras as they come, right out of the box.

And that's pretty much the point. We're interested in looking at how these cameras can be used in less-than-optimal conditions. A cloudy day outside is one of the better less-than-optimal conditions. An ersatz photo studio set up in one's home office is also a pretty good less-than-optimal condition. How will we do? How will the cameras do? Will these images be usable?

We'll find out, won't we?

Oh, by the way, the limitations of writing a black-and-white book on digital photography do mean that we won't be able to look specifically at things like color fidelity. So you'll have to take my word for the results we get. And would I lie to you?

Outdoor Shooting

If you can control the time of day you are shooting, you will have better success than if you are tied to a particular time. As you probably well know, outdoor lighting changes over the course of a day. Early morning, shadows are long and the light is diffused. High noon, when the sun is directly overhead, everything is a bit brighter, shadows are shorter, and the lighting is a bit more harsh. Things tone down a bit as we progress toward sunset, as you can see from the images on page 70.

In program mode, we let the camera make all settings with regard to shutter speed, aperture, and exposure. We also did not use the flash, as at the distances we were shooting it would have had little—if any—effect. We could have manually set the aperture and shutter speed, but we took a few preliminary shots and decided that we liked what the defaults gave us.

As we saw in the last chapter, you can adjust the brightness of the LCD to accurately represent how your images look on your monitor, which in turn can be adjusted to accurately—to a degree—display how images will print. We don't use a comprehensive color management system, although we certainly could if we were so inclined. Basically, we did quick-and-dirty calibration by printing a set of test images on an inkjet printer, then adjusted the brightness of the monitor to get fairly close brightness and color values in line with what came out of the printer. This was then compared with the images as they are displayed on the camera's LCD. True

Watch how the same scene can change over the course of a day, as the sun goes around.

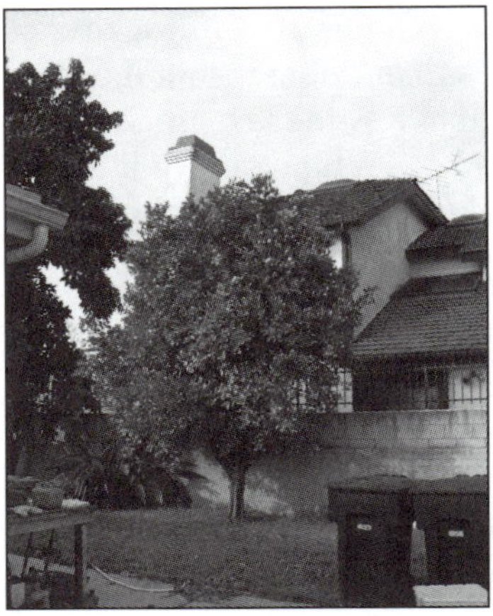

Approximately 9 a.m. on a January morning in Southern California, facing southwest.

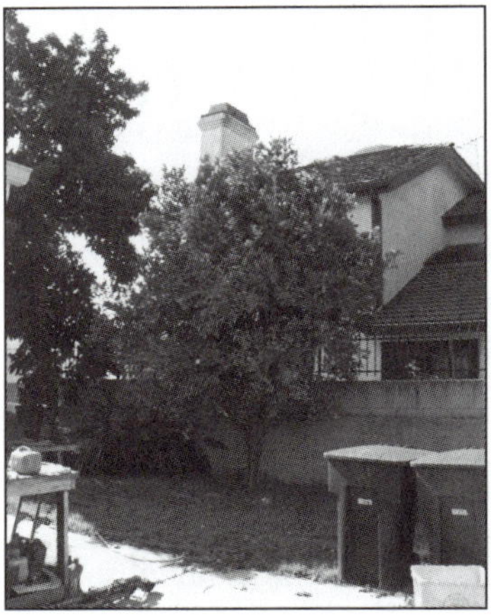

High noon in January in Southern California, facing southwest.

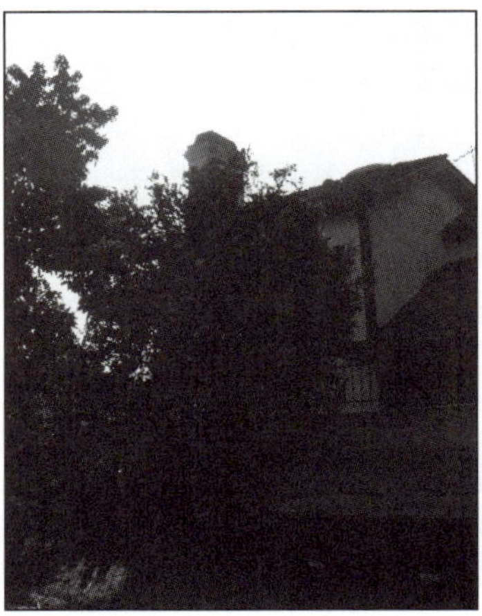

About 3 p.m. on a January afternoon in Southern California, facing southwest.

photographers or color experts would probably blanch at this feeble attempt at color management, but it works pretty well for our purposes.

If we wanted, we could nudge the exposure compensation a bit to compensate for the murk of the day.

We left the ISO equivalency (i.e., sensitivity) at 100. Since it was a rather dark day, we could have boosted the sensitivity to 200 or 400—which we did, and you can see what effect that had.

So, with an ISO equivalency setting at 100, we have a pretty decent image:

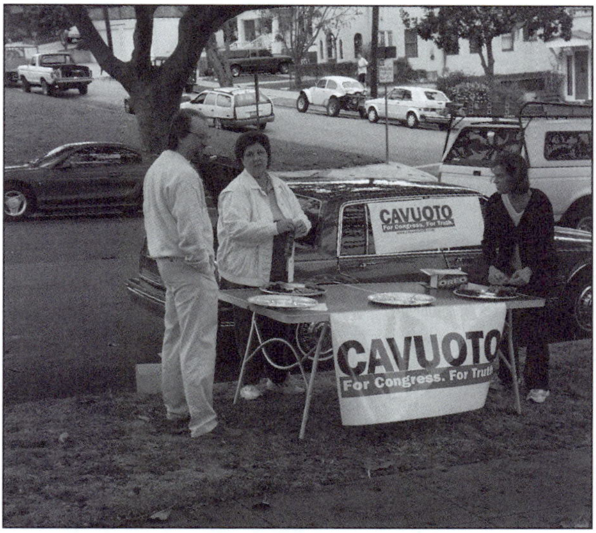

ISO 100

The two images on the next page show what results we get by changing the ISO to 200 and 400. As we saw in the last chapter, increasing the sensitivity can help compensate for low-light conditions. We noticed a slight bit of brightness increase in the ISO 400 image over the 100 and 200; there was little difference between the ISO 100 and 200 images.

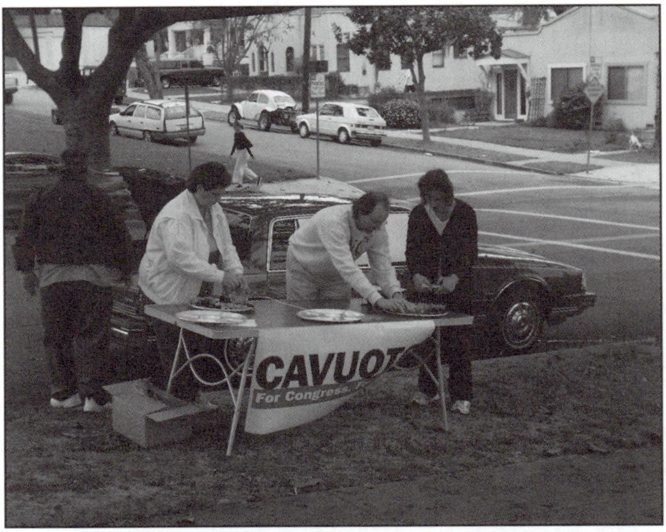

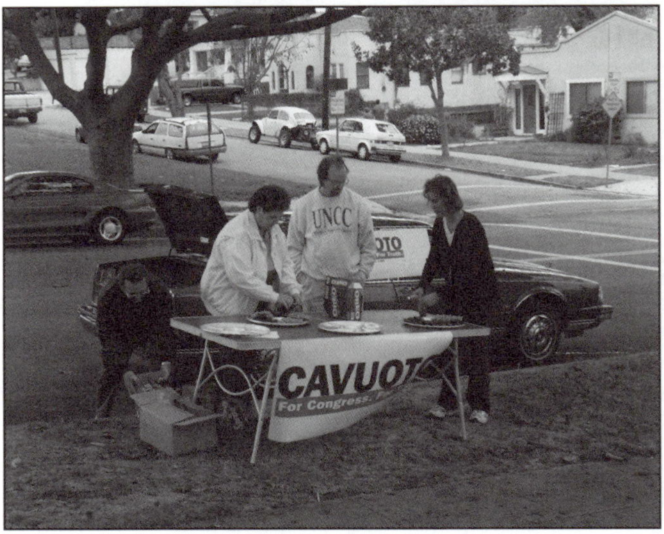

If you look at the banner on the table, you can see the difference in brightness that going from ISO 200 (top) to ISO 400 (bottom) equivalency gives us. However, boosting the ISO does tend to increase graininess, although that wasn't a problem in this case.

The physical act of snapping pictures digitally does tend to throw people. With these cameras though, especially in fully automatic mode, it is pretty simple. Basically, you point the camera at your subject and look through the viewfinder. We were lucky because the Olympus C-2500L has a through-the-lens (TTL) viewfinder. Basically, what this means is that you are seeing through the viewfinder essentially what the camera is seeing and what you'll get when you click the shutter.

Most other cameras at this price/quality level (especially those less expensive) use a separate viewfinder that tries to approximate what the camera sees. This brings up the problem of parallax, which refers to the difference in angle or coverage between what the viewfinder sees and what the lens sees. We saw from our sample spec sheet in Chapter 2 that that particular camera did not have a TTL viewfinder, and it provided approximately 80 percent coverage. That means that what you see is pretty close to what the camera sees. This is not unique to digital cameras, and if you've ever used an Instamatic-type camera, you know this problem very well. (It still doesn't mean you are completely innocent of cutting off Grandma's head, though.)

So we have our TTL viewfinder, and we see two lights inside, or just to the right of the viewfinder. These are usually red and green, although in this case they are orange and green. We aim, and hold the shutter button down halfway. This locks the auto focus on the subject, or what the camera assumes is the subject. In this case, the camera is right, and we can see in the viewfinder that our subject comes into focus as the auto focus does its work. When the auto focus is locked, and the camera believes there is enough light to snap a good picture, the green light comes on, and we hear a reassuring beep. We depress the shutter release all the way, we hear a click and a beep, and the picture is taken.

The captured image immediately comes up on the LCD, and we can review it. As we saw in the last chapter, we can set how long it displays; this is a battery-saving feature. Five seconds is usually sufficient. We decide that we don't like this shot, for whatever reason. Maybe someone walked in front of the camera as it was being snapped, or the photographer moved the camera and got a big blur. Whatever. We simply spin the mode dial to the play mode, and we can see the captured images come up. Depending on the camera, you can set your playback display to show a bunch of thumbnails two-up, four-up, six-up, nine-up, whatever, on the LCD. This saves time and keeps you from having to keep toggling through each image one by one, which you can certainly do.

So we maneuver to the image we don't like and hit the delete button. The delete command is sometimes selected from the menus, but in this case it is a button on top of the camera. We press it, the camera asks us if we really want to delete it (we do), and we hit OK. It is soon gone.

So we compose our next shot, and keep going, deleting the ghastly pictures and keeping the good ones. This editing is useful if you don't have a large number of memory cards or a very high-capacity card.

Choosing the Best Image-Quality Settings

All models of digital cameras let you set a variety of things that affect image quality. The settings you choose should in large part depend on your intended destination of the images. The most important of these settings, not surprisingly, is your image quality. What you choose here can either take full advantage of the capture capability of your camera or can be some sort of trade-off between image quality and other more mundane considerations, such as how many memory cards you have.

The Olympus C-2500L gives us five image-quality settings from which to choose, which are reproduced on pages 76–77. They are:

Mode	Resolution (pixels)	File Format	File Size	File Size on Disk
SHQ	1,712 × 1,368	TIFF	6.71 MB	6.71 MB
SHQ	1,712 × 1,368	JPEG	6.71 MB	1.8 MB
HQ	1,712 × 1,368	JPEG	6.71 MB	504 KB
SQ	1,280 × 1,024	JPEG	3.75 MB	384 KB
SQ	640 × 512	JPEG	960 KB	136 KB

You can see that different amounts of JPEG compression give you different file sizes. The greater the JPEG compression, the greater the chance you'll get some artifacting.

So the question you may be asking is: Wouldn't I want to use the highest possible quality setting and get the biggest file size I can? Isn't that why I bought the damn camera?

And that's a good point, but it depends on two factors: what you are going to actually do with the images, and how many memory cards you have. We'll look at memory cards in more detail in the next chapter, but you are probably going to be using either SmartMedia or CompactFlash. Most cameras have been shipping with 8-MB SmartMedia cards, even though there are 32-MB and even 64-MB cards out. And for those camera manufacturers that prefer CompactFlash, 8-MB cards are still commonly the ones that are bundled with the camera, although there are capacities available up to 128 MB.

If you do the math, you'll see that if you have only one 8-MB card, you will be able to take exactly one highest-quality image before the card is filled up. That may not be practical, unless you're looking for that one perfect shot. With a 32-MB card, you can fit four images. And even with a 64-MB card, you can fit only about nine images. But that's at highest quality mode.

So although you might want to shoot at the highest quality mode, you may not be able to do so effectively. There are, however, ways around that, such as carrying a laptop around with you and copying the images to it after the card is full. That can get really aggravating really fast, though. As we'll see in the next chapter, Iomega has a device out called a Clik! drive that is designed to let you download your images from a CompactFlash or SmartMedia card to a 40-MB Clik! disk. The Clik!s are cheaper than either flash memory card, but you still may find it a pain to keep copying images back and forth.

But as the memory cards increase in capacity and decrease in price, this problem may be alleviated in the near future.

The other issue is what you intend to do with the images. If your needs are modest, you can probably get away with a lower-than-optimal quality setting, especially if you're taking pictures that will end up only on the Web.

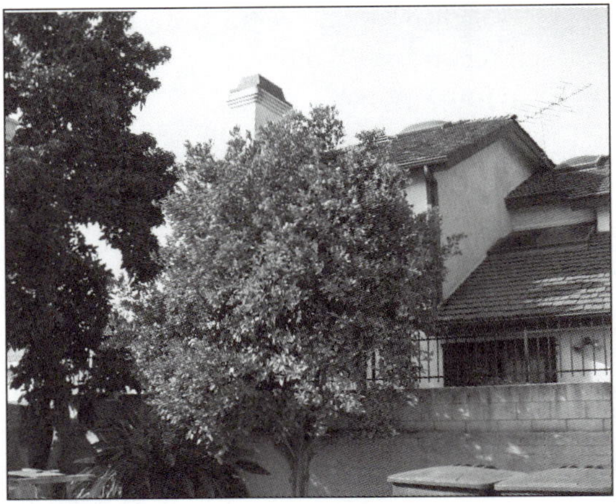

SHQ – TIFF
1,712 × 1,368 pixels
6.71-MB file
6.71 MB on disk
Maximum reproduction size at 300 DPI:
5.707 × 4.56 inches

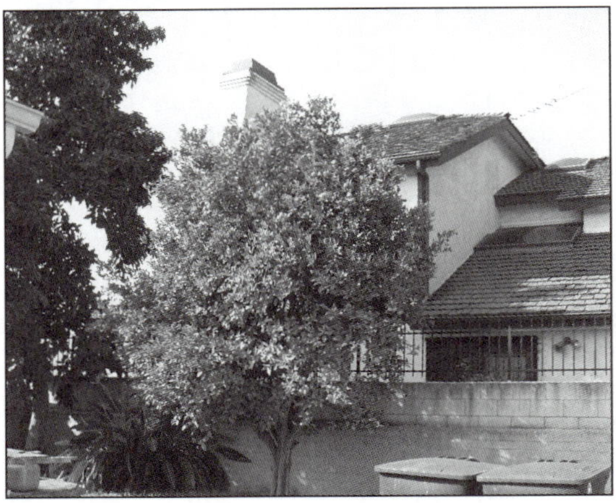

SHQ – JPEG
1,712 × 1,368 pixels
6.71-MB file
1.8 MB on disk
Maximum reproduction size at 300 DPI:
5.707 × 4.56 inches

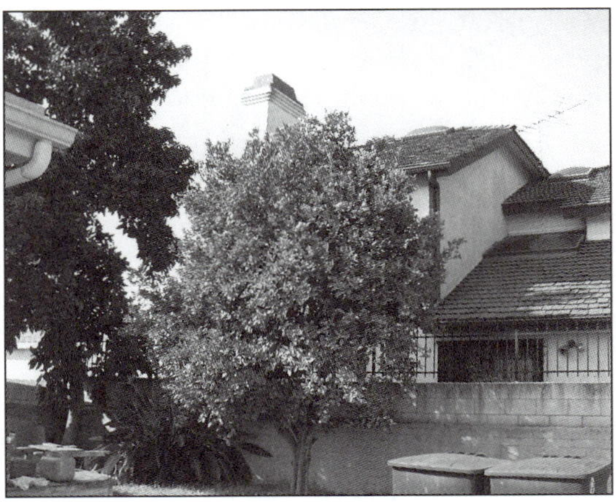

HQ – JPEG
1,712 × 1,368 pixels
6.71-MB file
504 KB on disk
Maximum reproduction size at 300 dpi:
5.707 × 4.56 inches

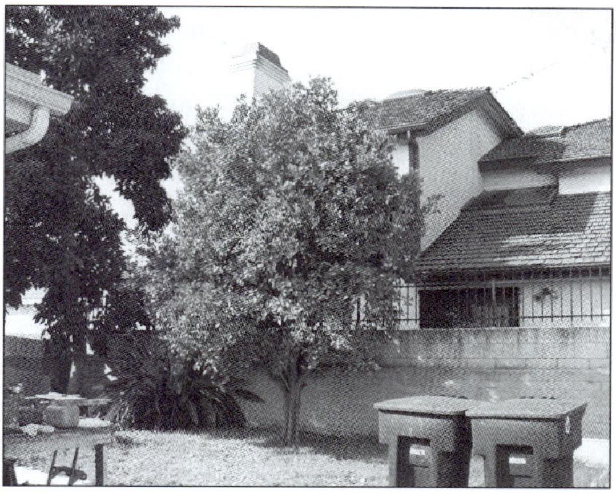

SQ—JPEG
1,280 × 1,024 pixels
3.75 MB file
384 KB on disk
Maximum reproduction size at 300 DPI:
4.267 × 3.4113 inches

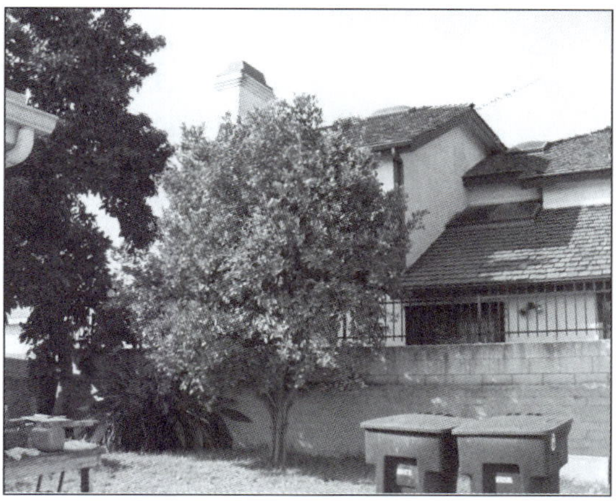

SQ—JPEG
640 × 512 pixels
960 KB file
136 KB on disk
Maximum reproduction size at 300 DPI:
2.133 × 1.707 inches

For those who need truly high-quality images, the choice may be between SHQ/TIFF or SHQ/JPEG. Uncompressed TIFF mode gives you a straight 6.71-MB file (by the way, the file sizes quoted here refer to the original color images out of the camera, not the grayscale representations reproduced here). However, SHQ with JPEG compression gives you a 1.8-MB file that unfurls into a 6.71-MB file. As you can see here (it is hoped), the compression doesn't do very many bad things to us. Some scant loss of detail is apparent in the color image (i.e., the blue sky is a tad washed out, and we're starting to lose some of the spines on the TV aerial), but it's not extraordinarily serious. It looks worse in grayscale than in color, which is a consideration; if you're going to reproduce in grayscale, you'll need to think about that as you're shooting (but not for too long). In sum, I would have no qualms about using SHQ/JPEG mode, unless my needs were truly high end.

Even the HQ mode is pretty good. As we can see, that creates a 504-KB file that unfurls to a 6.71-MB image. The TV aerial is continuing its trip into oblivion, but there is no more loss of detail or bad artifacting from the compression. If push came to shove, I would not be averse to shooting in HQ mode.

The two SQ modes are problematic. The first, with a pixel resolution of 1,280 × 1,024, is okay; that's actually the resolution at which many 1.X-Mp cameras capture, so we can't fault it, and many people do use that resolution for reproduction. The JPEGing doesn't do anything too unseemly.

The low-res SQ mode, though, has a resolution of 640 × 512. That's really not much better than VGA resolution, and it pixellates badly at sizes beyond about 2 × 2 inches. It would be useful for Web work but little else.

By the way, we'll see where the maximum reproduction size numbers came from in Chapter 6.

You can see that picking your image-quality mode is a trade-off among various things like image destination and how much removable storage you have. If you have a ton of cards, then by all means shoot uncompressed TIFF. But if you need to compromise, remember that all JPEG is not terrible.

Indoor Shooting

Well, I would scarcely call it a studio. We are going to be doing some basic "product" shooting, the goal being to see what noodling with various camera settings does for us. We are shooting at about noon on a bright sunny day. We have some ambient light coming through a window, but the bulk of the illumination comes from overhead incandescent lighting. If we are having white balance problems, we'll need to adjust the camera for one or the other, so we try to let the outside sunlight cause as little interference as possible.

To Flash or Not To Flash...

Let's assume we don't know what the image will end up looking like, so we'll use a flash. We're still working with general default settings at this point. So we snap the image.

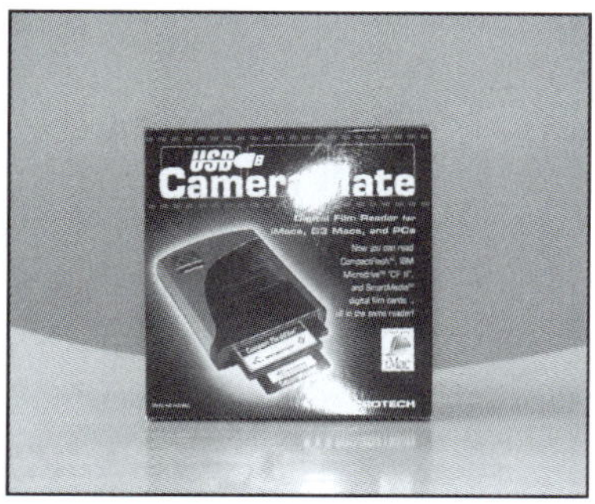

The color looks okay, but that flash! That's not going to cut it. We have a few options. I can run out and buy lighting equipment (not a real option right now), I can use a different flash (an option), or we can see how it comes out without a flash. Let's see:

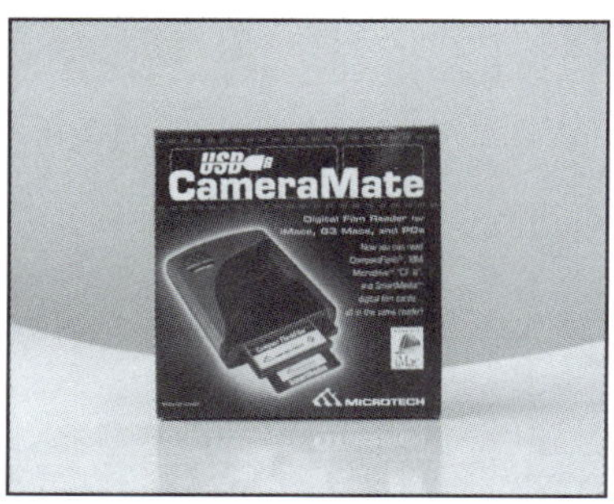

Okay, that's not too bad. But we remember that we can try to compensate for low-light conditions by boosting our ISO. Let's do it at ISO 400 and see what happens:

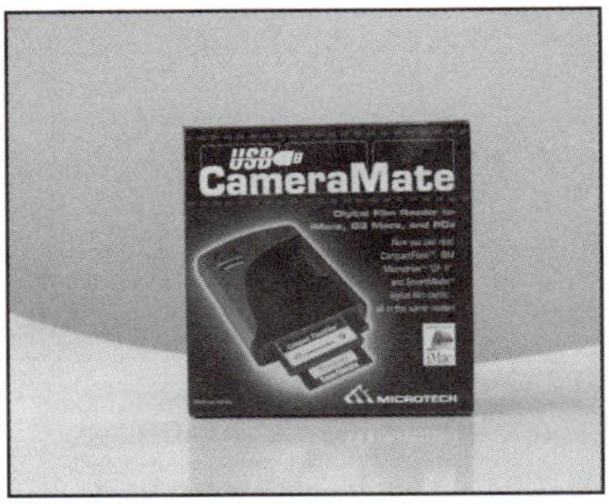

Not much of a difference.

Exposure Compensation

We can also adjust our exposure compensation. This particular camera lets us adjust it + or – in ⅓-EV steps, up to (or down to) +2 EV or –2 EV. Let's do one image at +1 EV and one at –1 EV, just to see what sort of effect that gives us.

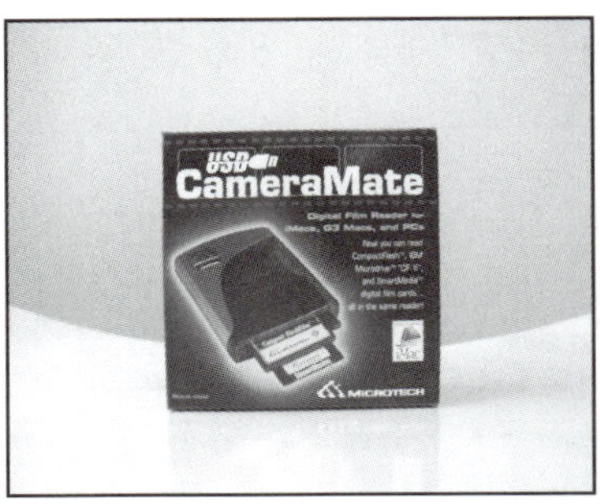

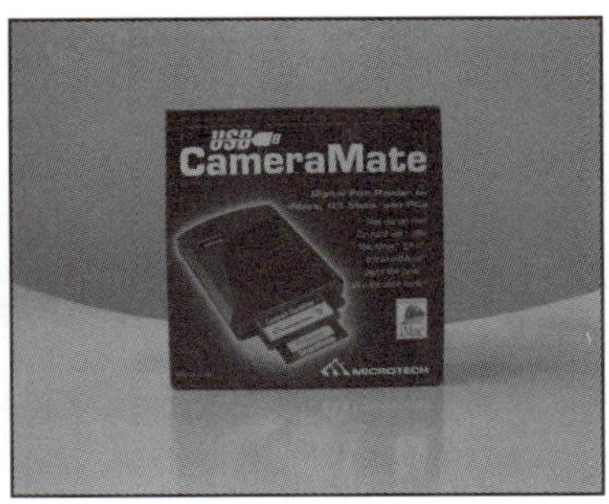

The image on the left is +1 EV and is a bit too light. The image on right is –1 EV and is way too dark. Thus, we know that our desired exposure compensation is probably +⅓ or maybe +⅔ EV.

Macro Mode

The product still seems a bit too far away. We need to get closer to it. We can try zooming, but this camera—like most digital cameras—has a macro mode, which lets us take pictures of objects very close to the camera—sometimes less than 1 foot, usually 12–14 inches or so. So let's use an exposure compensation of +⅓ EV in macro mode and see what that gives us.

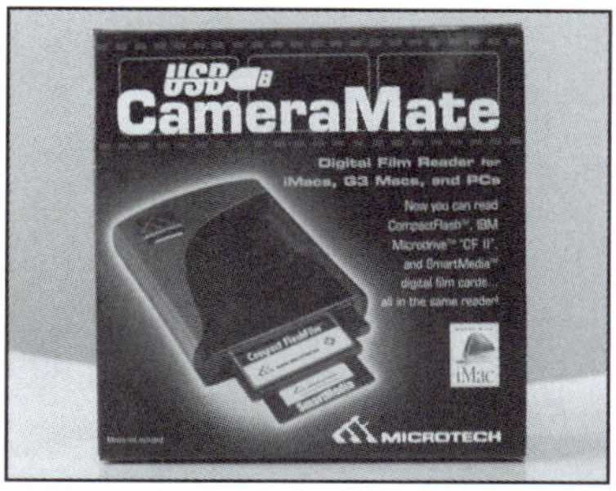

And what that gives us is the ability to get in really close.

Understanding Center versus Spot Metering

We can also use our spot-metering feature, which many digital cameras have. Metering is the means by which the brightness of the subject is measured and exposure automatically compensated for. The default, and most common metering, is center metering. What center metering does is meter the brightness around a wide area surrounding the center of the image. The alternative is spot metering. This lets you measure the brightness of the object in the center of the frame. It may help us in this case. Let's see. Cameras that have a spot-metering feature usually have a button that toggles between center and spot metering, as in fact our Olympus does.

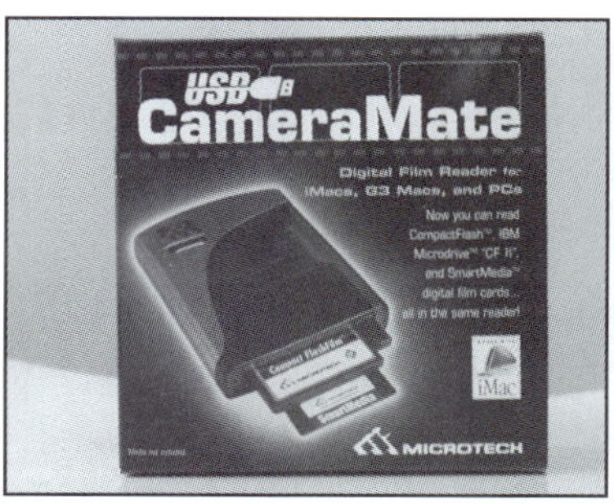

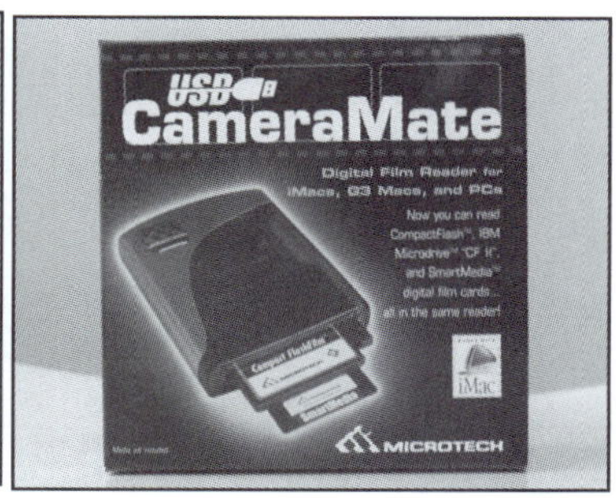

The image on the left on page 81 was taken with spot metering on. Notice that it is a bit brighter than the center-metered version on the right. We could even take our exposure compensation down –⅓ EV to darken it up, and since the background is very faint, it could be easily removed. But since we're likely going to want to put a clipping path around this image, it doesn't really matter what the background is like. (We'll touch on clipping paths in Chapter 6.)

Making Manual Settings

Some cameras give us the ability to adjust the aperture, focus, shutter speed, and exposure manually. You may or may not want to take advantage of these features—and you'll usually pay more for them. If the idea scares you, and you don't want or need such control, then that is a factor in your camera-buying decision to which you need to attach a heavy weight.

For those who do want it, let's just go over very quickly what some of these features are, and how changing them can be to your advantage.

Shutter Speed

Shutter speed is measured in fractions of a second—1/15, ⅛, ¼. As you can tell, the smaller the number, the faster the speed. For example, 1/2000 of a second is faster than a lethargic ½ second.

By increasing the shutter speed, you are increasing your ability to capture objects in motion. Quickly moving objects tend to come out blurry because they are moving across the frame as the shutter is open. They can't be caught "at a standstill." But if your shutter is fast enough, if you can snap a picture in thousandths of a second, the object doesn't get very far across the frame before the shutter has closed again.

The camera usually determines what shutter speed works best for the various exposure settings, since shutter speed is one of those interrelated factors that affect how an image is exposed.

Photojournalists, especially sports photographers, need fast-shutter-speed cameras. At the low end, not so much, and not at all if you're doing product shooting, unless the products you are shooting tend to move about quickly of their own accord. However, shutter speed adjustments also can be used to control exposure, if you need to.

Aperture
You can set the aperture to add various "special focus" settings to your images, such as taking images that are sharp from foreground to background, are deliberately out of focus, and more. When adjusting the aperture, you may also need to adjust the exposure compensation. Some cameras will tell you when the exposure is off by a certain number of EVs.

Sequence Mode
Some cameras also have a sequence-shooting, or burst, mode, that lets you shoot multiple frames in rapid succession.

Flashes
The lower-end cameras give you a slight bit of control over how the flash fires. Most cameras have at least three modes: flash on, flash off, and auto flash, the latter being the mode where the camera determines if a flash is required. Some also have what is known as "red-eye reduction," which helps to eliminate the problem of red-eye. Red-eye, as you probably know, is a rather eerie effect on the eyes that gives people and animals a kind of *Village of the Damned* look. Essentially, it is caused by the flash reflecting off the retinas at the backs of the eyes.

Red-eye reduction works by emitting a series of quick flashes before the proper flash is fired and the shutter clicks. What this does is contract the subject's pupils so that not as much light from the primary flash enters the subject's eyes, and not as much red light from the retina is reflected back out of the eye.

One flash feature that some of the Olympus (and other) cameras have is a flash synchronization effect, by means of which you can set first-curtain and second-curtain flash. Essentially, you use it with slow shutter speeds to achieve very stylized images. First curtain fires the flash at the beginning of a slow shutter. Second curtain fires the flash at the end of a slow shutter.

For Comparison's Sake
We've seen how we can use the Olympus camera to take pretty good-looking outdoor and indoor shots. Let's once again turn our

attention briefly to a lower-end camera, our old pal the Epson PhotoPC 750Z.

Let's begin by again juxtaposing the various image-quality modes.

The Epson PhotoPC 750Z gives us the following choices:

Mode	**Resolution (pixels)**	**File Format**	**File Size**	**File Size on Disk**
***	1,280 × 960	JPEG	3.52 MB	360 KB
**	1,280 × 960	JPEG	3.52 MB	196 KB
*	640 × 480	JPEG	900 KB	60 KB

We can see the results on the next page.

Even though there is no uncompressed TIFF mode (this camera came out before that was popular), we find the best-quality (***) mode to be adequate for a roughly 4 × 3-inch reproduction at 300 dpi. There is a slight amount of JPEG artifacting, but it's not horrible. In color, the tangerines on the tree aren't as vivid as they came out with the Olympus, but some of that could have been the lighting; the Epson images were shot in the afternoon, the Olympus ones in the morning. (This was designed in part to point out how time of day can affect your images.) We also weren't intending to compare the two cameras directly, which would be grossly unfair; I just want to point out that a less-expensive and less-featured model can suit a variety of needs just as well as a higher-end model.

The medium-quality mode (**) does cause us a few problems, but it's not woefully wretched. The details are a little softer.

And of course, the VGA-quality mode is pretty unusable except on the Web.

How does this camera do in our product-shooting scenario? Well, let's see.

On the top of page 86, there's a shot with all the default settings, in macro mode, and flash off (we've seen what flashes do):

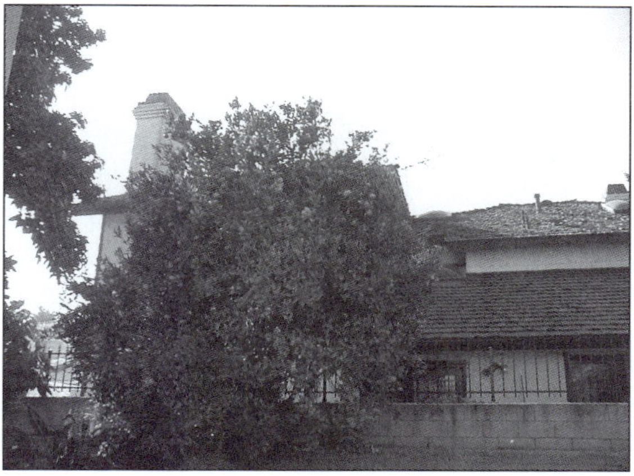

**** (Best) — JPEG*
1,280 × 960 pixels
3.52 MB file
360 KB on disk
Maximum reproduction size at 300 DPI:
4.267 × 3.2 inches

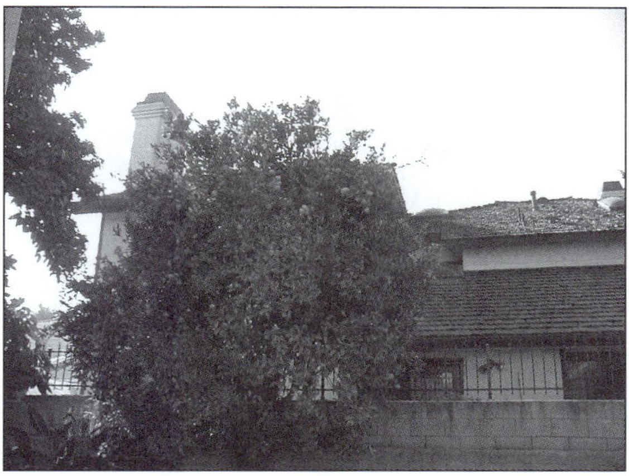

*** (Med.) — JPEG*
1,280 × 960 pixels
3.52 MB file
196 KB on disk
Maximum reproduction size at 300 DPI:
4.267 × 3.2 inches

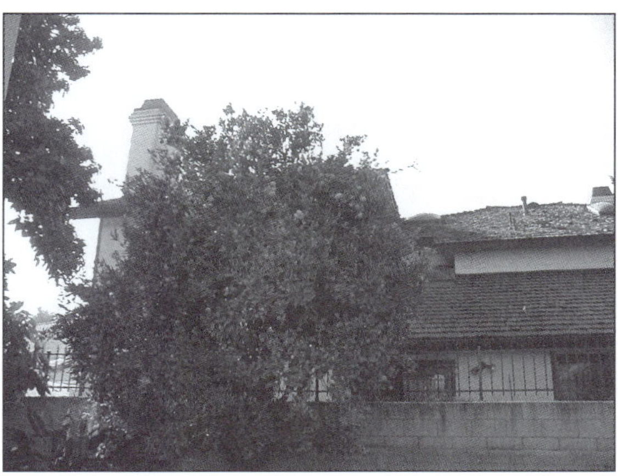

** (VGA) — JPEG*
640 × 480 pixels
900 KB file
60 KB on disk
Maximum reproduction size at 300 DPI:
2.133 × 1.6 inches

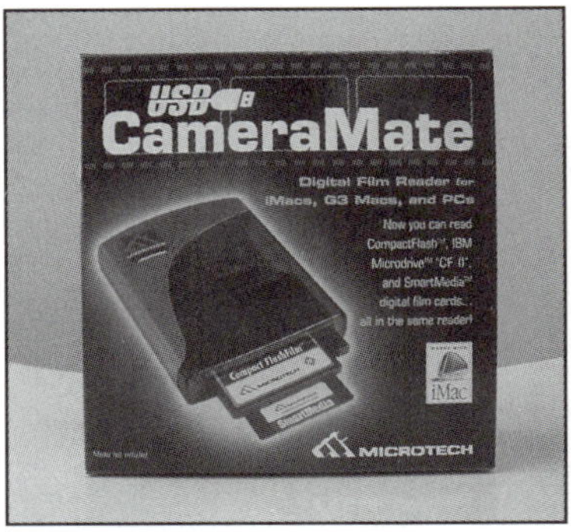

Now, that's not bad at all. A tad on the darkish side, so let's see if boosting the ISO to high will help us out:

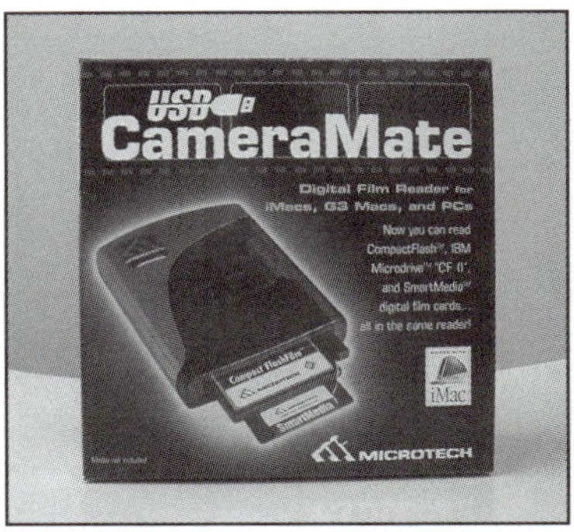

I don't know how much of this you can see on this printed page, but even on screen and on an inkjet print I can see the grain popping out. Yikes. Okay, let's put our ISO back down to auto and see if upping the exposure compensation to +.5 EV will help. Remember, the last time we had good success with a +⅓ (.3) EV.

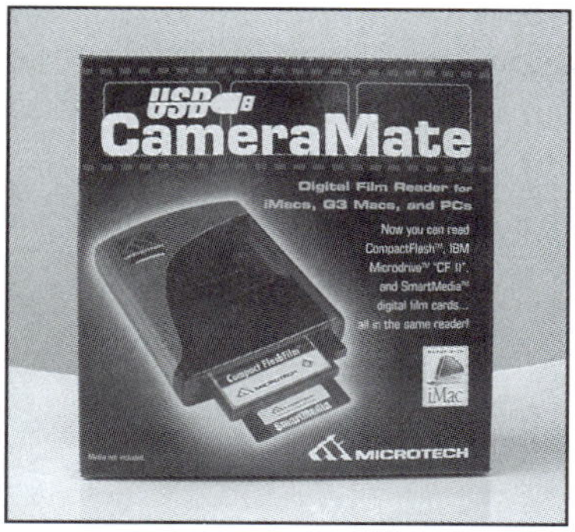

Okay, so that's a tad on the light side, but there's always our old friend dot gain.

But my point is basically that even a 1.X-Mp camera can suit a purpose nearly as well as a higher-end model. (Am I starting to sound like a broken record? Hmm ... does anyone remember what a broken record sounds like anymore? Maybe a broken CD...)

Wrapping Up

So we've seen how we can use our digital camera to take a variety of different shots, ranging from outdoor scenes to indoor product shots.

Many of the people who are getting involved in digital photography are not photographers. At *Micro Publishing News,* we don't have any on-staff photographers, per se; rather, when we cover events, we send the writer out with a camera, and he takes his own shots for the story. A lot of smaller magazine and newsletter publishers do this. And since I am one of our primary reviewers of digital cameras, I am the one who does the processing of images. Here are some common problems I've seen in "developing" digital film and suggestions for what can be done about it.

• *Images that are too dark*

There is a myth that digital cameras' images are darker than corresponding film images. I have not found this to be the case. Yes, digital camera images can be dark. But so can film images. But with digital, we have the advantage of being able to see what our images look like as soon as we take them, and we can take measures to lighten them up before bringing them back to the office to be downloaded. After all, if you've been covering a single-day event, you don't have a second chance to get more images.

That's why I mentioned earlier that it is a good idea to roughly calibrate your LCD brightness in tandem with your computer monitor—or better yet, the computer monitor of your production person. You don't want an LCD that indicates you have a great image when you don't.

As for dark images, you can try several things. We've seen in this chapter how boosting our exposure compensation can brighten images. This is a good solution. We can also use more powerful flashes; the built-in flashes with most point-and-shoot digital cameras can be woefully inadequate, especially for events like lectures and seminars where you may be several rows back in a dark hall.

You can also try upping the ISO. We've seen that this can get grainy in a hurry, but it may be a decent trade-off.

- *Images that are way too washed out*

This is a function of shooting where there is too much light, or into direct sunlight. (By the way, you never want to point a digital camera at the sun. It can damage the CCD.) We've looked primarily at how images can come out looking very dark and how we can rectify that, but you can fix an image that is too light in essentially the same manner. Try decreasing the ISO, if you have it set to anything higher than the lowest setting. You can take the exposure compensation down a few fractions of a EV. And so on.

- *Images with resolutions too low to be used in print*

Sometimes people grabbing a camera as they run out the door fail to notice what quality mode the camera is set on. This may sound like a no-brainer, but I've seen it happen. People come back and wonder why their images are all at VGA resolution.

- *Not enough storage space to hold all the images that need to be taken*

This is simply a case of not taking enough memory cards. Or setting your image quality too high to use your available memory efficiently. We've seen that very often your image-quality setting needs to be a compromise between the resolution you absolutely need for print and what you can physically store on the media you have. If you're unwilling to compromise, then buy more cards.

- *Images have a weird color cast, as if everything was photographed through soup*

This is a white balance issue. We looked at white balance briefly in Chapter 3, and we talked about how different light sources have different color temperatures—the cause of the soup-like color cast. Most cameras give you at least the ability to adjust the white balance for some typical sources of light, such as natural sunlight, fluorescent lighting, and incandescent lighting. (Usually the lower-end cameras give you these settings as straightforward words similar to what I just described; some of the higher-end ones prefer to use degrees Kelvin.)

Either way, adjust your white balance settings, and if you're still getting soup-like images, you may have more than one light source (i.e., if you're shooting under fluorescent lights but are near a window), making it difficult to set a white balance that is completely accurate. You can either try to eliminate one of the light sources or you can set the white balance manually by focusing the camera on a piece of white paper. By setting what the camera knows is pure white under that specific lighting, it can then figure out what is normal color.

Onward

One more question that may need to be asked:

- *How can I get my images into a computer, which is where I really want them?*

Boy, am I glad you asked that question, because that brings us to the next chapter, in which we explore all the myriad ways of getting an image from camera to computer—and where it can go from there.

Photo Shoot Checklist

When going out (or staying in) to shoot digitally, remembering to take a few accessories can make the difference between getting all the images you want and need and coming back ready to slap someone.

- Digital camera (well, duh!).
- Enough memory cards for as many images as you plan on shooting.
- Make sure the cards are formatted for the camera you're taking, if you have more than one.
- Make sure the cards don't have images you'll eventually need before you reformat them.
- Strap, either a wrist strap or a neck strap, to keep from dropping the camera. I've seen people drop cameras, and it ain't pretty.
- Flash, if you're using a external flash.
- Extra lighting, if required or desired.
- Additional lenses, such as wide-angle, telephoto, or what-have-you, if you have and want them.
- Extra batteries, fully charged.
- Tripod, if your camera has a tripod mount.

5

Getting the Picture (Out of the Camera)

Remember when life and photography used to be simple? You shot a roll of film with your camera, then you took the film down to the local drugstore or photolab, and an hour or a day later you had a batch of 4 × 6 prints with which you could bore friends and coworkers. Or even better, you had a Polaroid camera that delivered the finished image to you right out of the camera.

Things are a little bit more complicated for digital cameras—getting your captured images from inside the camera to some tangible form has sprung up several cottage industries. At one time you didn't have too many options; you had to tether your camera to your PC (usually through the serial or parallel port) and transfer them onto a hard drive. And at one point, you didn't even have anything removable; images were stored solely in the camera's internal memory.

Serial/parallel connectivity is still a popular way of downloading images today, but there are increasingly better and faster options.

Serial/Parallel Transfers

Just about every camera you are likely to buy features serial or parallel port connectivity as an option. The process is very simple. The camera comes bundled with a cable, and you connect one end to a port on the camera and the other to the serial port (Mac) or parallel port (PC) on your computer. You turn on the camera, and there is usually a wheel or switch on the camera that turns on the "PC View" mode. On the PC, you launch the software that comes with the camera. The software varies, but usually it gives you the option of viewing the images in the camera as thumbnails, and then you can pick which ones you actually want to download.

Download Utilities and Other Bundled Software

The software then downloads the images. Most software lets you retain a thumbnail view, or open an image (or some multiple thereof) and view it full-screen size. Most software also gives you some rudimentary image-editing abilities, too, such as changing the brightness and contrast, cropping, rotating, and sometimes changing color spaces. You can then save the image as either a JPEG (with varying degrees of compression), a TIFF, a BMP, and sometimes even a Flashpix file.

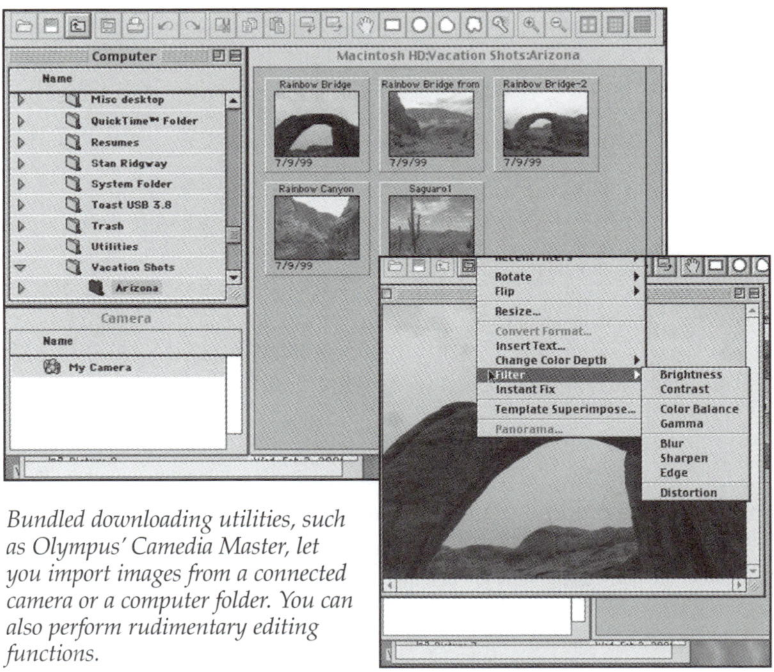

Bundled downloading utilities, such as Olympus' Camedia Master, let you import images from a connected camera or a computer folder. You can also perform rudimentary editing functions.

Camera manufacturers, especially those targeting their products toward a more consumer-oriented market, often include other programs that let you work with images. Adobe's PhotoDeluxe is one of the most common and popular, but others, such as Ulead's PhotoImpact, are also available. Most software bundles are also including ways of easily e-mailing images to friends and relatives or posting your images on Web sites. We'll look at these tools in more detail in the next chapter.

Other Connectivity Options

One of the problems with direct serial and parallel connections is that they are extremely slow ways of transferring data. Especially on the Mac, the serial port is a staggeringly slow transfer. Another problem with this type of connection is that it differs on both Mac and PC. Manufacturers, needless to say, grumble enough about having to develop both Mac and Windows software, never mind also having to provide two different cables.

The latest rage in connectivity is what is known as the Universal Serial Bus (USB). The advantage to USB is that not only is it designed to be the same on both Mac and PC, but it is also a faster transfer. USB has caught on in a big way, especially among hardware manufacturers, nearly all of whom are developing USB adapters. The technology is still in its infancy and is starting to catch on with PC users—especially as the number of peripherals that support it is increasing exponentially. In fact, the new Macintosh models, including the consumer-level iMac and the high-end G3s and G4s, have eliminated serial ports in favor of USB. This annoys those who have older "legacy" devices such as serial port printers, but it is very forward thinking of Apple. Look for USB to be commonplace in the very near future.

Users who dislike the software that comes with a camera may also have another option on the download side of things. Some manufacturers include a TWAIN driver in their software bundles. TWAIN is a standard image-capture interface, often used to allow an image-editing program to link to a scanner. The origin of the term is variously given as "it's a technology with which the twain shall meet" or as an acronym for "Technology Without an Interesting Name." Both etymologies may be apocryphal.

Be that as it may, with a TWAIN driver you can download your images directly into Photoshop or whatever other imaging program supports the TWAIN standard. It can be a quick way of acquiring images if you're only going to bring them into Photoshop eventually anyway.

Not all camera bundles include TWAIN drivers, so if that is a must-have feature, be sure to check with your seller.

Digital Film

I said before that digital-camera connectivity issues had spawned a whole cottage industry. Well, the digital film market is definitely that cottage industry. In fact, there is one company in particular, Lexar Media, that bills itself as The Digital Film Company, and all they do is develop storage options for digital cameras and related devices. The are many other companies that are developing digital film, such as Delkin Devices, Simple Technologies, and others. All the major camera manufacturers use memory cards from Toshiba and SanDisk, and those two also have their own brands of their respective cards.

The idea of digital film isn't revolutionary; it's just a smaller version of the type of removable storage we've known since the invention of the floppy disk. In fact, the first digital film was the floppy disk. The Sony Mavica stored captured images on a 1.44-MB, 3.5-inch floppy diskette.

Today's cameras take pictures that are too large to fit on a floppy—although depending on your level of JPEG compression, you may be able to get one image on a floppy. But do you really want to have a ton of floppies around, each with only one image? (Then again, you may finally have a use for that trunk full of old AOL diskettes.)

SuperDisk

That said, Imation has developed a "next-generation" floppy that it calls the SuperDisk. Consisting of a drive and media, the SuperDisk is essentially a 3.5-inch floppy disk whose capacity has been boosted to 120 MB. The drives also read older 1.44-MB floppies. The latest SuperDisk drives are also USB-compatible and are a good option for users of new Macs who need floppy drives but also need a larger storage option.

The SuperDisk hasn't really caught on as a storage medium for digital cameras, although Panasonic has developed the PalmCam PV-SD4090 SuperDisk, which has a built-in SuperDisk drive. Although it does have a lot of storage space for images, the drawback is simply the physical size of the 3.5-inch media. It certainly makes the camera very large, much larger than those that use flash memory cards.

Flash Memory

The most popular types of "digital film" are flash memory cards. Flash memory is a type of memory that is a middle ground between RAM and ROM. Computer RAM (random-access memory), as you know, is what is known as volatile memory. That is to say, data remains stored in it so long as it receives power. Shut the power off, and the data stored in RAM disappears. The advantage of RAM, though, is that it can be erased and new things stored in it. It is also very quickly accessed.

ROM (read-only memory), on the other hand, is nonvolatile memory. It retains the data that is stored in it even when the power is shut off. This is how your computer remembers how to load the operating system; the data stored in ROM tells the computer what to do next to get the operating system going. The disadvantage to ROM is that it cannot be erased or recorded over.

Flash memory is based on the same storage technology as RAM and ROM, but it incorporates the best features of both. It is nonvolatile like ROM, which means it doesn't need a constant power source, but it is erasable like RAM, so it can be reused. Flash memory also has a very fast access time, measured in nanoseconds. (A hard drive, in comparison, accesses media at speeds measured only in lethargic milliseconds.)

PC Cards

One of the first types of storage media based on flash memory is the PCMCIA card, more commonly referred to as a PC card. (PCMCIA stands for Personal Computer Memory Card International Association.) PC cards, which are still popular, are about the size of a credit card and hold up to 64 MB of data. PC cards are often used in notebook computers and in higher-end digital cameras. Their high capacity makes them ideal for the large file sizes produced by

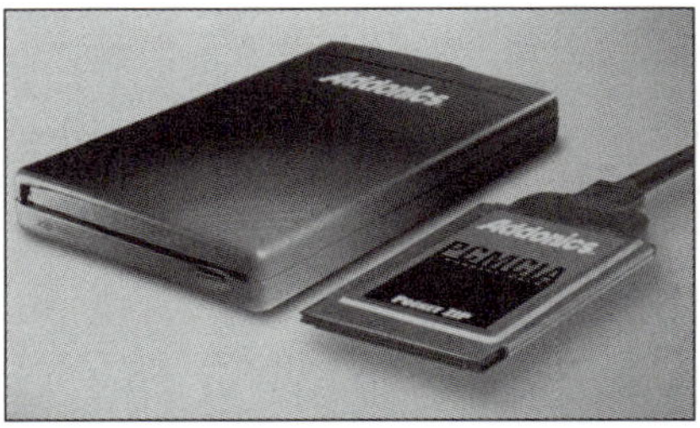

PC cards are a popular option for digital camera images, especially cameras that produce large file sizes. PC cards are high-capacity, and readers are often built into laptop computers.

high-quality digital cameras. Also on the plus side, many notebook computers have built-in PC card readers, which means that it can be fairly easy to get your images off the card and into the computer. However, the large size of the cards makes them somewhat unsuitable for lower-end point-and-shoot cameras. In fact, PC cards are almost as large—if not larger than—some of the new cameras coming out!

CompactFlash

The PC card yielded another type of flash memory card, the CompactFlash. CompactFlash, developed by SanDisk but made by many other manufacturers, is smaller than a PC card, and is about the size of a matchbook. Standards for the CompactFlash card are defined by the CompactFlash Association (CFA), which means that, say, a Nikon CompactFlash card will function exactly as any other type of CompactFlash card. They're all interchangeable, which is nice. They are also high in capacity. Only two years ago, there were only 8-MB CompactFlash cards. Now, sizes of 16 MB, 24 MB, 32 MB, 48 MB, 64 MB, 96 MB, and 128 MB are available. (That's as of this writing; look for capacities to increase.)

Another advantage to the CompactFlash format is that for less than $20 you can buy an adapter that will let CompactFlash cards

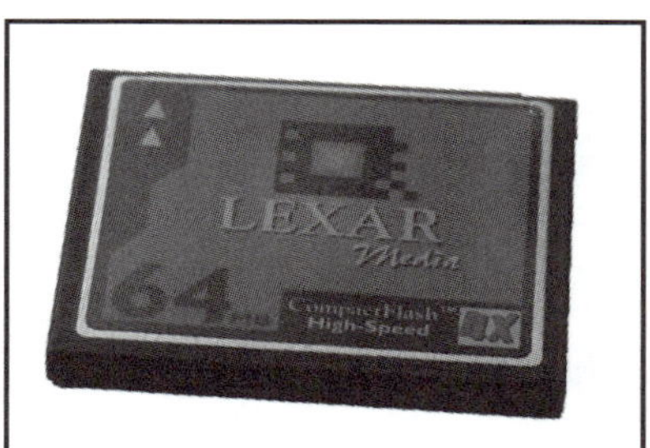

CompactFlash is a popular form of memory card for digital cameras.

be read by PC card readers, which are often found in notebook computers.

That may be a moot point, as there are now inexpensive CompactFlash card readers (see below). It depends on what hardware you already have.

CompactFlash cards are not cheap; an 8-MB card costs somewhere in the neighborhood of $40. The 128-MB card is about $400. (You could get a 9-GB hard drive for that.) But prices are dropping.

SmartMedia

Consumer-level and mid-range digital cameras are the site of a turf war between CompactFlash and another flash card developed by Toshiba but made by others: SmartMedia. Even smaller than CompactFlash—SmartMedia cards are about the size of a small Post-It Note—SmartMedia are also extremely popular among digital camera manufacturers. Although SmartMedia lags behind CompactFlash in storage size (SmartMedia cards range from 4 MB to 8 MB to 16 MB to 32 MB to 64 MB, but needless to say, more are on the way), their small dimensions make them favored by manufacturers who don't want to waste a lot of camera real estate with a big, thick memory card.

SmartMedia cards are also slightly cheaper than CompactFlash, but not by much and then only at the lower capacities. According to the latest MicroWarehouse catalog, you can get a 4-MB SmartMedia card for $25, an 8 MB for $30, and a 32-MB card for $130. Many

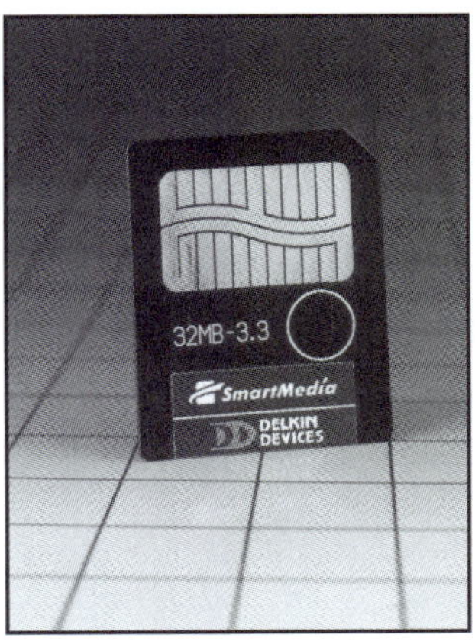

One common alternative to CompactFlash is SmartMedia. SmartMedia is gaining ground in the PDA, palm computing, and MP3 player markets, so may have the upper hand.

experts predict that both CompactFlash and SmartMedia will be comparable in price and capacity in the very near future.

The upshot of the SmartMedia/CompactFlash dichotomy is that both are excellent camera storage media. The higher-capacity CompactFlash makes that an ideal choice for those who take a lot of pictures or use cameras that take big files. (Depending on the camera, you can get about seven or eight "super-high-quality" images on an 8-MB storage card. On our 64-MB CompactFlash card, we can fit about 147 highest-quality images from one of our cameras.)

However, one drawback to SmartMedia is that higher-capacity cards aren't always compatible with older cameras and/or card readers. You may need to purchase what is known as a "firmware" upgrade from your camera or card reader manufacturer if you want to use the newer cards in older devices. The new 32-MB SmartMedia cards caused system crashes when inserted in our older card reader—and caused problems in our older Olympus digital camera. CompactFlash does not have this problem.

The other upshot is that the media you use will be determined by the camera you buy, and it's not really a decision that should heavily weigh on any digital camera purchase.

Some cameras have slots for both types of flash card, and many readers (see below) also have slots for both. Both media have their good points and bad points. SmartMedia cards have the storage surface exposed, and it is believed that data can be easily damaged, although in all our experience we've never actually had this happen. As for CompactFlash, the readers and writers connect to the card via a series of very small pins, which can become bent or broken off, rendering the reader unusable. We've never had this problem either, but it is possible.

One developing market that may impact this battle is the palm computing market. New palmtop computers and PDAs have seized on SmartMedia, as have the new breed of MP3 audio players. As all these niches strive for standardization, it is likely that one media type that can be used interchangeably will prevail. But then again, look how many storage options there are for desktop computing.

Digital Film Readers

Okay, I hear you say, how do I get images from the digital film to the computer? Even though you can download images from your CompactFlash or SmartMedia card via the serial/parallel/USB connectivity we discussed earlier, some pretty elegant options have debuted. These are the digital film readers.

SanDisk came out with a CompactFlash card reader a couple of years ago, and Lexar Media has followed suit. Essentially, the CompactFlash card reader is a drive that can be connected to a PC's parallel port. A software driver is included for Windows 95/98/NT, and essentially the drive shows up as a removable disk drive in your My Computer zone. You insert the card in the device, and images can be copied right to your hard drive—and very quickly, too. Unfortunately, there is no Mac version of the device as of this writing.

Lexar, an equal-opportunity digital film manufacturer, also has a SmartMedia version of the device, which operates in the exact same way.

Meanwhile, Microtech, an industry veteran that cut its teeth on the first generation of SyQuest drives in the late 1980s, has a USB

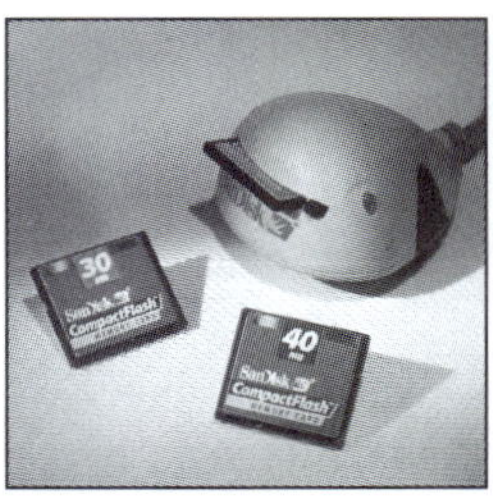

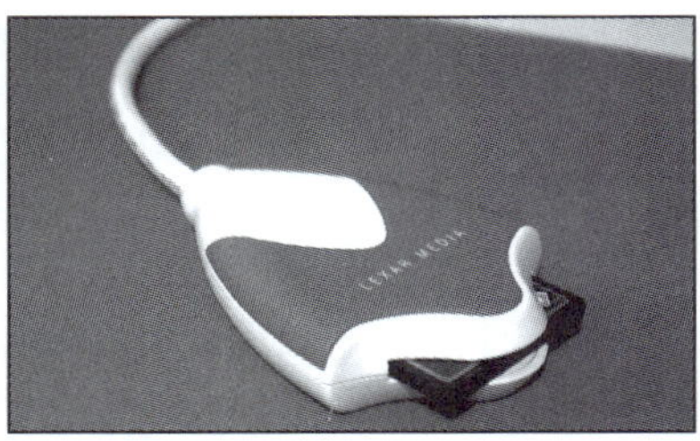

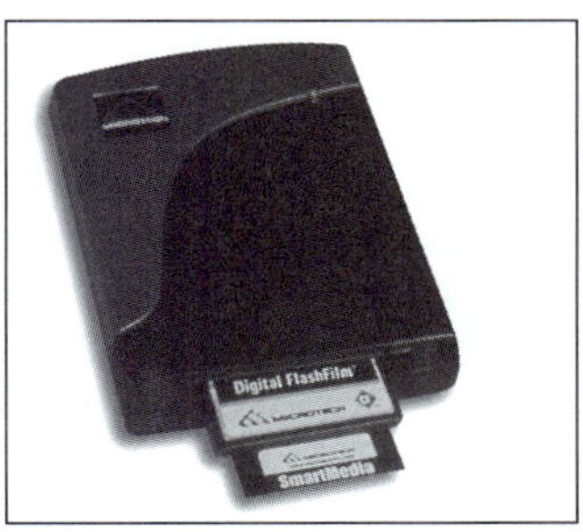

Above left: SanDisk's original ImageMate CompactFlash card reader. Above: Lexar Media's CompactFlash card reader. Lexar also has a similar model that reads SmartMedia. Left: Microtech's USB CameraMate is a great little device that lets you quickly and easily bring both SmartMedia and CompactFlash images into the computer via the USB port.

digital film reader that has slots for both SmartMedia and CompactFlash. It plugs into the USB port on both Mac and PC, and (on the Mac) either or both cards show up right on the desktop, just like any other removable disk. Images can be copied to and from it. It's a marvelous little device; it was my workhorse during the production of this book, as it let me quickly and easily get all my assorted SmartMedia and CompactFlash images into the computer.

However, this was the device I mentioned earlier that caused problems when I tried to use it to read the 32-MB SmartMedia cards.

Other manufacturers are going the USB route as well, and these devices are usually available for less than $80 or so.

Floppy Disk Adapters

Another transfer method that Toshiba had originally developed is the floppy disk adapter. Taking advantage of the thinness of the SmartMedia card, the floppy disk adapter is essentially a floppy diskette "shell" that features a slot for a SmartMedia card and electronics that let the card be inserted in a PC's floppy drive and transferred that way. The computer needs drivers, of course, but it works pretty well, and there is a Mac version of the driver.

However, this doesn't help if you've bought one of the new Macs that lack a floppy drive. And like the floppy, the SmartMedia adapter is a slow transfer method. As floppies themselves go away, there may be less of a market for these adapters in the near future.

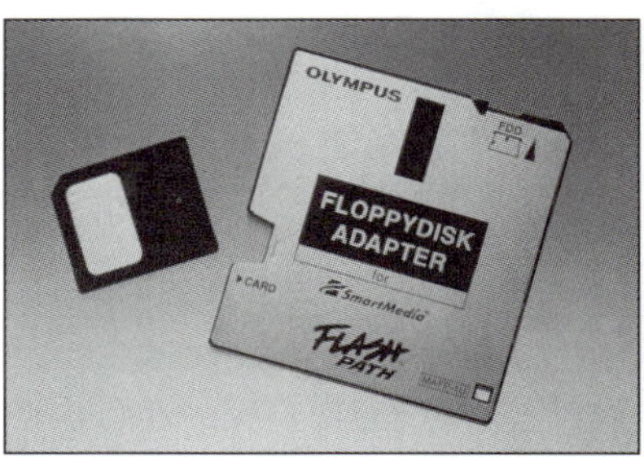

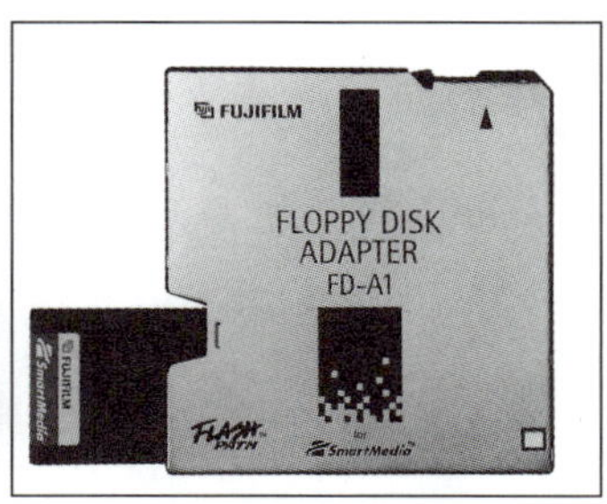

Both Olympus (left) and Fuji (as well as others) make floppy disk adapters that let you read SmartMedia cards via the computer's floppy drive.

Clik!

One other unique product that is good for those who don't want to invest in a ton of SmartMedia or CompactFlash cards is the Iomega Clik! drive. The Clik! is a small, hand-held drive that reads and writes to small, 40-MB disks. The drive features a rechargeable battery, and it can be left in a cradle to recharge or toted around in a carrying case that hooks to one's belt. The cradle can be connected to a PC's parallel port, and the Clik! disks can be copied to one's hard drive as one would other Iomega media, such as Zip or Jaz cartridges. The unique aspect of the Clik! drive is that the drive has a snap-on module that features slots for both SmartMedia and CompactFlash cards. When a card is inserted, it can be copied to the Clik! disk with the push of a button, and the LCD readout tells you how full the Clik! disk is.

The advantage to this is that if you are on location and taking a lot of different shots, you need to buy only one CompactFlash or SmartMedia card. When it is full, you simply dump the images onto the Clik! disk, erase the card, and continue shooting. The drive is priced at $249 and the media at $10 per disk, when purchased in packs of 10. As you can see, this is an economical option in lieu of buying a bunch of $400 128-MB CompactFlash cards.

Whether that will remain economical for long, as the price of the flash memory cards comes down, is anyone's guess. But for now, the Clik! may be a good intermediate solution to the problem of needing to take more pictures than your media can handle.

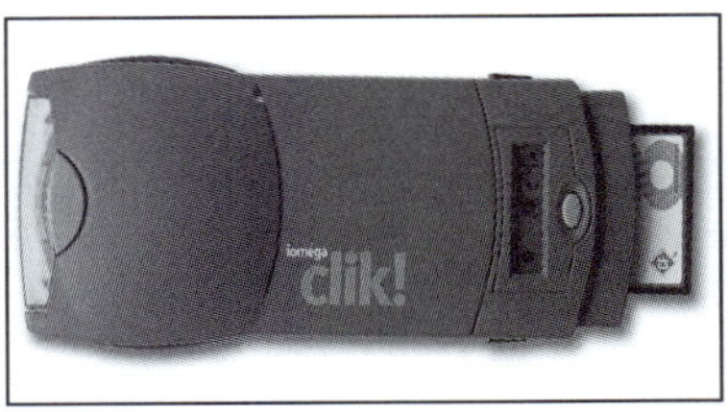

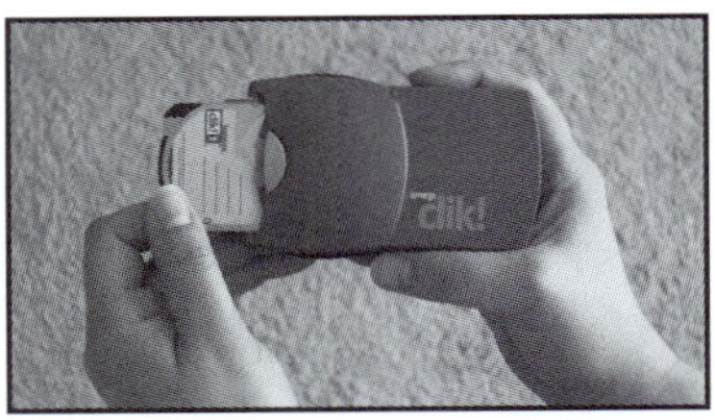

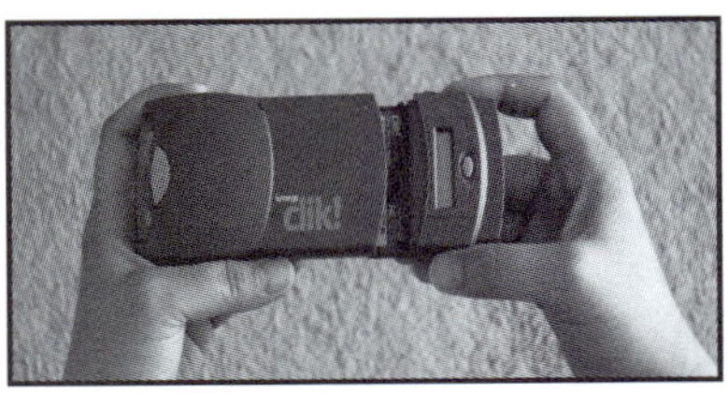

Iomega's Clik! drive reads its own 40-MB disks, which are priced fairly inexpensively. The device also reads SmartMedia and CompactFlash, which it can copy to its own disks. It can also connect to a PC. (Photos courtesy of Joe LiPetri.)

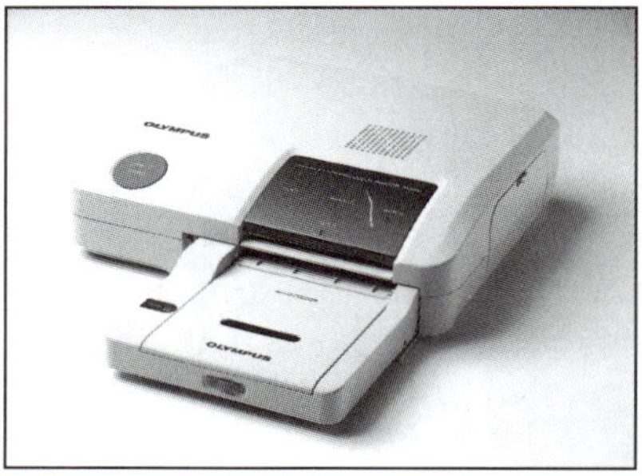

Olympus has a line of inexpensive dye-sublimation printers that can print directly from its cameras. Other manufacturers have various types of direct-connect printers, as well.

Direct Printing

Some manufacturers are going one better and are seeking to take the PC out of the digital imaging chain completely. So far, many camera manufacturers, including Sony, Epson, Olympus, Fuji, Kodak, and others, sell low-end dye-sublimation or inkjet printers that can be connected directly to a digital camera (sorry, you can't use one manufacturer's camera with another manufacturer's printer). Software in the camera lets you pick which image(s) you want to print, or even if you just want to print several rows of thumbnails. At the press of a button, the printer prints the selected images.

The printers typically sell for around $400–$500, and as you can imagine, the quality varies. But generally speaking, it's a good solution for those who want quickie prints of the images. The advantage also is that some—if not most—of these printers can be connected to a PC and can function as general-purpose color printers, if you need one. The best choices are the ones that print on paper that is larger than 4 × 6 inches, since then you don't need to dedicate a printer just to generating images from your digital camera.

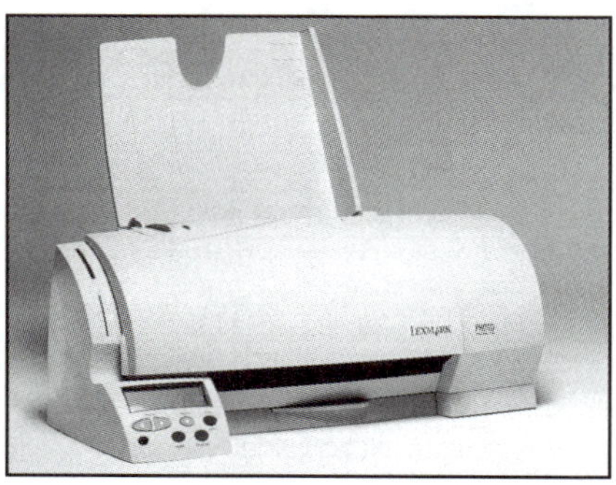

The Lexmark Photo Jetprinter 5770 is able to print directly from a CompactFlash or SmartMedia card without any computer intervention.

Another interesting approach to the direct printing idea was undertaken by Lexmark about a year or so ago. Called the Photo Jetprinter 5770, it was an inkjet printer that had slots for SmartMedia and CompactFlash cards. It could print images directly from the card, which meant that your printing wasn't tied to any one vendor. The printer also allowed basic image cropping or scaling, and let you add a variety of basic effects to images as they were being printed. The key to it was keeping the device updated with the latest digital camera drivers, which could be downloaded free from Lexmark's Web site. Near as I can tell, it never made much of a splash.

As nice as the direct-print features are, they really haven't caught on, primarily because the point of digital photography is to keep the images in electronic form. In other words, you take digital images because you want them on a computer, either to e-mail, post on the Web, or incorporate in other digital documents. Bypassing the computer does seem to miss the point of digital photography.

Media

That said, though, often you do want a print of your digital images, even if they are destined for some primarily digital medium. One of the sticking points with output options for digital images has been that of longevity. One of the least expensive and highest-quality options of desktop color printing is inkjet. But the dye-based inks used in inkjet printing had very short lives before the image faded away. However, as this book was being finalized, a new set of inks and media designed for a new series of inkjet printers from Epson addresses this problem. We'll look at printing issues in more detail in the next chapter, when we discuss what to do with images.

Summary

As you can tell, there are many options for storing your images, transporting them, and getting them from the camera to either a PC or a printer. What's reassuring is that some of these technologies are also being implemented in other areas of technological development. For example, flash memory cards like SmartMedia and CompactFlash are used for file transfer and storage for PDAs, PalmPilots, and other such devices. If you play your cards right (pun intended), you may be able to consolidate your removable storage with other aspects of your life.

Onward

Now that we've got some images into the camera (at our photo shoots), and we've figured out how we can get them out of the camera into the computer, let's go ahead and do just that, and explore our image-editing, enhancement, and output options.

6

Working with Images

Now that we've captured our images and brought them into the computer, it's time to begin working with them. There are many, many applications available for you to edit, manipulate, save, and print your images. These range from very inexpensive utilities, often bundled with the cameras themselves, to programs costing hundreds of dollars. In general, the program you use will be a function of what you ultimately want to do with your images—be it print them to an inkjet printer, import them into a page-layout program for print publishing, or post to the Web. In fact, you may want to do all of these things.

Image-Editing Applications

Before we start working with images, let's take a brief look at what applications are available. (For more information on these and other products, see the Resources section on page 214.)

Adobe Photoshop

This is the granddaddy of all image-editing programs. It is one of the oldest (version 1.0 appeared in 1990) and is the de facto standard for graphic arts pros. At version 5.5 (as of this writing), it has almost every conceivable tool for manipulating images. Chances are, if it's not in Photoshop, you don't need it. Well, that's not entirely true, but you get the idea. Photoshop lets you resize images, scale images, upsample or downsample images, change the color spaces of the images, crop images, improve (or worsen) color balance, contrast, and other qualities, sharpen images, composite several images, draw on images, or apply any or all of thousands of different filters and effects. These filters and effects are available as *plug-ins*, small subapplications that operate from within the Filters menu in Photoshop.

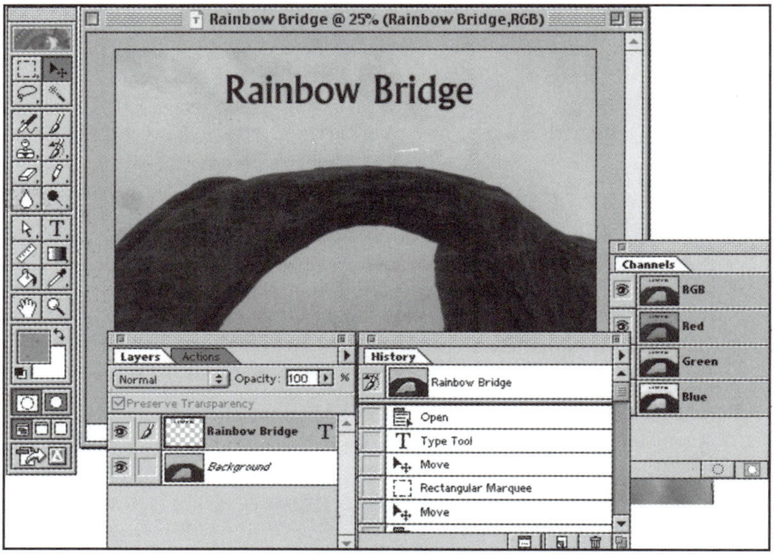

Although it can seem a bit like a fever dream to the uninitiated, Photoshop has a wealth of tools that has made it — quite rightly — perhaps the de facto standard for image editing for professional graphic arts pros.

Photoshop lets you optimize images for print, and it can save images in any of many different file formats. Version 5.5 also comes bundled with ImageReady, a complementary program for optimizing images for Web publishing.

Photoshop is available for both the PC and the Macintosh and works fairly seamlessly in most cross-platform environments.

The drawback to Photoshop is that it can be very complicated, especially to casual or new digital imaging users. It is also more expensive than most casual users may be willing to spend; in fact, the program itself can cost almost as much as a digital camera! Fortunately, there are simpler and cheaper applications on the market, many geared specifically for the casual user.

Corel PhotoPaint

A less expensive program than Photoshop, and currently available only on the PC, Corel's PhotoPaint, now at version 9, is part of Corel's graphics suite of programs that also includes CorelDraw as well as many other utilities and royalty-free stock photography. PhotoPaint does many, if not most, of the things that Photoshop can do, but doesn't have the market share that Photoshop enjoys.

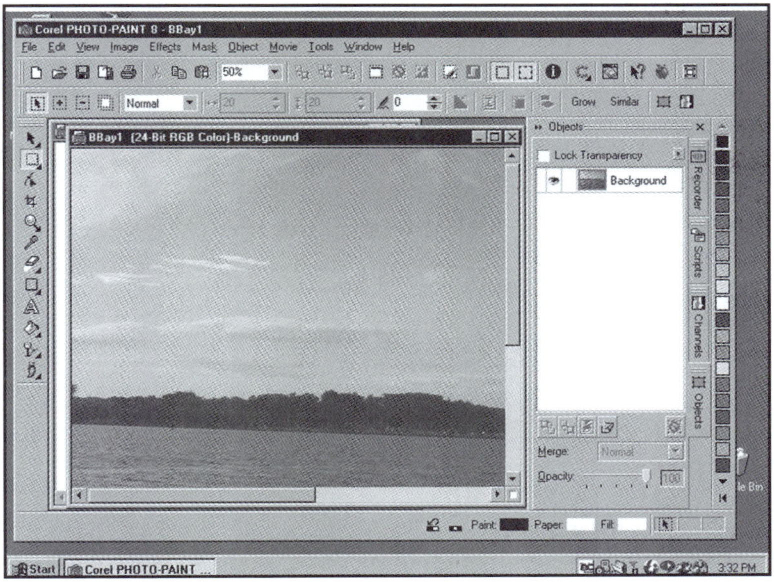

Corel's PhotoPaint is bundled as part of the Corel Graphics Suite that also includes CorelDraw.

Microsoft PhotoDraw 2000

Not to be left out of any software niche, Microsoft has recently released PhotoDraw 2000 version 2, designed as a complement to Microsoft Office. Although very different in its interface than many of the more popular high-end graphics programs, PhotoDraw does make working with images pretty easy, especially if you're a neophyte. It has a number of templates and can access a connected digital camera or scanner fairly easily. It comes with a bunch of stock

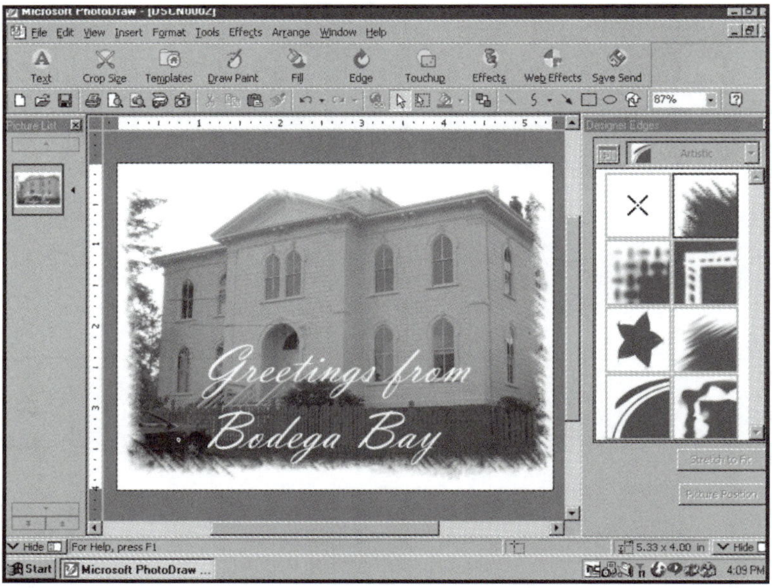

PhotoDraw makes it pretty easy to import digital camera images and add a variety of border, text, and other effects.

images, which range from fairly usable to godawful. It has a very Photoshop-like layers approach, and it does a lot of nice things with text and borders, as well as other effects. Its biggest drawback for print publishers is that it does not handle CMYK images.

Ulead PhotoImpact

One PC-only program that is bundled with some digital cameras is Ulead's PhotoImpact, now at version 5. Originally designed as a low-rent competitor to Photoshop, PhotoImpact has retooled itself as a primarily Web-only application, and it includes many creative tools for spiffing up Web images. And at $80, it does an awful lot.

Adobe Photoshop LE

Perhaps oddly, one of the cheapest alternatives to Photoshop is … Photoshop. Huh? Actually, Photoshop LE (Limited Edition) has been around for a long time and was originally available only as part of a software bundle included with many scanners. Recently, Adobe decided to market the program in its own right at a cut-rate price ($99, as of early 2000).

Photoshop LE is essentially the same program as the full version, but as its name implies, it has some limitations. Most notably, Photoshop LE lacks the ability to work with CMYK images. CMYK—short for cyan, magenta, yellow, and black—is the required color space for print publishing, as these are the colors a printing press prints. In contrast, most digital images are by default in the RGB—red, green, and blue—color space, which are the three colors that a computer monitor displays. If your images are destined for print, you'll need to use a program that handles CMYK images.

Adobe PhotoDeluxe

Not to be left out of any imaging niche, Adobe has PhotoDeluxe, an inexpensive, consumer-oriented imaging program. Bundled with many digital cameras, PhotoDeluxe boasts a simpler interface than Photoshop.

MetaCreations Painter

What can I say about Painter? I started playing around with Painter several years ago when version 4 came out (it's now at version 7) and it is one of the most fun programs to play with I have ever seen. Painter is a "natural media" painting program, sort of a fine-art version of Photoshop. Painter lets you paint images from scratch, giving you a wealth of pen, brush, ink, and paint styles to choose from. You can also import digital images—such as those you've shot with your digital camera—and turn them into art. Painter also has what is called an Image Hose, a tool that lets you "spray" repetitions of a single image into another image. You can save your digital images so that they can be imported into the Image Hose.

Plug-ins and Effects

Photoshop's plug-in architecture has spawned an entire industry of plug-in and effects manufacturers. One of the first and most powerful was Kai's Power Tools, developed by noted designer Kai Krause in the early 1990s. Originally produced by HSC Software, HSC became MetaTools, which merged with Fractal Design to become MetaCreations, which recently released version 6 of Kai's Power Tools (KPT).

One of my favorite plug-ins, which started out as a PC-only tool but is now Mac compatible as well, is called Deep Paint, from New

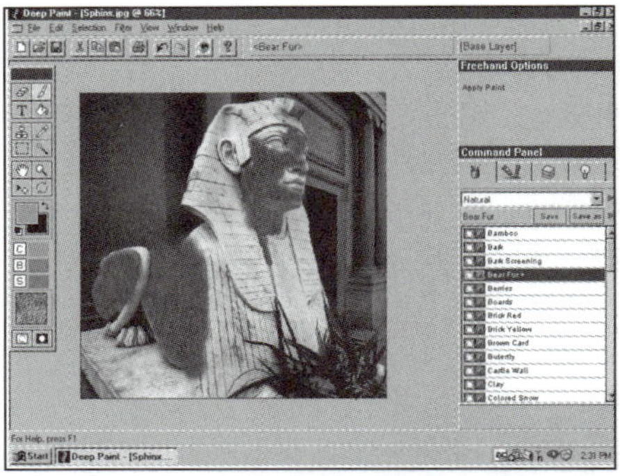

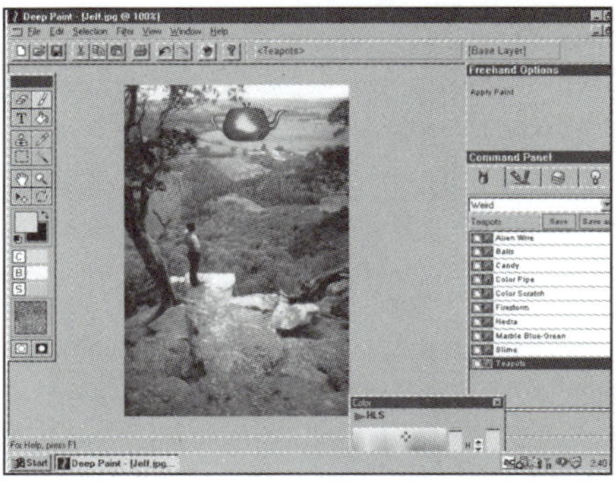

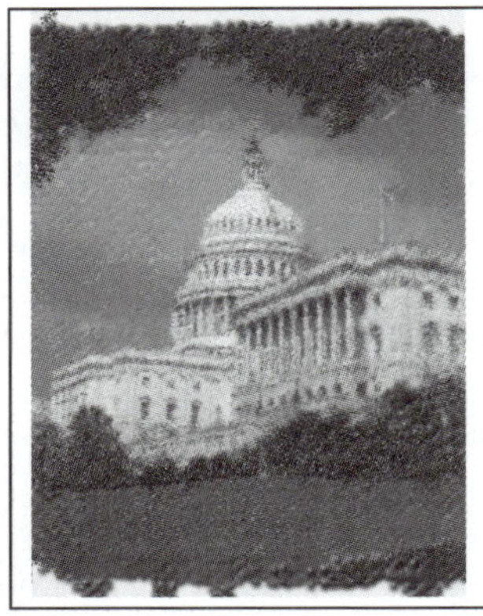

Deep Paint, from Right Hemisphere, is a combination plug-in to Photoshop and stand-alone program that functions a lot like MetaCreations Painter. You can add a variety of painterly (or just plain bizarre) effects to your digital images, such as bear fur, a Seurat-like pointillist effect, or just do something silly.

Zealand-based Right Hemisphere. Deep Paint functions as both a stand-alone program and as a Photoshop plug-in and works very much like Painter, giving you a variety of "natural" media, inks, and paints to work with. It also has a number of presets built in. Like Painter, it is also staggeringly fun to play with, and it is possible even for those of us who are artistically challenged to get great-looking—or at the very least very odd—results.

Photoshop plug-ins are also a cottage industry. See the Resources section for a more extensive list of what's available.

Editing Images

Probably the first thing you're going to want to do with a captured image is edit it in some way.

By the way, let me just say at the outset that although there are many programs for editing images (as we've just seen), we will be concentrating on Adobe Photoshop in the rest of this section. There are a couple of reasons for this. The first is that I know it better than the others. The second is that this book is skewed more toward graphic artists, and Photoshop is arguably the de facto standard for image editing and manipulation. (We'll touch on the other programs in passing throughout this section, though.) And to answer that cynical question you're no doubt framing, no, I don't get kickbacks from Adobe for mentioning their products.

Anyway, one of the first things you might need to do is rotate your image. For example, if you have taken a shot that is in "portrait" orientation (taller than it is wide, usually accomplished by turning the camera at a 90-degree angle), it will come into your image-editing program horizontally, or in "landscape" orientation.

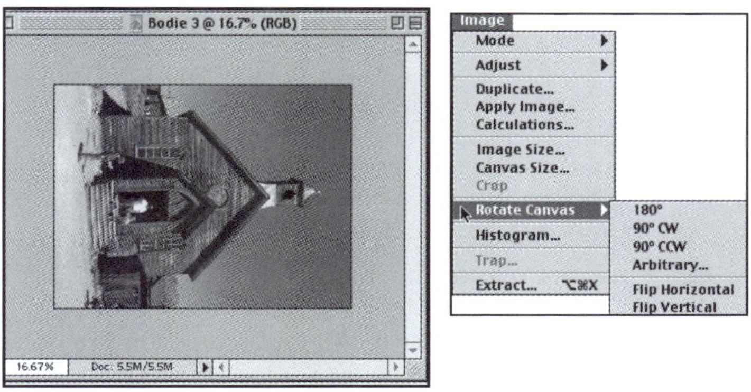

Most programs give you the ability to rotate an image.

This may be a no-brainer, but this is accomplished by using the rotate command (in Photoshop, it is Rotate Canvas). The image can be rotated clockwise or counterclockwise. Often you can flip an image horizontally or vertically, or rotate an image at the arbitrary angle of your choosing (i.e., 47 degrees), if you want to.

Contrast and Brightness

Depending on your photographic skills, you may have an image that is over- or underexposed. For example, outdoor shots taken in bright sunlight can be very washed out, while those taken indoors can look very dark. As you get better at making pre-exposure adjustments in the camera, or adjusting lighting, you'll begin to obviate many of these problems. As you remember from the days of film, you were often at the mercy of the prints you got back. But modern image-editing applications give you a great degree of control over the image, and you can clean up a lot of user error.

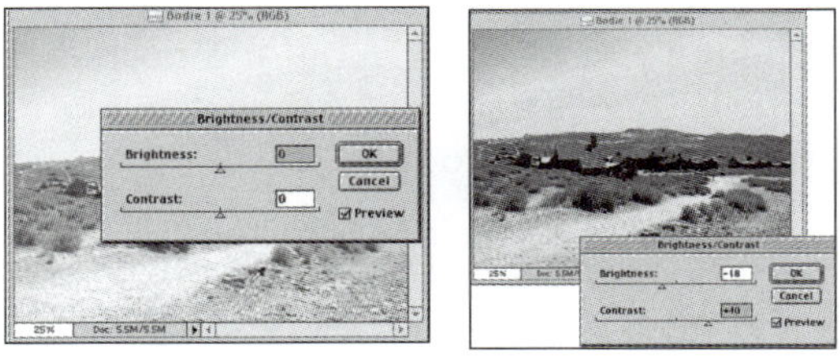

Adjusting brightness and contrast is a good, quick way to save slightly over- or underexposed images.

The most basic way of doing this is via the Brightness/Contrast box. Most programs offer a live preview that lets you see what specifically you are doing to an image, which lets you stop before you ruin things irretrievably. Brightness, as you would expect, makes an image brighter or darker. In Photoshop, for example, moving the slider in the positive direction (to the right) lightens an image, while moving it in the negative direction (to the left) makes it darker. Contrast boosts the difference between light and dark.

Often, if you make an image brighter, you'll need to boost its contrast to keep it from becoming washed out. If you decrease the brightness, you may need to decrease the contrast to keep the image from getting too murky. There are few hard and fast rules here; adjust the image until you like the way it looks.

How Not to Be Done In By Dot Gain

If you are taking digital images destined for print reproduction, there is one thing you need to worry about, and that is *dot gain*. Dot gain has a number of causes, but what it refers to is that the halftone dots that comprise a continuous-tone image (such as a photograph) get larger when printed.

What does this mean? Well, it means that images will tend to print a bit darker than they may look on screen or on an inkjet print or proof. Dot gain tends to vary with the type of paper on which you print. Uncoated or matte papers tend to absorb more ink, thus the dots expand as they are absorbed into the paper. Glossy and high-quality papers don't absorb so much. The upshot is that when you are editing your images for print, you may want to boost the brightness a little bit beyond what looks good on screen. You don't want to make it *too* washed out; I've had good results with a brightness boost of +10 or +15. And we usually complement that with an equivalent boost in contrast. This will vary by image, of course, but this is a pretty good rule of thumb.

Levels

If you are a graphics pro—well, you don't need me to explain levels to you. If you have some proficiency with Photoshop, you have a number of other options for improving the quality of your images. You can also adjust what are known as levels. This is a bit more precise than simply adjusting brightness and contrast. For example, you can adjust the brightness and contrast of the individual color channels (red, green, and blue), as well as the entire composite image itself.

Levels adjustment is based on the image's histogram. A *histogram* is a graph that shows the distribution of image density. A "good" histogram resembles—or at least approximates—a bell curve; the densities are distributed somewhat evenly from light to dark, with a bulge in the midtones. A "bad" histogram, or one that describes an image that is too light or too dark will have density "bulges" at either the light (highlight) or dark (shadow) ends.

By using the levels adjustment, you can set the light and dark points, either using eyedropper tools to select the whitest part of an image or the blackest part of an image, or by moving sliders, much

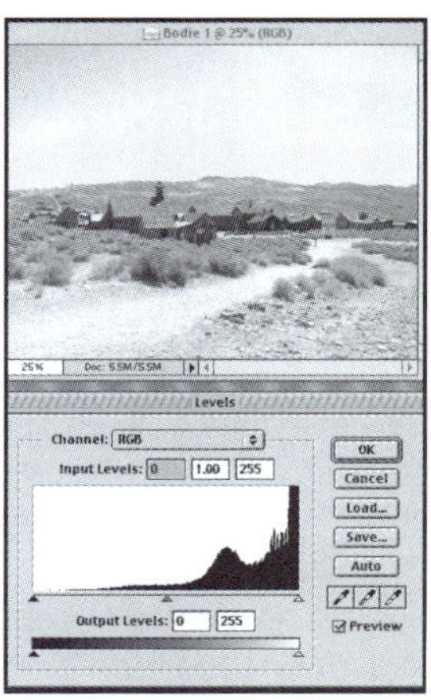

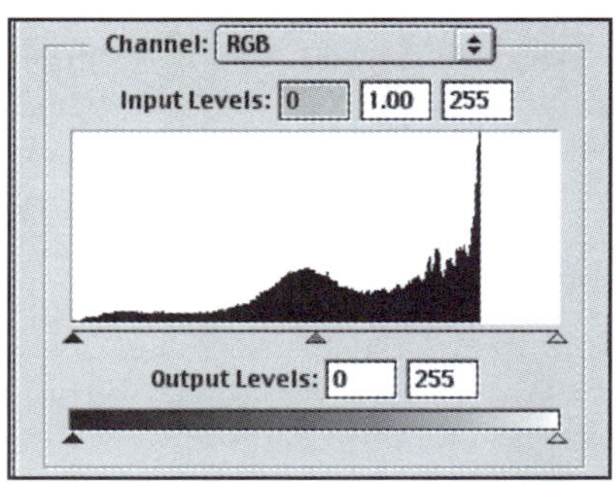

If you have a very underexposed, washed-out image, you can try moving the white point toward the dark end. It may or may not help.

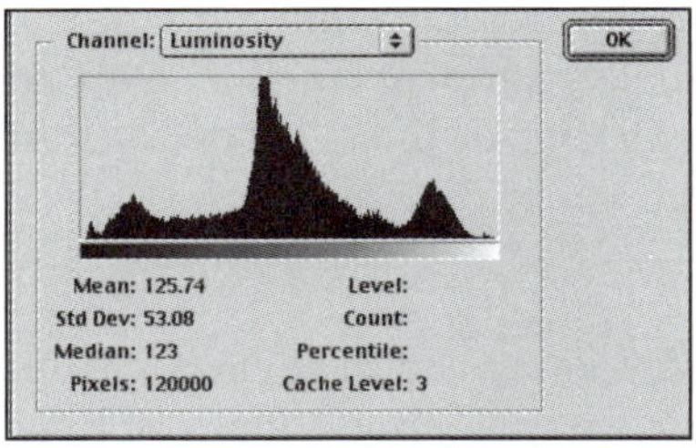

An image histogram in Photoshop.

like we saw in the Brightness/Contrast box. Moving the highlight slider to the left makes an image darker; moving the shadow slider to the right makes it lighter. Often you'll have better success by moving the midtone slider. It will depend on the image. Again, the rule of thumb is not to worry too much about rules of thumb; adjust it until you think it looks good. Most programs also have an auto-levels feature that works reasonably well.

The Pros and Perils of Sharpening

As you may also recall from film-based photography, pictures often come out blurry. You were often stuck with the results—a faint, indistinguishable blur that was supposed to be Grandma. Well, sad to say, even in the digital world, you may still be stuck with the result. Image editing is only so powerful, despite what television shows like *The X Files* depict; I love it when they have a "forensic imaging expert" bring an image into a software program and resolve almost infinite levels of detail from an indistinguishable blur. It's just not possible.

Be that as it may, if the blurriness isn't too bad, you may be able to yield a usable image after all, using some of the sharpening filters these programs make available to you. The best of these is called Unsharp Masking. This may sound like it blurs an image (unsharp?) but it is actually a sharpening tool.

The term and the basic concept date back to traditional graphic arts photography. The original "unsharp mask" was a somewhat blurry, low-contrast photographic negative produced from a transparency and placed on top of that transparency (i.e., like mask) when making color separations. The light passing through the mask was altered, which resulted in a color correction to compensate for hue errors inherent in process color inks. One side benefit of unsharp masking was that it enhanced (actually, exaggerated) the edges on the image, yielding greater detail on the color separation negatives.

It is this latter aspect of unsharp masking that made the transition to the digital world. Essentially, unsharp masking is a filter in a pro-

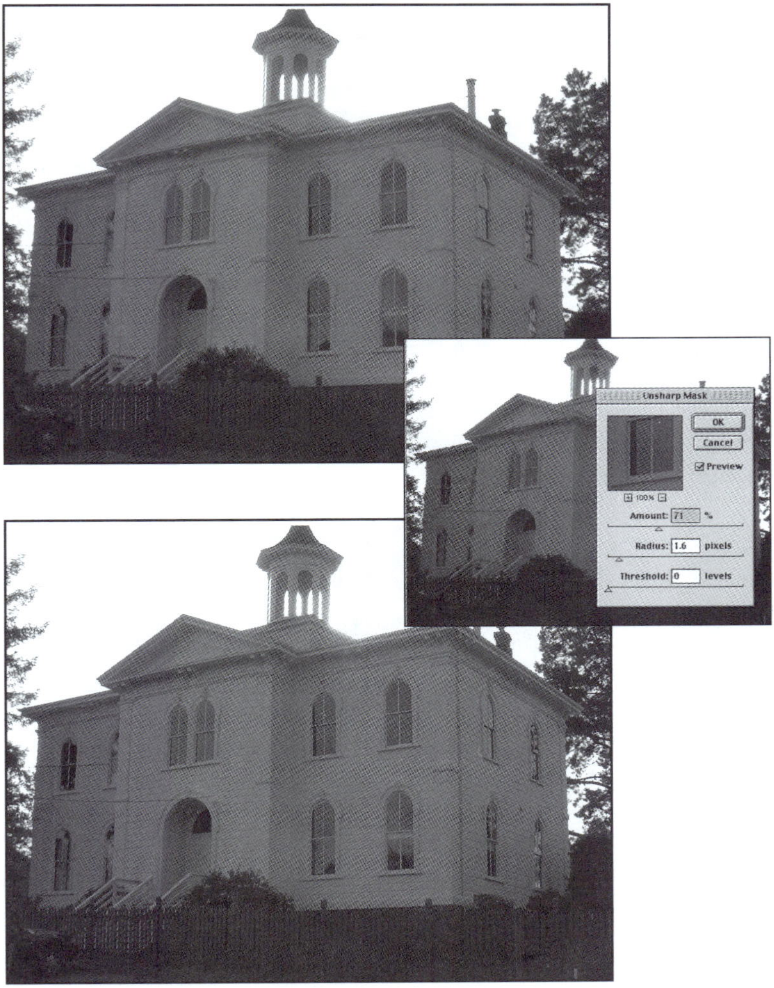

Unsharp masking can help you sharpen a slightly blurry image or bring out subtle detail. The top image is un-unsharp masked; the bottom image has had a little bit of unsharp masking.

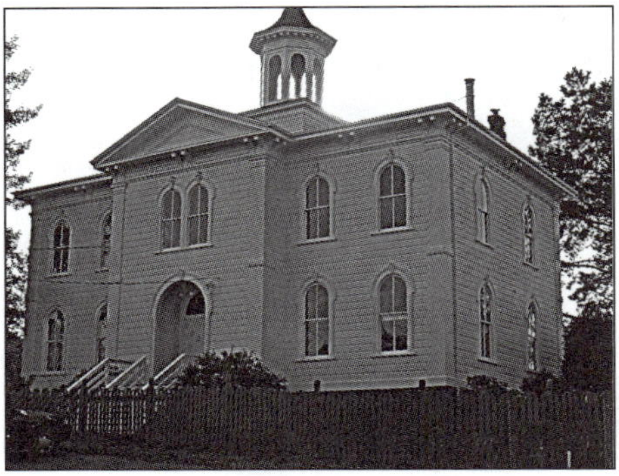

Too much unsharp masking can make an image look very grainy.

gram such as Photoshop that analyzes adjacent pixels, locates the edges of objects, and adjusts the tonal values of the pixels on either side of the edge in opposite directions, increasing the contrast. Unsharp masking (as well as somewhat less-powerful filters such as Sharpen and Sharpen More) can help save an otherwise unusable image, but remember that it has its limitations. The Unsharp Mask filter should also be used judiciously, as it tends to give images a very grainy effect, especially when used in large doses.

Some digital cameras automatically apply unsharp masking filters to an image upon capture, with varying degrees of success. Some users think the result is just fine; others report that the effect is exceedingly grainy for their tastes. As with most aspects of imaging, use these tools to make an image look good to you.

Know Your Color Spaces

If your image is destined for print, you'll need to change its color mode to a print-friendly color space. If you are printing in color, you will need to convert to CMYK. The default color space of most if not all digital cameras is RGB. If RGB images are imported into

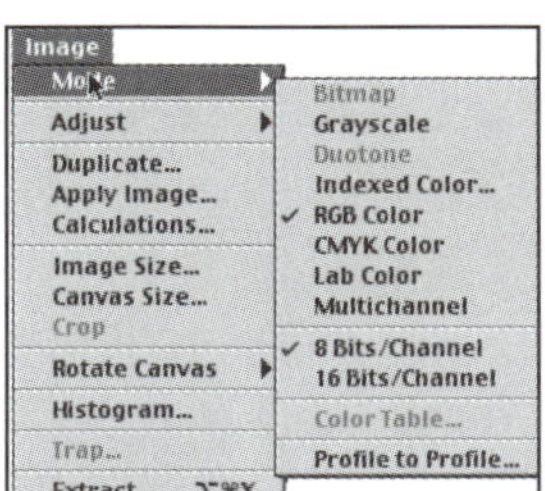

The Color Mode pop-up menu in Photoshop easily lets you convert to CMYK — or a variety of other color spaces.

a page layout (such as a QuarkXPress or InDesign document), you will get a blank box when you get your film back from the service bureau. This is bad juju. Consequently, you will need to convert to CMYK, which will allow the images to separate properly. In most programs, this is a simple process involving selecting the CMYK option in the Color or Color Mode pop-up menu. (Be careful, though; some low-end graphics programs do not support CMYK.)

Sometimes, your service bureau will want to do its own conversion to CMYK, sometimes your printer will. Whole books have been written about color management—of which converting to CMYK is but a small part—and it is a very complex and nettlesome subject. Compounding the problem is that different experts will tell you different things about the need for it. Suffice it to say here (and color management is beyond the scope of this book) that there are a variety of tools that enable you to manage color from input to output.

If you are printing in black-and-white only, you will need to convert to grayscale. If you will need a color image in the future, it is a good idea to save the grayscale version with a different name, or tack on a "-g" to the file name. Make sure you import the correct file into your layout, needless to say (but I'll say it anyway).

In some programs, there is a very striking difference between what is called "black-and-white" and what is called "grayscale." Grayscale refers to images that have many (usually 256 or more) gradations of gray on a scale from white to black. Black-and-white can sometimes refer to 1-bit images, or images that are described only as black or white. If you convert to this, you'll get something resembling a fax.

Depending on your editing program, you may have other colorspace options. One cool one is duotone. As you would expect from its name, a duotone is a two-color image. The two can be any colors you want; one is usually black. In Photoshop, you need to convert to grayscale first, then go back to the Color Mode pop-up and select duotone. You can then pick which colors you want. The second color is often a spot, but it can be a process color as well. You can adjust the duotone curve, or how much of each color is added. Duotones are good for giving a sepia-like or old-world effect to images. In a black-and-white-only book such as this, it's hard to show you the effect of this, but you get the idea.

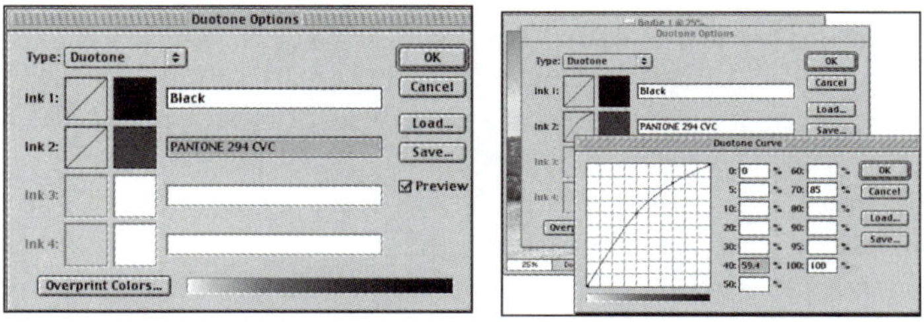

Converting an image to a duotone lets you add any color to black (or any other color) to give your images nice effects, such as a sepia, old-world look.

Other Editing Options

Once again, depending on your image-editing program, you can have a wealth of filters and effects to choose from. As the screen grabs below show you, Photoshop itself has seemingly zillions of stylistic options, and entire books have been written on these alone.

There are also many different plug-ins available, most notably Kai's Power Tools (KPT) from MetaCreations, as well as a variety of op-

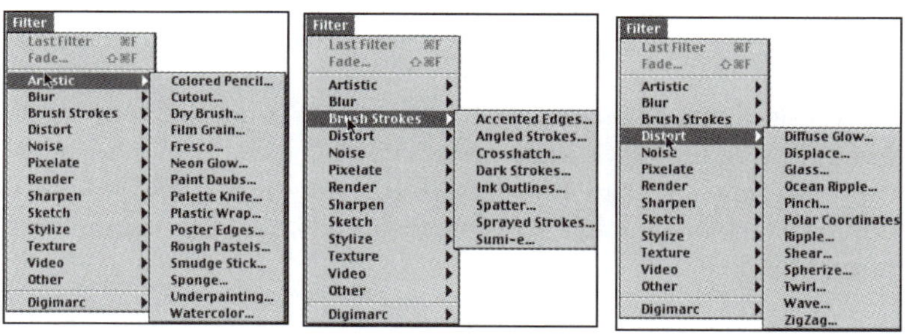

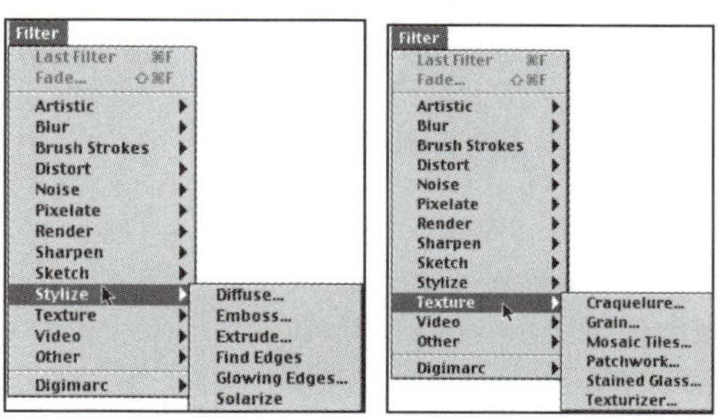

This is but a small sample of the types of filters that are available in Photoshop.

tions from Extensis. Rather than go into all these filters here, I encourage you to play with them yourself and see what they can do. You may not get much productive work done, but it's fun.

Another image-editing option is compositing. This essentially lets you insert other images or portions of images into a single image. Depending upon your skill, this can look quite realistic indeed. And some folks are so skilled at it that photographs are losing credibility as evidence in court trials.

Compositing can be done in a variety of ways. One simple way is to use what are variously called clone or rubber-stamp tools. These let you copy portions of an image elsewhere in the image, such as adding a separate house (or cactus), another "clone" of a person in the image, or what-have-you. Cloning is often done to clean up images, such as remove a stain on a shirt, lengthen a tie on the sartorially challenged, or clear up someone's complexion.

You can also clone from different images, such as taking a shot of Uncle Ned—who was unable to go with you to the Grand Canyon—and actually inserting him in a shot of the canyon itself. Ned may deny that he was ever there, but you can easily show him proof that you didn't take off without him. (Well, if you're mean, you can.)

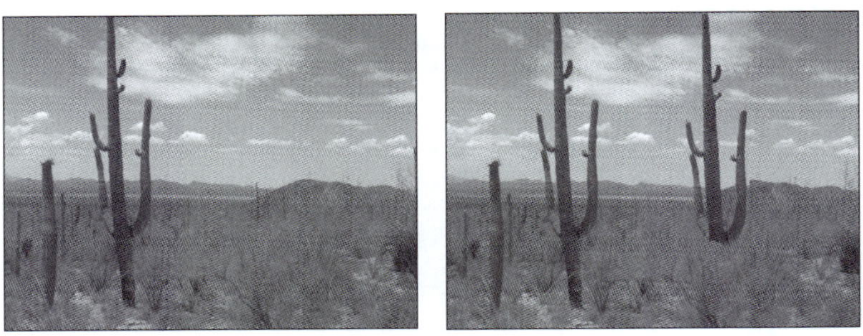

If we wanted, we could use the Photoshop Clone tool to solve problems of deforestation, as we found by simply "planting" a second saguaro.

At any rate, you get the idea.

Depending on what your ultimate use of a digital image is, you may or may not be excited by filters and compositing.

This is all a bit more impressive in color, but here is a random, brief sampling of some of the effects you can achieve in Photoshop — and this is without benefit of third-party plug-ins. (I shot this saguaro image in the Arizona desert with an Olympus C-2000Z digital camera.)

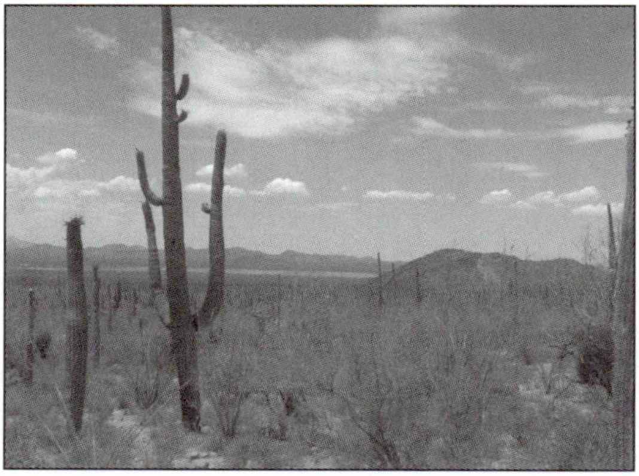

Original image

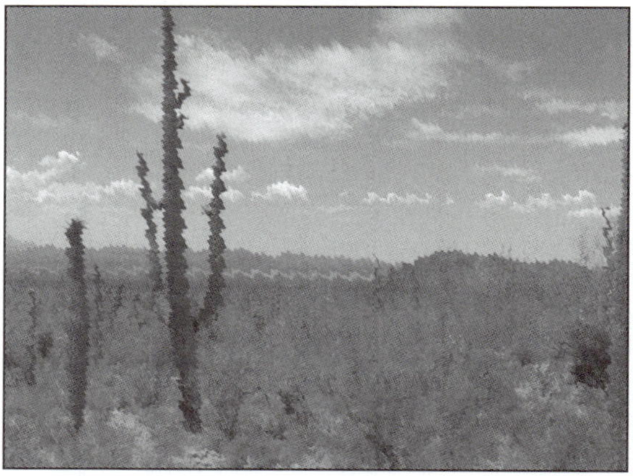

Ripple

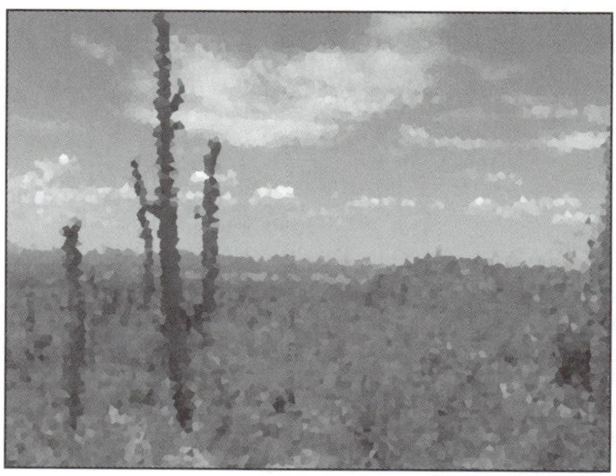

Crystallize

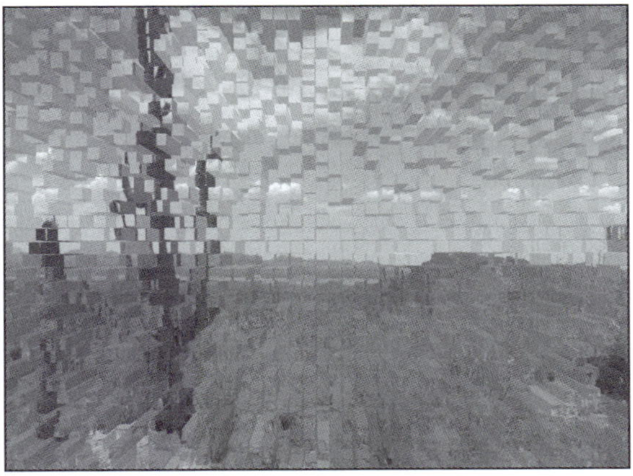

Extrude

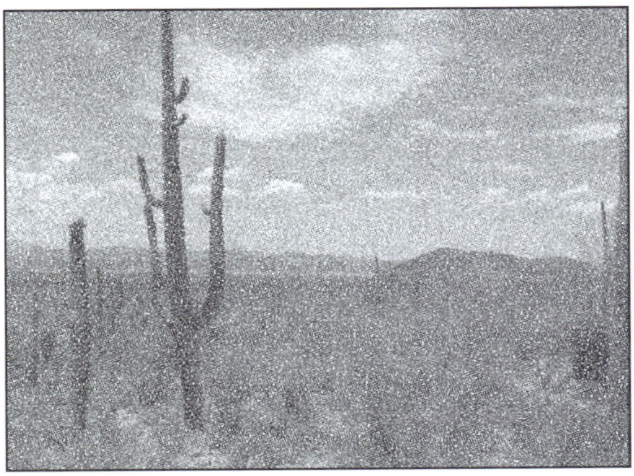

Pointillist

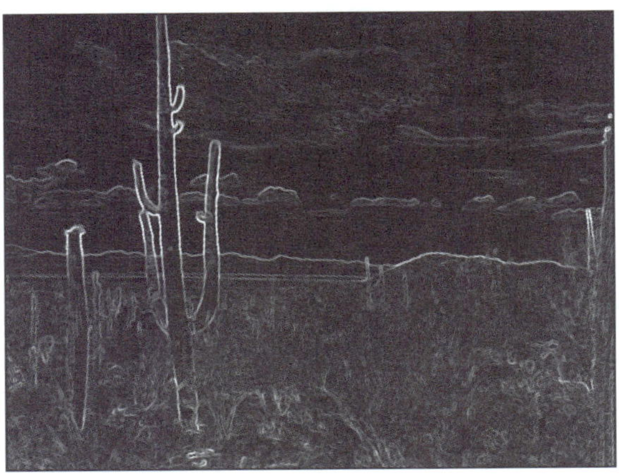

Glowing Edges

If you are a catalog publisher, you probably don't want pointillist images of products (or you may; who am I to judge?), and if you are a photojournalist, I certainly hope you won't be looking too longingly at the clone tool. But if you are a digital artist or illustrator, these tools can give you a lot of flexibility and ample opportunity to let your imagination go wild.

But sometimes (well, most often), our image editing needs to be decidedly more prosaic. So, I give you clipping paths.

Clipping Paths

One feature that is often useful when taking product shots for catalog publishing (or any product shots, as for hardware and/or software reviews) is the clipping path, usually created via the pen tool. This essentially lets you draw around an object, creating a "path." You can then isolate an object from its background or, indeed, the rest of the image. The "clipped" image can then be imported into a page-layout program, and this focuses the reader's attention on the object. It is often cleaner looking and, when enhanced with a subtle drop shadow, can make objects look quite fetching indeed.

The upshot with image editing is that you have a lot of power to take images "beyond the image itself," if that makes any sense. No longer are you stuck with what you get back from the photo lab—or even what actually exists in nature. Your photos can be accurate depictions of reality—or fanciful depictions of your imagination.

Lifelines

As is invariably the case, especially among amateurs, your imagination can sometimes be more powerful than your skill with image-editing programs. So before you say, "Yes, Regis, that's my final image," you may need to avail yourself of a variety of lifelines. One good feature that most image-editing programs have is an undo command that, as you would expect, lets you undo something that you did. So, for example, say you beefed up the contrast, hit OK, but you decide that you don't like it. Well, you can hit undo (usually found in the Edit menu, or often command-Z on the Mac or control-Z on the PC).

However, remember that if you did something else *after* the command you want to undo, you may be out of luck. Usually, you'll only be allowed to undo the very last thing you did. And if you hit save after you did something, you'll also be unable to undo it.

Photoshop 5, however, has added a history palette, which lets you undo just about anything you did to an image. (In the technical literature, this ability is called multiple levels of undo.)

Another lifeline that image-editing programs give you is the revert, or revert to saved, command. As you would expect, this closes out the image you're working on and reopens the version that was saved to the disk—or essentially, the image as of the last time you saved it. Often, you can hit save, then do something, or some combination of things, and if you truly loathe the result and undo won't help, you hit revert and you can start over again.

Other lifelines you have involve the save-as... command. If you're trying something truly wacky, you can save an image as a separate file with a different name. If you hate what you did, you can go back to the original file.

Output

Okay, so we have captured our images, we've transferred them to the computer, we've brought them into Photoshop and cleaned them up and color-corrected them. Now we want to actually do something with them.

We touched on several of these options in the last chapter, but let's look at them in more detail here.

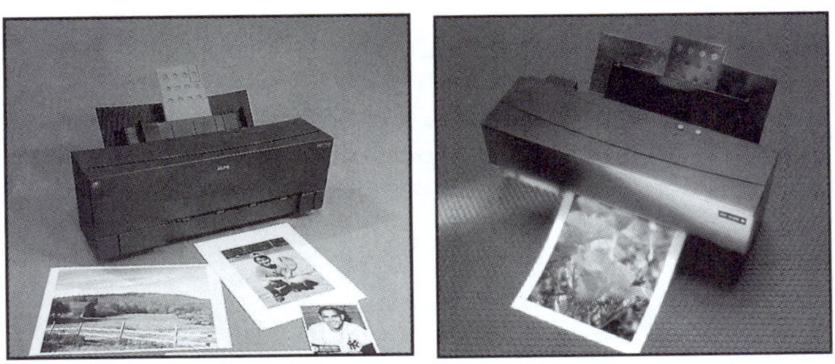

Alps Electric has the MD-1500 (left) and MD-5000, low-priced printers that can emulate dye-sublimation.

Inkjet Printing

One of the first things you might want to do with your images is print them. This is understandable. There are several options for printing your digital images, and the good news is that they're getting cheaper and better. One good option is inkjet printing. Several manufacturers, such as Alps, Epson, Canon, and Hewlett-Packard, to name but a few, have many models of low-cost inkjet printers. These devices can range from less than $200 to around $500–$600. Many are starting to be designed specifically for digital photography applications.

One of the drawbacks to inkjet printers, by many accounts, is that their dye-based ink sets do not generate very long-lasting output. In fact, most inkjet output is deemed to be extremely transient indeed.

As you would expect, manufacturers are working on this very problem, and Epson was among the first to introduce (in early 2000) a new inkset and media (and, naturally, a corresponding line of new printers) that, it is claimed, give inkjet prints the longevity of silver halide film. Other inkmakers also have long-lasting inks.

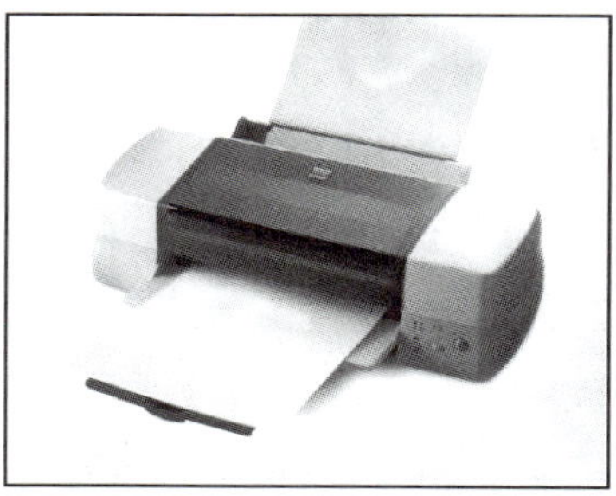

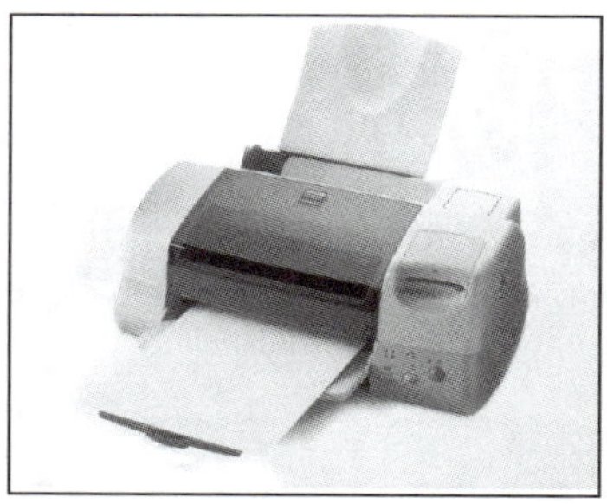

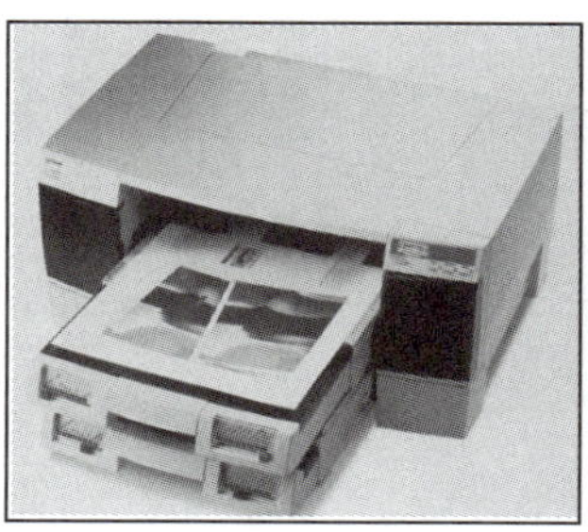

Epson's new Stylus Photo 1270 (top left) uses a new inkset and media that are gauged to provide inkjet prints that will last as long as prints made from film. The new Stylus Color 875DC (top right) uses the same inks and media but has a CompactFlash card slot. The Stylus Pro 5000 (left) began life as a $10,000 inkjet proofer, complete with Fiery RIP. Epson introduced a RIPless version. It can handle paper sizes up to 13 × 19 inches.

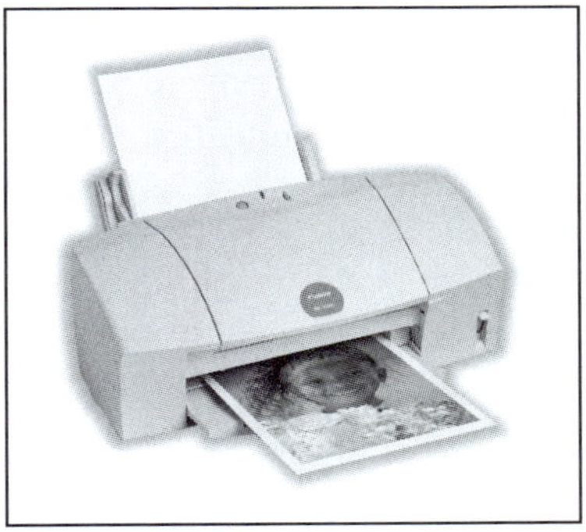

Canon's recently introduced BJC-8200 BubbleJet printer has been found to be a high-quality, low-cost means of printing color images captured from digital cameras.

Look for a great deal of activity on the "long-lasting inkjet prints" front.

Dye-Sub/Thermal Transfer Printing

There are, of course, other output options than inkjet printers, but nothing with the vibrant color coupled with the inexpensiveness. Some digital camera manufacturers have small desktop dye-sublimation or thermal-transfer printers that are designed to work with digital cameras. These aren't usually that expensive, but image quality is not as vibrant as inkjet, although they can be longer-lasting.

How Many Pixels Do I *Really* Need?

This is probably the most common question asked in relation to digital photography. And the answer is: It depends.

Okay, that's a cheesy answer. Let's look for a better one. We'll start with the Image Size box in Photoshop.

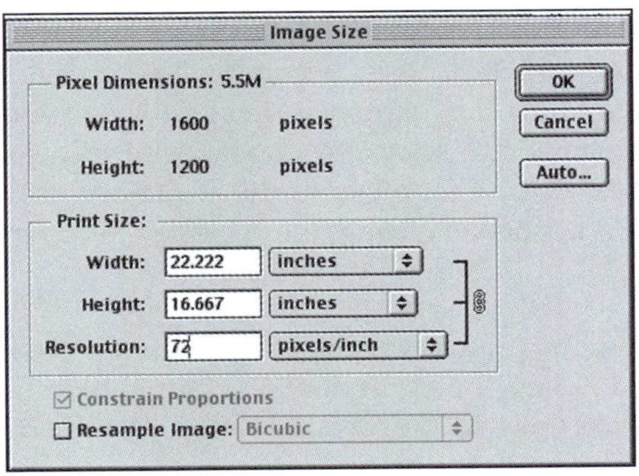

You'll notice that this box has several sections, and if you have been in this dialog box before, you know that these numbers are related to each other. For example, changing one often results in a change to another. Well, there's a reason for that.

The three most important numbers are: file size, resolution, and height / width. However, typically, file size is the most important, but since they're all interrelated, they're all equally important.

You'll notice in the screen capture on the previous page that the file size of the image that was captured by our camera is 5.5 MB. We'll touch on upsampling later on, but for the time being let's accept that number as the constraining factor on the upper limit of our image size.

You will also notice that the resolution is 72 DPI, and that the width and height are, respectively, 22.222 inches and 16.667 inches. These numbers represent the maximum output size and resolution possible with the file size we have. Remember, output size is a function of how much data is in an image. And the file size tells you how much data you have.

So what we've got here is an image that, if we kept its resolution at 72 DPI, we could output as large as 22.222 × 16.667 inches. That seems big, but it's a very low resolution. Essentially, it's computer screen resolution. If we were to put this image on the Web, you can see that we could make it quite large indeed.

But assume we want to print it. Let's pick an easy example. We're going to import the image in a page layout that will ultimately be printed on an offset press. If you have ever dealt with offset printing, you know that halftones—continuous-tone images broken up into small dots that can thus be printed—are printed at a certain *line screen*. This refers to the frequency of the halftone dots, which is a function of what the printing press in question can manage.

Let's assume our printer or production manager said they were printing at 150-line screen. In digital imaging, the rule of thumb (which can be violated on occasion, but let's not go there right now) is that the image resolution needs to be twice the line screen. So we know that our resolution should be:

$$150 \times 2 = 300$$

So we can enter 300 DPI in the resolution field in Photoshop. Let's see what happens:

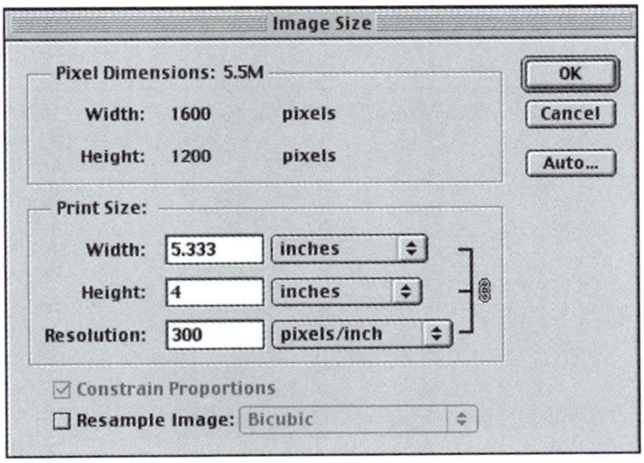

Aha! See how the width and height have changed to 5.333 inches and 4 inches, respectively? This tells us that with the image data we have, we can reproduce this image at 300 DPI as large as 5.33 × 4 inches.

We needn't have entered anything in this box to have figured this out. See the Pixel Dimensions at the top of the box? That tells us that we have captured 1,600 × 1,200 pixels. We can divide those two numbers by 300 DPI to yield our highest possible dimensions:

width: 1,600 pixels ÷ 300 pixels/inch = 5.333 inches

height: 1,200 pixels ÷ 300 pixels/inch = 4 inches

So we know that if we want to print this at 300 DPI, we can go as big as 5.333 × 4 inches. But many printing presses use a 133-line screen. Thus, we only need 266 DPI as a final resolution. Using the same methodology, we can see that at 266 DPI we can go as big as 6.015 × 4.511 inches.

Not only does this let us determine how large we can go after we've taken images, we can also use these relationships to inform our digital-camera buying decision. Let's take some common digital-camera pixel dimensions and see how big we can go with the images they produce.

The least expensive and lowest-end digital cameras can capture a maximum of 640 × 480 pixels (VGA resolution). So we see that that yields a file of about 900 KB.

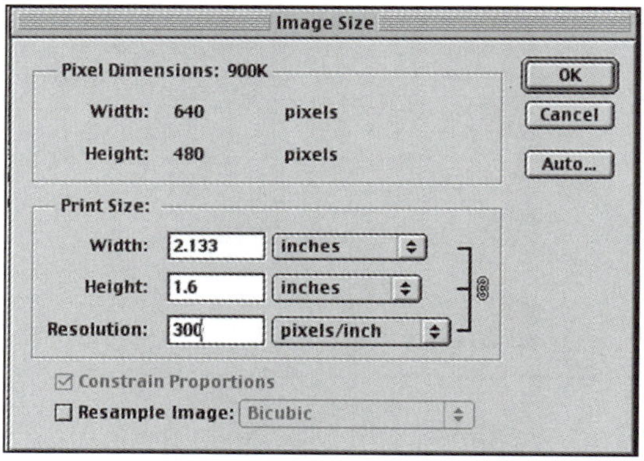

At 300 DPI, we could go as large as 2.133 × 1.6 inches. That's about postage-stamp size and will not be sufficient for print work.

But if you are strictly doing Web imaging, at 72 DPI that same 900-KB file would let you go as large as 8.889 × 6.667 inches, which is certainly large enough for the Web.

Let's see what the 1.X-Mp cameras get us. These tended to yield images in the neighborhood of 1,280 × 960 pixels.

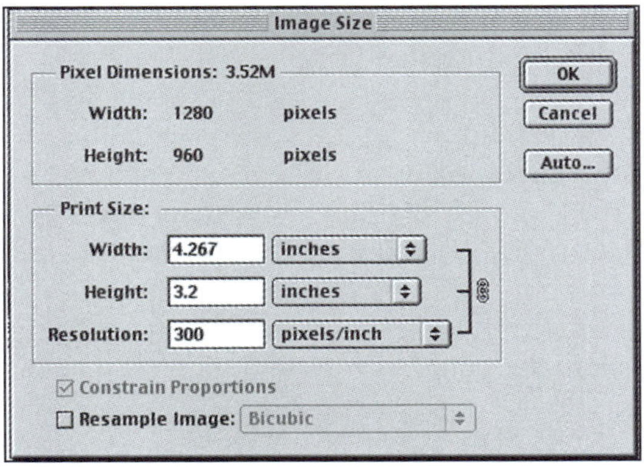

We can see that 1,280 × 960 pixels represent a 3.52-MB image. This, in turn, translates to a 4.267 × 3.2-inch image at 300 DPI. That is suitable for print publishing, if your needs are modest.

We can also take what we want our reproduction size to be, and work backward. Let's say we want the ability to reproduce our images at 8.5 × 11 inches—for example, as a full magazine page. How many pixels would we need?

Well, let's upsample the image we've been working with and see.

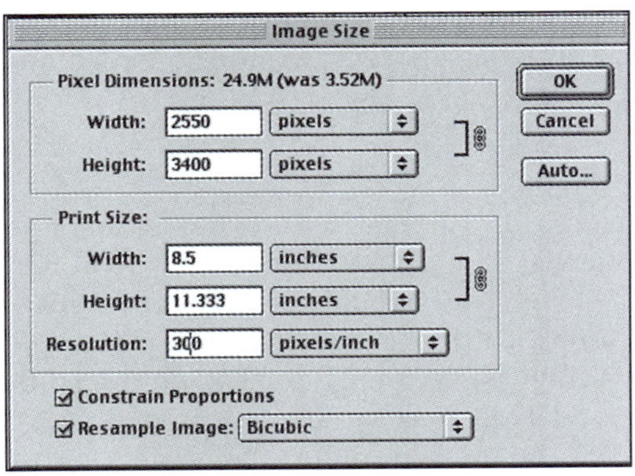

Zoinks! Photoshop tells us that to reproduce an image at 300 DPI and 8.5 × 11.333 (the closest we can get given the proportions of our original image), we would need an initial pixel resolution of 2,550

× 3,400, or a file size of 24.9 MB. We would obviously need a higher-end camera to reproduce that large.

Upsampling Revisited

We dealt with this subject in an earlier chapter, but let's look at it in a bit more detail here. Upsampling essentially refers to adding data to a file. For example, say you want to reproduce an image at 8 × 10 inches, but you only have enough data to reproduce it at 5 × 7. If you were to upsample, you are letting the image-editing program insert pixels into the image. It tries to do this by matching adjacent pixel values.

As you can imagine, this may be a hit-or-miss process, and you often don't get very good results. It can depend on the image and on how much you're upsampling. For example, things like screen captures (such as for use in a book or magazine article on a software program) can often be upsampled quite a bit without any horrible artifacting. And besides, they're only screen captures, so who cares? Well, that's perhaps a bit cynical. But screen captures certainly don't require the same quality as, say, a photograph. Suffice it to say, if you were doing a glossy magazine cover, you would definitely not want to upsample a 5-MB image. It would look really lousy.

Some programs, such as Image Alchemy from Handmade Software, do a pretty good job of letting you go big with meager images. And some RIPs for large-format printers have enlargement software that allows you to output bitmapped images at very large sizes without noticeable pixellation.

Downsampling

On the converse side, you may want to downsample your images. Downsampling, as you can well imagine, involves removing data from a file. Why on earth would you want to do this? There are a couple of reasons. The first is that if you are intending to e-mail an image to someone, you certainly don't want to send them a 5-MB file, unless you both have a superfast connection. Granted, if you've got DSL, T-1, or some proprietary system such as WamNet, all of which are designed for high-speed transfer of large image files, you do not need to downsample, especially if your service bureau or printer is at the other end of the pipe.

But if you are sending vacation pix to Grandma, who only has a 28.8-Kbps or 56-Kbps modem, you'll want to make them as small as possible. Also, if you are creating graphics for a Web site, you don't want images to be very big, or you'll surely test the patience of visitors to your site.

And even if you are working with images destined for print, too much data isn't necessarily a good thing. For example, you don't need 20 MB if you are only reproducing something at 3 × 4 inches, for example. Data far in excess of what you really need can sap system resources, such as memory and processing power, especially while opening, working with, printing, or RIPing files, not to mention taking up a lot of hard disk (or transfer disk) space. Can't fit all your images on a Zip? Well, make sure they're large enough to work for your target application but small enough so that they're not unwieldy and cumbersome.

Seeing a Real Workflow in Action

So how does all this work in the real world? Let's delve into all these issues in more detail here. In this section, let's construct a fictitious but completely plausible workflow. (And the fact that I actually did it for this book proves that it is perfectly plausible!)

A typical graphic arts workflow may go something like this: You send your intrepid photographer out with a digital camera to capture images of something or other. A trade show. A lecture or seminar. A rally. A sporting event. An outdoor location. An indoor product. Whatever. In this case, it is a campaign rally at a Redondo

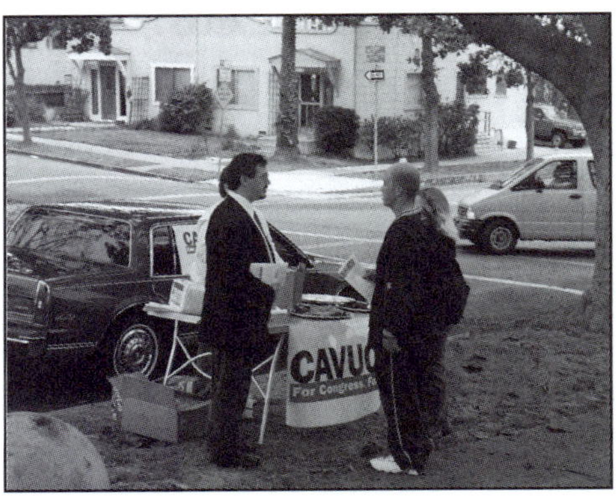

Step one involves sending our intrepid photographer out to shoot images of an event.

Beach high school, and the intrepid photographer has our old friend the Olympus C-2500L.

The intrepid photographer returns and downloads the images in one of the ways we mentioned in Chapter 5. In this case, he is using the Microtech USB CameraMate. The SmartMedia card from the camera is inserted in the drive, and it shows up on the desktop. The images are then copied into a "Digital Camera Images" folder on a file server. (Or an individual workstation, as the case may be.)

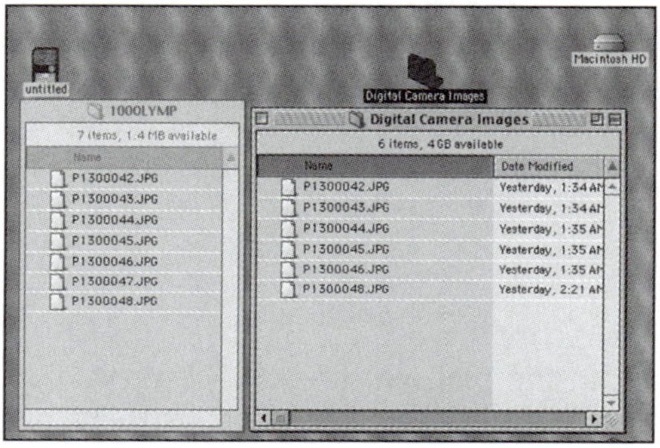

Downloading an image from a SmartMedia card to a workstation via the Microtech USB CameraMate.

The image is opened in Photoshop and "cleaned up." The brightness and contrast are played with, the levels are adjusted, etc., until the image looks pretty good on screen. In this case, it looks a little dark, so we'll boost the brightness and contrast a tad.

A quick check of the levels indicates that things look reasonably okay. And we do this for all the other images in the bunch that have been deemed "usable." As we all know, not all images from

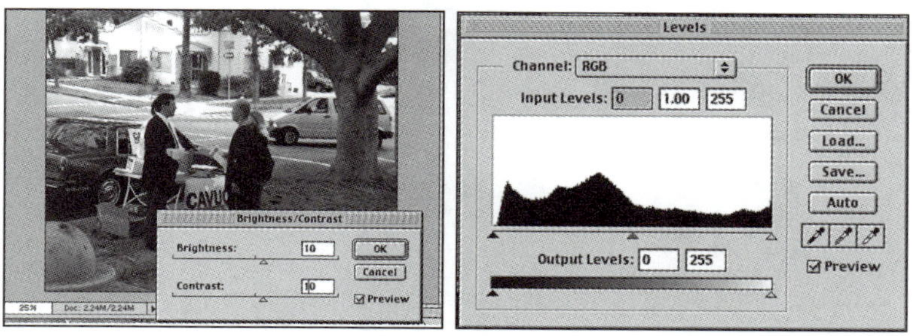

A brightness/contrast boost, and a quick check of the levels in Photoshop tells how our image is coming along.

a shoot come out well—for a variety of camera- and subject-related reasons. So from the 12 images that were shot, perhaps six or seven are deemed usable.

But remember, many of the glaringly poor shots were weeded out before this point. As our intrepid photographer was shooting, he could review the shots immediately after they were snapped, and delete the truly hideous ones. The ones that were weeded out after the photographer returned were those that the art director thought were not very good.

Other images may require some level adjustment; some may require some unsharp masking. And so on. We may even want to clone a cactus into one. Whatever.

The next issue is that of image size. At this point, the person working with the images needs to determine the purpose for which they're going to be used. As it turns out, they're going to be used for two purposes. In the first case, they are going to be e-mailed to a webmaster to post on a Web site. In the second case, they are going to be printed as part of magazine coverage of the event.

Now, there are file formats and programs that will allow you to create an image once and repurpose it in a variety of ways. LizardTech's MrSID application and file format springs immediately to mind. So does Flashpix. But our small shop doesn't have these, so we are left with the old way of doing things: Create one set of images for e-mailing to the webmaster, and create another set to give to the magazine production department.

The image editor saves the cleaned-up images in high-res, RGB format, which will give him flexibility later on. The webmaster has been calling all afternoon wanting the images. Fine.

So, the image editor will reopen them, keep them in RGB, and adjust the image size to 72 DPI. He will also reduce the dimensions to get the file down to a reasonable size, say about 1 MB. This is what the webmaster asked for, though it's likely that a different webmaster would ask for something else. All our intrepid image editor needs to worry about now is how to get them small enough to e-mail.

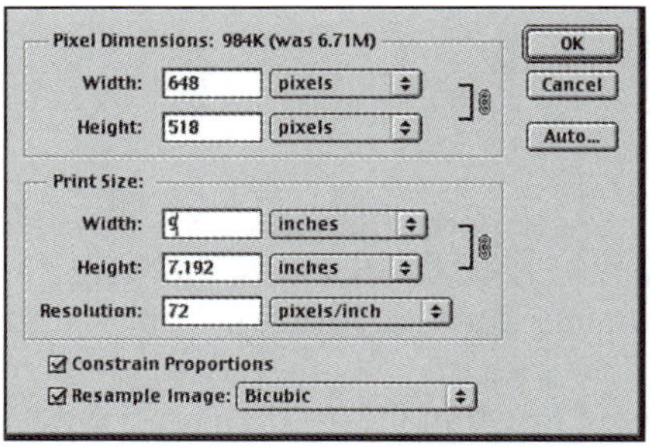

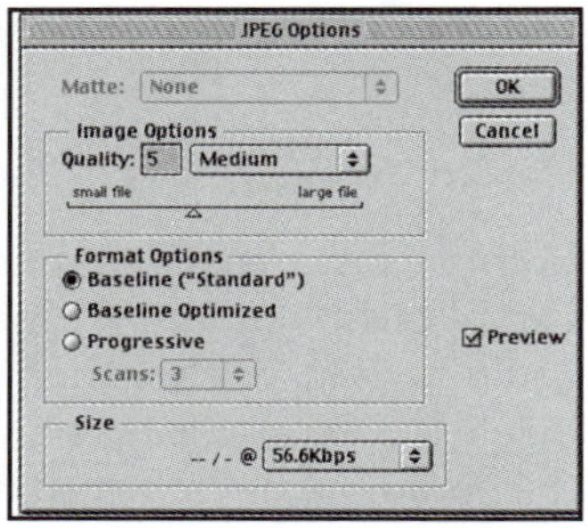

In Photoshop's Image Size dialog box, we can reduce the resolution and dimensions of our image to something a bit more Web-wieldy, getting the file size down to 984 KB. Then we can save the image as a JPEG with medium compression.

The image size was reduced to 72 DPI with width and height of 9 × 7.192 inches, respectively. That's probably larger than needed, but the file size is about right—984 KB. Notice that it came down from an original file size of more than 6 MB.

The image was then JPEGed, or, essentially, saved in the JPEG format, using medium compression. There might be some artifacting, but it's a good trade-off between small file size for e-mailing and image quality. And the final file size on the disk ended up being 92 KB, which is fine.

So all the images were processed in this fashion, and they were all saved with different names, with perhaps a .jpg suffix or "Web" indicator in the name, so as to keep the original, high-res files untouched. (Before e-mailing, we also need to see if the recipient is using a Mac or PC so the folder of images can be compressed using StuffIt or Zip, respectively.)

Now that the webmaster is happy, the images can be processed for print. The process is much like above, with the differences being the image size and color space need to be changed accordingly.

In the meantime, the hosts of the rally have called and would like some prints. So the image editor, who would like to see how the images look in print form anyway, outputs them to a desktop inkjet printer—in this case, an Epson Stylus Color 900. Since that is also a USB-compatible printer (and he hasn't invested in a USB

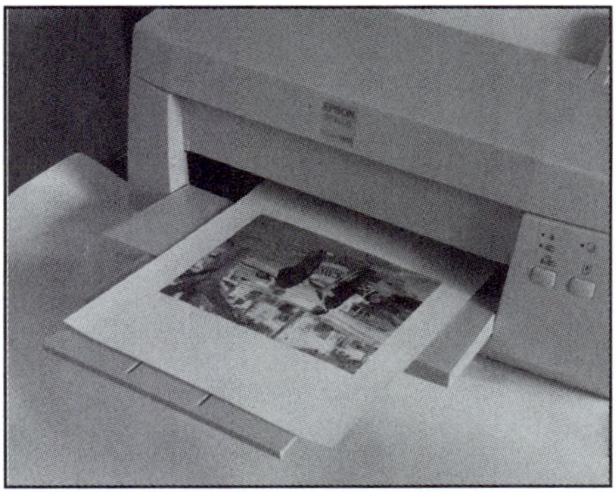

Making inkjet prints of your images is a good way to check image quality. If your images are destined for print, using Adobe's PressReady with an inexpensive inkjet printer is also a good, quick proofing system.

hub yet), he can easily swap out the Microtech USB CameraMate with the printer, without needing to reboot. He selects the printer in the Chooser, and in a few minutes he has an inkjet of the images. And they look great.

He hears back from the production department: Provide the images at 266 DPI (they'll be printed with a 133-line screen), and don't downsample them. The designer may need to run them big or small, and may need to go as large as possible. Save them as CMYK TIFFs.

Easily done. They can be reproduced as large as about 5 × 7 if need be (there is a bit of wiggle room; you can go a little bit larger than what the pixel dimensions strictly allow). The conversion to CMYK is easily handled, and they are all saved as TIFFs and placed on the production department's file server.

From there, it is up to the production department. Most likely, the images will be imported into a QuarkXPress or InDesign layout

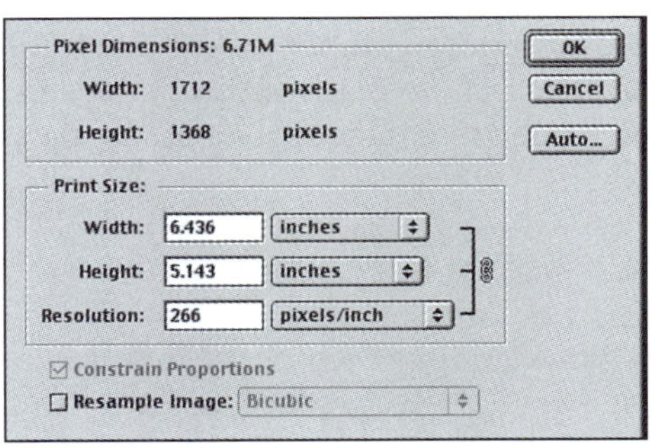

The original image is then resized for print output — again in the Photoshop Image Size dialog box.

and incorporated with text and other graphics. After layout and proofreading, color proofs will be output on an Epson Stylus Pro 5000 proofing system (or other proofing system). These color proofs will be inspected, then sent with the electronic file to a service bureau for negative film output, or more likely to the magazine's computer-to-plate department.

If the image editor wanted, he could also have seen pretty much how the images would reproduce from the desktop, if he knew what type of press his publication was printed on. The Epson Stylus Color 900 is supported by a program from Adobe called PressReady, which is essentially a software RIP that works with the inkjet printer to produce calibrated output that will match the final printing press output. Many other inkjet printers are supported by PressReady, as well.

At any point in this process, different paper could be put in the printer. Photo-quality glossy paper could have been used, to produce more vivid output. Smaller paper sizes could have been used to output 4 × 6-inch prints.

Summary

You have seen in this chapter how images captured by digital cameras can be used. We picked a fairly low-rent graphic arts workflow, because many graphics workflows are low-rent. A large portion of the graphic arts market is small office/home offices (SOHOs). In fact, all the processes outlined above were performed in a one-person (i.e, a book author) "studio" (of sorts), which is essentially a two-bedroom apartment. This could have easily been done in a larger production environment as well, perhaps more or less easily, depending upon the production environment.

The point is, you don't need a huge investment to do many of these things. Here's a complete list of the hardware and software that was used in this chapter (all prices taken from the January 2000 MicroWarehouse catalog):

- Olympus C-2500L digital camera ($1,500)

- 8-MB SmartMedia card (supplied with camera)

- Microtech USB CameraMate ($80)
- Apple Macintosh Blue G3 with 300 MHz and 256 MB of RAM ($1,500)
- Adobe Photoshop 5.5 ($600)
- Epson Stylus Color 900 inkjet printer ($400)

Total investment: $4,080.

But is it fair to count in the cost of the computer? I probably had one already. Or I could have bought a less expensive PC for less than $1,000. And I could also have easily used a less expensive digital camera. Similar cameras with about the same resolution but fewer hard-core photographic features cost about $900–$1,000. In fact, the new 3.X-Mp cameras are clocking in at about $1,000. These two factors could just as easily knock $1,000 off this investment. And if I didn't need CMYK color support (or some other features), I could have used Photoshop LE ($100), for more savings, or whatever software was bundled with the camera.

The point is that digital photography really isn't exorbitantly expensive, especially if you have a lot of the equipment already in place. And if you are even a small graphic arts concern, chances are you do.

Onward

Now that we've looked at different types of cameras, how to take pictures, how to transfer images, and what to do with images once you've got them, let's now turn, in the next chapter, to some of the applications for digital photography. Who is using it and why? Who could very well be using it? Who should be using it? And who *shouldn't* be using it?

7

Applications for Digital Photography

The foregoing may all be well and good, but you may be thinking: How can I use digital photography? And is anyone else using it? If you believe the analysts and pundits (and how could you not?), everyone will be shooting digitally in the next few years. I doubt that'll be the case, but there are many applications for which digital photography is well-suited.

Consumers

As I've mentioned before, digital camera manufacturers see the consumer as the Holy Grail, and that's understandable. Think of the money to be made. In the consumer space, digital cameras are still in the early-adopter phase (you know, the folks that love gadgets), but they're beginning to catch on—at least to the point where many people have heard about them. In the past year, many people in and out of the industry have asked my opinion about what camera to buy or what to look for. The volume of these questions has increased, which is heartening.

But the consumer market can be a very dodgy proposition. As we've seen in previous chapters, the quality, ease of use, and cost are reaching a point where the time is ripe for consumer acceptance. But there still needs to be a "killer app," and at the outset, that has been the Internet. We've seen that it was not until recently that good desktop output options for digital photographs existed. And why do consumers who take holiday snaps really want to have their images in digital form?

Remember when Kodak came out with the original Photo CD in the early 1990s? It was targeted as a consumer technology. Basically, the principle was this: You shot your pictures on film, took the roll down to a photo lab, which then printed images and then scanned them onto a CD-ROM. You could then see them on computer or get a Photo CD "player" that connected to a TV. That didn't take off (although it was an idea ahead of its time), but the graphic arts industry seized on the technology, especially since at that time desktop flatbed scanners were pricey and not very good. The Photo CD was a good, reasonably inexpensive way of getting print images in digital form for electronic publishing. or at least until (a) flatbed desktop scanners got cheaper and better, and (b) digital cameras got better and cheaper.

So the Internet is playing a very large part in consumer-based digital photography. People can e-mail images back and forth or use them as desktop pictures or "wallpaper" on their computers. Many people have personal Web sites and often post their images there for friends and family to log on and see.

There is even a service called Club Photo, which is geared for those who may not have their own Web site. Essentially, members can log on, and Club Photo will host the images in their own personal, password-protected photo albums. Club Photo also has a photo-printing service whereby you can order prints of your digital im-

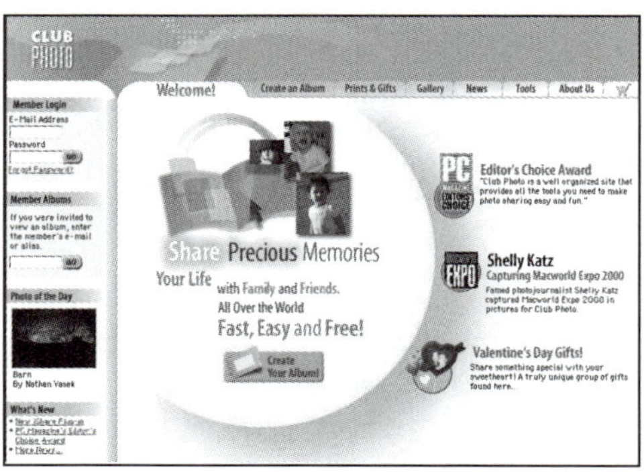

Club Photo is a service that lets you create Web-based photo albums, as well as order prints of your digital camera images.

ages. It also released a plug-in to Photoshop that will let you upload your images directly to your Club Photo album.

As the growth of the Internet and "dot com" companies has proliferated toward the end of 1999 and beginning of 2000, a number of "on-line photo labs" have turned up. Many have been around for a while, but for whatever reason (probably lazy shiftless technology writers not paying attention), they have kept a fairly low profile. That is now changing, and there are plenty of services available on line that will let you not only post your images to online albums but will also provide you with prints, CD, and so forth.

There are also inexpensive shareware and freeware programs that let you make slide shows of your images. In fact, many software bundles with digital cameras will feature software for creating slide shows. These can be small enough to e-mail or send along on a floppy or Zip disk. Artists and designers often create portfolios of their work in this fashion, and digital photographers can take advantage of this as well.

One thing I personally like to do, in one of those "practice what you preach" instances, is take a digital camera on vacation with me. I snap all my pictures (and as we've seen, discard the wretched ones

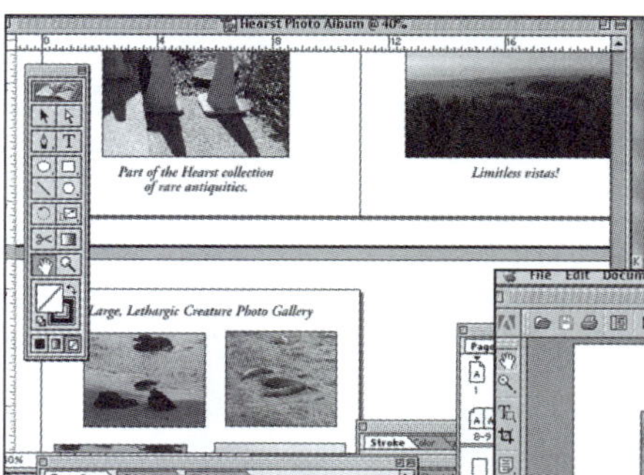

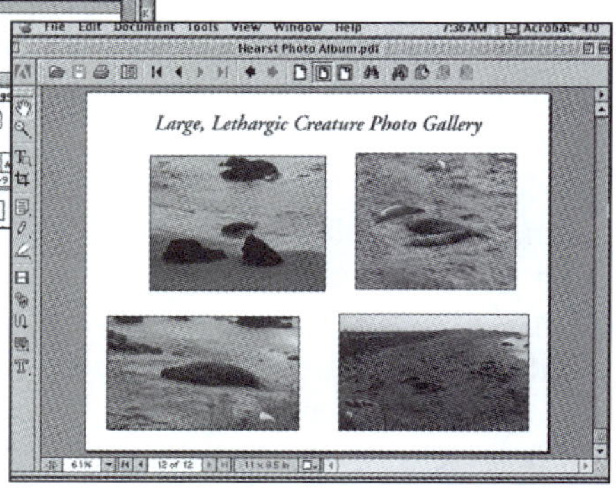

After a vacation, I like to create a "photo album" of my digital camera images in InDesign, then save the lot as a PDF, which I can then electronically inflict on unsuspecting friends and family.

as they happen), and when I get back home, I download them, clean them up in Photoshop, import them all into a QuarkXPress (or, more recently, an InDesign) layout, add captions and other snide remarks, and export the lot as a PDF photo album that I can e-mail to friends. If I had a Web site, I could post it there for download. It works really well. And it's fun.

I can also output the images on any of the new brands of long-lasting inkjet paper with long-lasting ink sets and have prints that will last a long time. Or since I've still got the images in digital form, I can print them again on el cheapo paper if I need to.

So at the consumer level, there are infinite numbers of applications for digital imagery.

Professional Applications

Okay, this book isn't about my vacation snaps. But any of the processes mentioned above can certainly be done on a professional level, especially in the creation of portfolios. Assume you're not in the graphic arts, but you have a computer and a digital camera. You restore antique furniture either as a hobby, a side business, or even as a professional business. You can take digital pictures of the pieces you've restored and e-mail them (or a slide show/photo album/etc.) to prospective buyers or appraisers. You can shoot from various angles, or if you are into QuickTime Virtual Reality (QTVR) you can even make the experience more "immersive." (We'll get to immersive media later in this chapter.)

It needn't be antique furniture restoration. It can be anything, really. If you are an artist, you can shoot your own work and do pretty much the same thing.

Digital Art

Speaking of art, a comparatively recent development in the art world is the advent of "digital art," or artwork created digitally (rather than with oil on canvas or more "traditional" media). It's taken a while for digital art to catch on, and many of the snootier people in the art world instinctively flinch at anything that smacks of digital, but digital art is exciting, and is becoming even more so. For the past seven years, *Micro Publishing News* has sponsored a digital art contest—and this year the pieces were more diverse and better than ever. Our first-place winner was a Delaware-based photographer and artist named Thomas Bulat, whose winning entry, though not shot with a digital camera, was a composite of many different photographs of a restaurant fire. It's quite an amazing piece; I cannot reproduce it with any justice here, but you can check out our story in the February 2000 issue of *Micro Publishing News* at www.micropubnews.com. You can also see our runners-up, which ran the gamut from completely hand-drawn art created in Photoshop to unusual treatments of digital photographs.

One sort of "artists' collective" is the Digital Atelier, a group of artists and lecturers—Dorothy Simpson Krause, Bonny Lhotka, and Karin Schminke—who tour the country (and the world) demonstrating their techniques. Tirelessly inventive, they have experimented with printing digitally created art on frescoes, as well as other unusual substrates. Often, the art does not end at the printer; they often paint on the print, or add other materials, to give each piece more of a sense of singularity, or something that simply can't be mass-produced from a printer. Their most recent work comprises their experiments with lenticular imaging. Check them out at www.digitalatelier.com, or watch for them at an upcoming Seybold Seminars show, where they usually have a booth.

There are infinite numbers of methodologies (as in traditional art), but typically an artist will begin with a graphics program and either draw from scratch or import a digital image and begin "tweaking" it. The results can look painterly, abstract, realistic—whatever the artist's imagination can conceive, the tools will allow him or her to create. The result is often output on a large-format printer.

Digital cameras are playing a larger and larger role in digital art. Many professional photographers who work digitally no longer have to be content with leaving an image as it was captured—or even be limited by the various effects you can achieve in a conventional darkroom. By working digitally, you can make a photograph look like a painting (and vice versa) and add an infinite number of effects to the image. It's all pretty cool.

Art is always wonderful, but there are more prosaic—but important nonetheless—applications for digital photography.

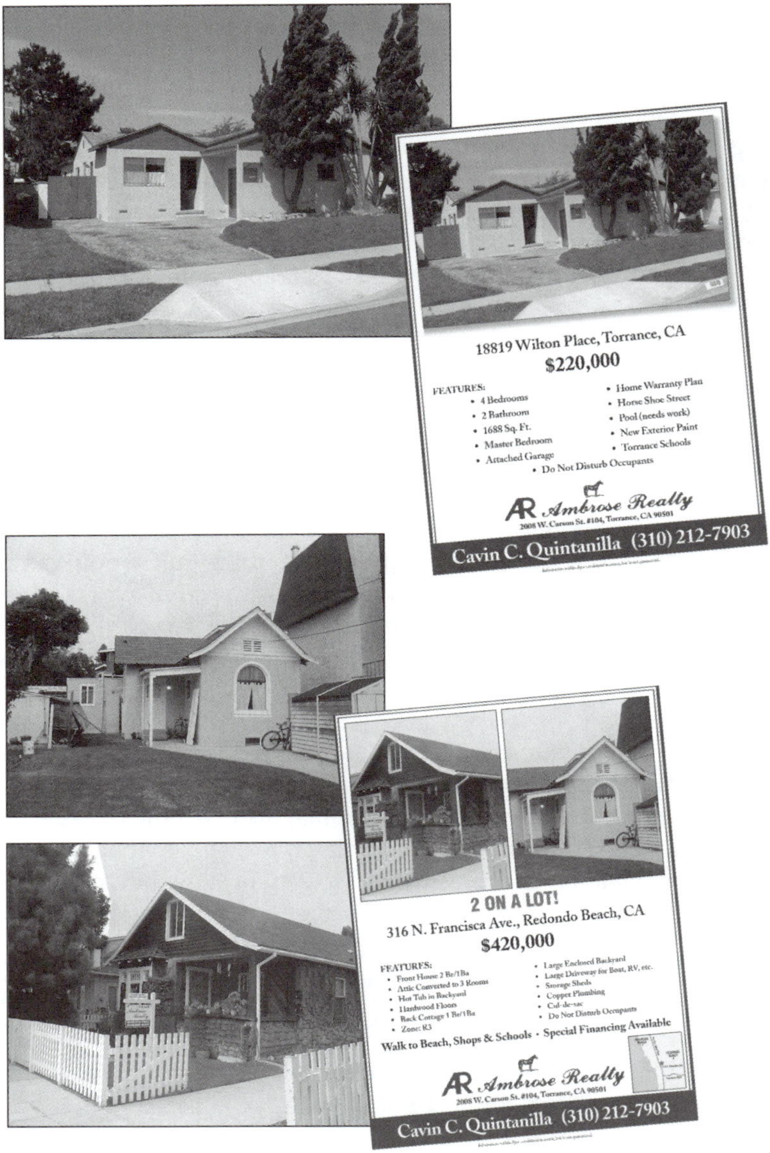

For real estate flyers, images of properties for sale are shot with a digital camera — in this case, an Epson PhotoPC 750Z — and handed to a designer who incorporates them into eye-catching flyers. (Images courtesy of Cavin Quintanilla and Ambrose Realty.)

Real Estate

At the risk of lapsing into cliché, let's look at real estate. Since the first digital cameras appeared, analysts and manufacturers alike always singled out real estate as one of the archetypal examples of how digital photography can greatly benefit a industry. This amused me for many years. Always real estate. But was it true? Were realtors using digital cameras?

As it happens, yes. In Torrance, CA, Ambrose Realty has been using digital cameras for more than a year to capture images of homes, which can then be incorporated into flyers. The realtor goes out to the home with a camera—in the case of Ambrose, an Epson PhotoPC 750Z—snaps some pictures of the home, downloads them, and hands them to a designer, who then creates brochures and flyers advertising the property.

As more real estate agencies move onto the Web, digital camera images can be posted there, as well, to create "digital flyers." It is not even inconceivable that PDF-based brochures can be created also.

One popular application that is starting to find a niche in real estate is immersive media. We'll look at immersive media later in this chapter, but by means of digital camera images, panorama stitching software, and a technology from Apple called QuickTime Virtual Reality (or QuickTime VR, or even more succinctly, QTVR), you can create interactive walkthroughs of a property, where the user can log on to a Web page and "click" through the home, being able to wander around the inside and outside of the property.

Immersive media is used for many other applications, as well, which we will get to in a bit.

Publishing

One of the workflow bottlenecks in electronic publishing was that of getting images from a camera to Quark layout. Typically, publishers would deal with prints, slides, or transparencies, and send them out to a service bureau for high-end scanning. The high-res scans were then returned and popped into the layout (either directly or via an OPI system). It can be kind of unwieldy and takes a while—you have to get the film developed, then scanned, and all of this costs money. Essentially, you were paying twice for the same images—developing and scanning.

The Photo CD, as we mentioned earlier, cut some time and expense off the process. But things still have to be sent out for Photo CD creation.

Enter flatbed scanners. In the mid-1990s, inexpensive flatbed scanners could do a reasonably good job of scanning reflective media if your needs were modest. (They had—and still have—some trouble with slides, but there are now inexpensive and pretty decent side scanners you can buy.) This is still how a lot of publications work.

But many are now adopting digital photography, which is a fantastic time saver. In our own case, if I may be allowed to toot our own horn, *Micro Publishing News* uses a variety of 1.X- and 2.X-Mp digital cameras to shoot a variety of images for publication. For example, when we go to a trade show, we'll get overhead floor shots or shots of booths with a digital camera. Similarly, when we cover a lecture or seminar, we'll get shots with the same cameras. Or when we do profiles of designers or other creatives, we'll take a digital camera to get shots of the profilees or their shops. These are very easily downloaded back at the office and cleaned up very quickly. They are not typically reproduced very large, and we are not *National Geographic,* so these cameras suit our needs extremely well, and the workflow is much more efficient than when we needed to get film developed and the prints scanned.

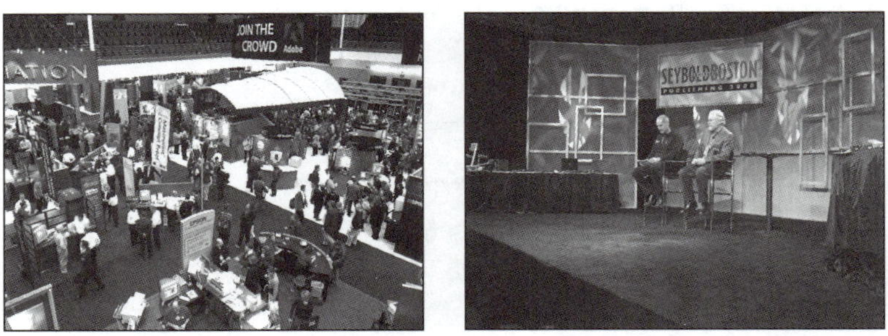

Point-and-shoot digital cameras are often useful for taking shots of trade shows and keynotes, such as Seybold Seminars. The cameras are small enough to be carried around while also reporting on the events, and at the small sizes at which they are typically reproduced, the images work well. (Photos courtesy of Joe LiPetri.)

We now have the ability to cover events much closer to our production deadline, because the images can be imported into the page literally minutes after the event, if need be.

Other publications also use digital cameras, and not just graphic arts magazines. *Time* magazine uses the megapixel point-and-shoots for book covers, CD covers, and other small, spot art that appears throughout the magazine. Higher-end publications use higher-end digital cameras to capture higher-quality images, depending on their specific needs.

Catalogs

One popular application for digital photography is catalog publishing. Let's face it: In catalog publishing you often don't need to reproduce an image very large, and with carefully controlled lighting, you can use a pretty inexpensive digital camera to get quick, Photoshop-ready images.

In fact, if you remember Chapter 4, our less-than-optimal studio setup worked pretty well. Obviously, Land's End or Victoria's Secret is not going to come around my home office asking me to do their catalog photography (unfortunately). Depending on what it is you're creating a catalog for, you may need a higher-end camera. If you're doing a high-quality clothing catalog, you'll want something better than a 1-Mp camera. But for many less stringent requirements, a point-and-shoot will do quite well.

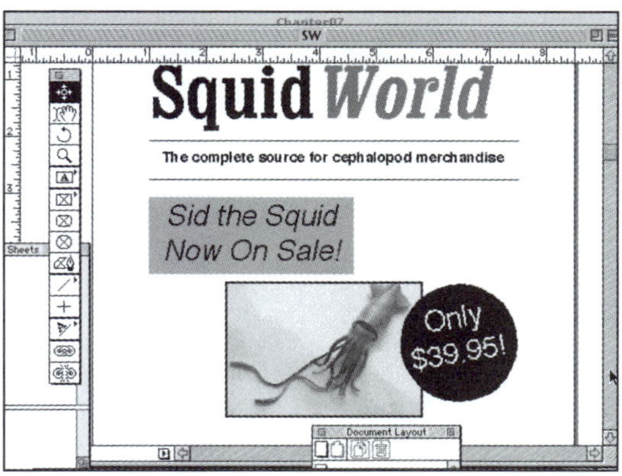

With a combination of a digital camera and a page-layout program like QuarkXPress or InDesign, you can easily create your own catalogs.

For example, we can easily throw together a small catalog by taking some digital camera images, importing them into a QuarkXPress layout, and adding some text and graphics.

This, however, is merely a reversion to our quick-and-dirty way of working. Serious catalog photographers and publishers have a much more high-end setup than what we looked at in Chapter 4. We'll look at that in more detail in the next chapter, but suffice it to say here that in catalog photography, much is being done digitally these days. The digital workflow eliminates the need for preview prints (usually done with a Polaroid) as well as print processing. It also is having a strange effect of moving the entire imaging process to the front end of the production cycle.

Catalog photographers use high-end scanning backs with view cameras, as well as controlled lighting. Clients drop their products off with the photographer, who then brings them into the studio, lights them, and can preview the shots on a computer monitor. When the client is on hand, decisions can be made on-the-fly, and if everything looks good, the shots are taken. The products themselves can be composited with background or other objects, color can be managed, and proofs can be made—all in the course of one single process.

But we're getting ahead of ourselves here.

Newsletters

Another good use for lower-end digital cameras is newsletter photography. Newsletters are usually not as well printed as a magazine, and they tend to be very small. Many trade organizations, associations, and other groups produce their own in-house newsletters, monthly, bimonthly, etc. They often include shots taken of recent organization events and parties. You've no doubt received many of these, typically after the holidays, where you can see fellow association members frolicking in some sort of state of inebriation. (They can also be more prosaic and include pictures of a seminar or lecture.)

Be that as it may, many times these images are snapped on a conventional film camera, and the prints are scanned. There is little reason why a $500–$800 camera couldn't work fine for applications such as these, especially since they are often printed in black-and-white.

Photojournalism

At a level beyond what we have been talking about in this chapter, professional photojournalists have been taking advantage of some of the mid-range professional digital cameras. Sports photographers, as well as those shooting for news outlets, are using Kodak DCS systems in the field. Coupling the professional photographer's skill at composition with the ease of self-editing, as well as the native digitization of images that need to be digital at some point anyway, you have a serious application for digital photography. As the mid-range cameras—such as the Kodak DCS 520, which was one of the first models designed with the professional photojournalist in mind—have the image quality and the seamless integration of essential features and optics found on professional film cameras, they are being used more and more.

Fashion

Fashion photography was slow to adopt digital photography, primarily because many photographers and clients felt that the quality wasn't there. In a well-publicized event in late 1999, however, a new high-quality digital camera from Scitex's Leaf—the Cantare—won some converts. The Cantare captures 3,072 × 2,048-pixel, 14-bit image files, and participants in the event—held in October 1999 at New York City's Pier 59 studio complex—feel that with the new device, the image quality is finally there for fashion applications.

Up-and-Coming Applications

Print and Web imaging based on digital camera workflows is really only the beginning of a story that is continuing to unfold. Other, purely digital applications and technologies are evolving that need digital camera images as raw material.

A couple of years ago, there was much hoopla about what was called "immersive imaging." Essentially, the basic point of immersive imaging was to combine a variety of technologies—digital cameras, panorama-stitching software, and QuickTime VR—to create Web sites or other distributed multimedia that could provide the user with an "immersive" experience. Basically, you opened up a panoramic image, which you can navigate around—essentially clicking through a 360-degree image. At certain points, there would be "hot spots" that, when clicked on, could take the user to another panorama, and so on. You could get up close to objects, turn them over and around, examine them, and so forth.

The QuickTime VR technology that allowed this first gained popularity in 1994 with the release of the *Star Trek Interactive Technical Manual*, a CD-ROM that "immersed" the user in the *U.S.S. Enterprise* and let you wander through various decks and rooms, pick up objects like Klingon knives, and so forth. It was a Trekkie's delight, and even non-Trekkies were awed by the technology.

Immersive imaging was touted for all sorts of consumer applications—like virtual tourism and such. But as it turns out, most people preferred actual tourism, so immersive imaging never got very far. It still exists, though, and has found a niche in on-line advertising. The process works something like this. An automotive manufacturer, for example, wants to give prospective car owners a tour of a new model. So, the interior and exterior are photographed from a variety of angles, or the car is placed on a turntable, and several photographs are taken as it rotates, so you can essentially capture a complete 360-degree view of a car. The images are converted to QuickTime VR 9 (or some other similar program), and when the result is posted on the Web—or distributed on CD-ROM—the user can "walk around" the car, "get into" it, check out the upholstery, examine the dashboard up close, etc.

There is a company in Long Beach, California, called Evox Productions that has made this sort of immersive imaging its stock in trade. They primarily do immersive imaging for advertising clients but have done some interesting things with live Webcasts. One Webcast of an Emmy Awards program involved placing actress Florence Henderson on a turntable and spinning her round. You can check them out at www.evox.com and see what that's all about.

Panoramas

It's hard to show you in print what we mean by immersive imaging, but one element of it we can show fairly easily is the panorama. There are a few manufacturers making what is called "stitching" software. What panorama stitching software does is let you take a bunch of adjacent images of a 360-degree scene, then the software analyzes these images, finds out where the common bits are, and "stitches" them together to give you a 360-degree (or 180-degree, or however thorough your source images) panorama.

One of the first applications for stitching images into panoramas was PhotoVista, which was made by the now-defunct Live Picture. I remember playing around with the decidedly consumer-level PhotoVista in 1997, and it did a reasonably good job. I basically stood in a park with a camera and rotated through 360 degrees, snapping pictures all the way. The software was rough, and you really needed to plan out your shooting in advance (and a tripod would have helped), but it wasn't too bad.

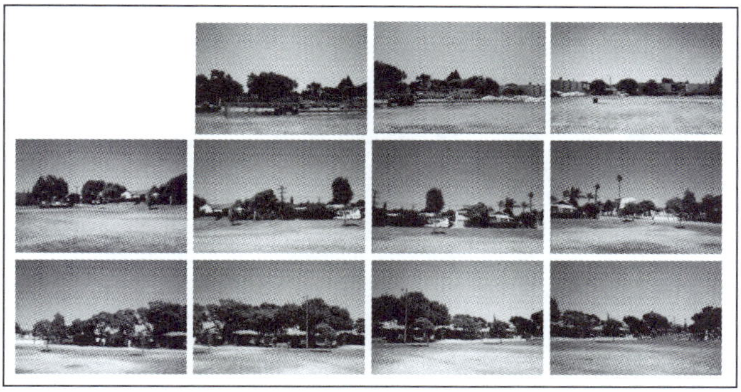

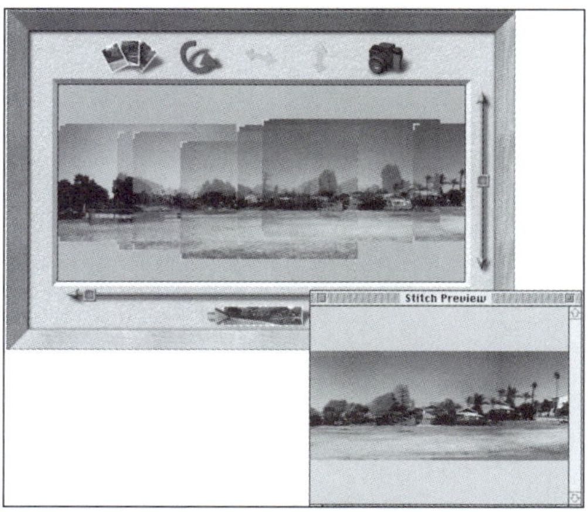

Live Picture's original PhotoVista let you import a number of adjacent photographs — such as you would take by standing in a park with a camera and rotating — and "stitch" the lot together into a panorama. It was designed primarily for Web applications, since the final file size and resolution the program supported were not very large.

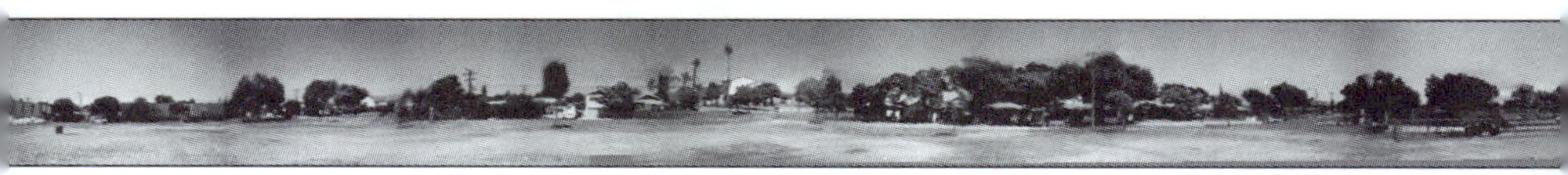

PhotoVista may have been an idea ahead of its time—or maybe the time just hasn't happened yet. At any rate, there are other panorama packages available. Ulead introduced one a couple of years ago, which I have not seen since, and Enroute Imaging came out with QuickStitch and QuickStitch 360 some time ago. QuickStitch is often bundled with Olympus digital cameras, and in early 2000, Enroute began shipping PowerStitch, a decidedly high-end approach to panorama stitching.

Basically, QuickStitch lets you take a bunch of JPEGs and import them into a grid. The interface is very clean and intuitive. You place your source images in the proper order, and away you go. The application automatically finds the common points in each image and

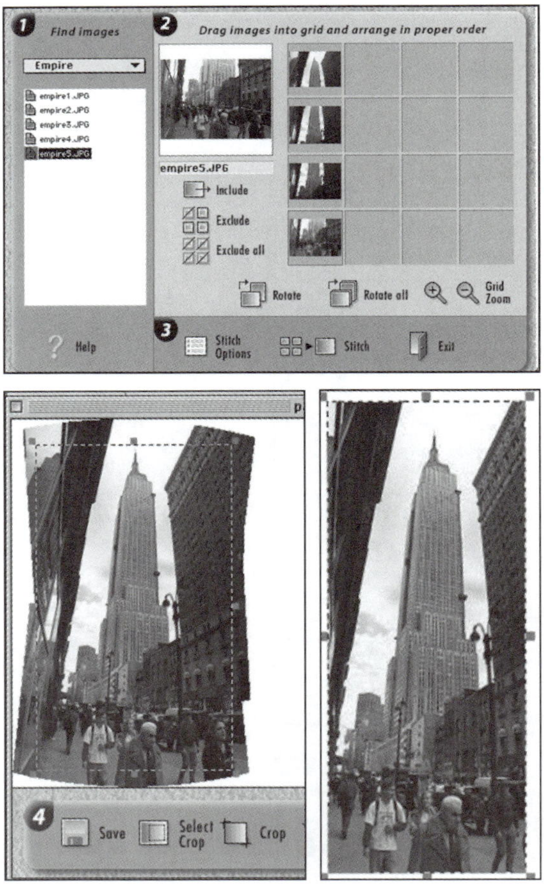

Enroute Imaging's QuickStitch, bundled with Olympus digital cameras, lets you stitch together a bunch of small shots to create a panorama — either wide or tall. Later applications from Enroute include QuickStitch 360 and PowerStitch.

sticks the lot together. You can then save your panorama as a JPEG, albeit not one with a great deal of resolution. Later Enroute programs let you export higher-resolution panoramas, as well as QuickTime VR movies.

What can you do with these panoramas? Well, if they're of high enough resolution, and you have big enough paper, you can print them out. In some cases, they can be used to create a larger image for print publishing than you normally would get. In lieu of getting a wide-angle lens for your camera, simply take a few adjacent shots and stitch them together.

We actually tried this a few years ago. We went to a trade show, took a few adjacent shots of the show floor, and tried to stitch them together. The experiment didn't work; we somehow didn't take the source images properly, so they didn't line up well. Essentially, it looked like an earthquake had hit the hall. At any rate, we remain confident that at some point we will get that approach to work.

3D Modeling

One interesting product from MetaCreations—whose future seems uncertain, at least at the time I am writing this—is Canoma, a program that lets you build 3D models out of 2D images such as digital camera images.

Skeptical? I was, too, but it works pretty well. Here's how it works. You bring in your source image. Canoma lets you build your model based on underlying shapes, to which you then "pin" your image. Think of it as putting a cardboard box together, then pasting a printout of a photo of your house on it to represent a 3D version of your house. Basically, you have what are known in 3D modeling parlance as "primitives"—your rectangles, your boxes, your cubes, etc. You then import a picture of a house, say. You then start pinning a box to the house. You hit the render button, and the surfaces of the house are applied to the sides of the box, and you can rotate it as well. It being a one-sided, 2D photo, you'll have a blank back, but Canoma gives you a couple of options for rectifying that. You can either take a second photo of the back of the object you want to model, or you can simply duplicate the front of the model on the back.

The problem with Canoma version 1.0 is that you are stuck with excruciatingly angular objects—no cones, spheres, etc. But it works pretty well.

The model you create in Canoma can then be imported into another 3D program, such as MetaCreations' own Bryce, or many other commercially available applications. If you work in 3D, or

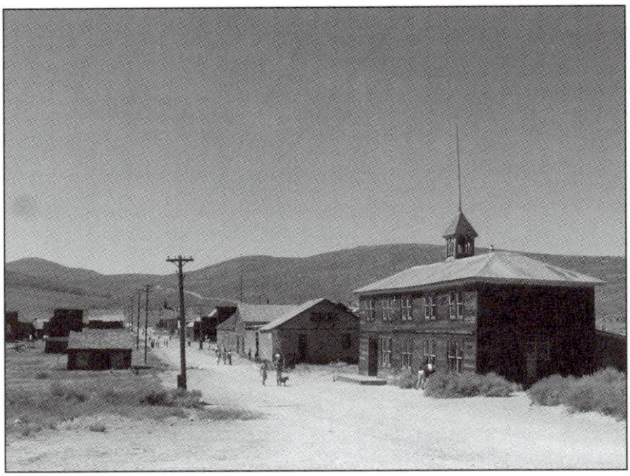

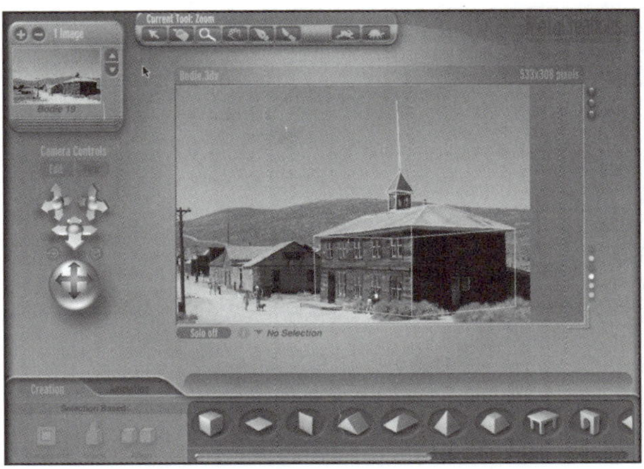

MetaCreations' Canoma 1.0 lets us take a digital camera image (top) and import it into our workspace. The row of primitives at the bottom of the screen are the shapes to which we can pin our image. We do so, and …

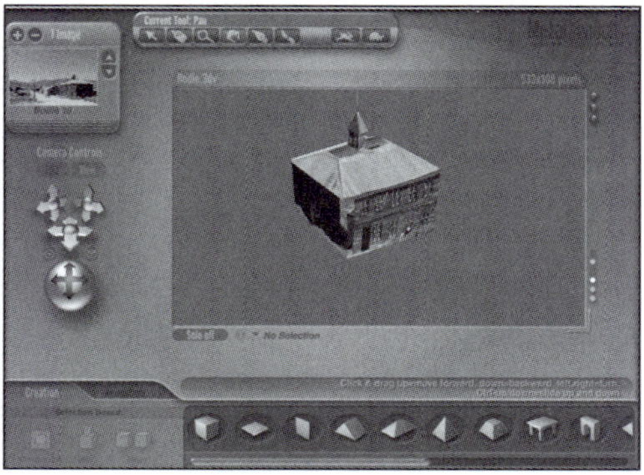

. . . voilà! One 3D model.

want to combine 3D models with QTVR or other "immersive" elements, Canoma is an interesting—albeit expensive—tool.

The Web

We touched on some of the applications earlier for digital cameras as part of a Web imaging workflow. There are many applications available for not only optimizing images for the Web but also for creating Web pages. These are beyond the scope of this book, but suffice it to say here that if you are taking photographs for Web sites, it is silly not to be digital. Even if the mid-range to the high end of the print publishing market will benefit little from lower-end digital cameras, Web imaging—by virtue of the less stringent resolution and data needs of the Web—is ideally suited to digital photography.

This is not to denigrate Web publishing as a low-quality medium; far from it. Color and image quality are still crucial concerns, regardless of what medium you're publishing for.

When Work Is Over

When you have finished with your images, the issue of archiving becomes a crucial one. Although many computers these days are shipped with many-gigabyte hard drives, digital images—especially if you save more than one version—can chew up a lot of hard disk space. So what the heck are you to do with them? We need to take this opportunity to touch on the issues of cataloguing and archiving.

Asset Management

In terms of cataloguing, there are many programs available for asset management—far too many to mention here. "Digital asset management" was a buzzword a couple of years ago, and although the bloom is off that rose to an extent, many options still abound. They can range from very inexpensive tools like Portfolio from Extensis to the different varieties of Cumulus from Canto Software.

Asset managers can be divided into roughly three levels: client, server, and enterprise. A client asset manager is a single program that runs on a workstation. Essentially, it lets you create a database of images. You can drag and drop your images into the database, and you can define what fields you want to include. You can save information about an image, such as file type, copyright info, the date the image was created and/or modified, and other content-related information—such as who is in the pictures. The new version of Canto Cumulus also lets you add a short voice annotation to an image, so if you don't want to enter text, you can simply record yourself saying, "This is Uncle Ned shortly before the tiger escaped" or something like that.

You can also add keywords, which then can be used as a search-and-retrieval aid if you want to find an image having specific things

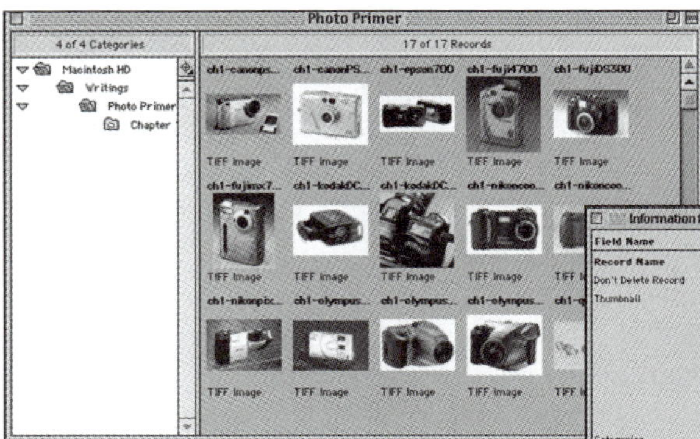

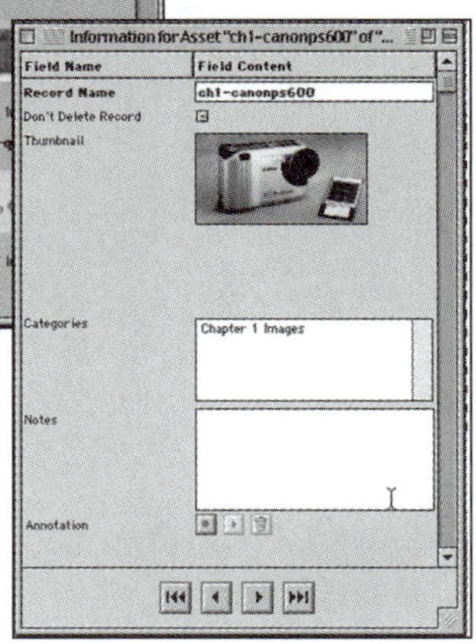

Canto's Cumulus (version 5 as of this writing) lets me drag-and-drop all my assets into a database, the fields for which I can customize however I'd like. I can add keywords for later searching, and I can even add a short voice annotation if I want.

in it, such as all images with Uncle Ned in them. The database can also display thumbnails of the images, as well.

Server editions of asset managers are designed for workgroups or smallish organizations, where the image database is stored on a central server, and several different workstations—or "seats"—can access them. Usually, the administrator can set various access privileges for images or the database as a whole. Different individuals can be granted or denied certain types of access. These can include "read only," where an individual can look at an image but not make any changes; and "read and write," where the individual can open as well as edit an image. Or an image can be barred completely from certain individuals.

Enterprise versions of asset managers are kind of like server versions, only writ much larger. Often the database can be accessed via the Internet, and in this case the idea of access privileges becomes even more crucial.

Asset management can be a complex topic, and there are lots of issues involved, which go far beyond the scope of this book. In fact, it could very well be a book unto itself—although arguably not a very interesting one. Your asset management needs should address some very basic concerns, regardless of how high-powered you need the system to be. You should be able to easily find images you need; you should be able to search for images either by photographer, name, subject, or other data related to content—or by whatever criteria you think you'll need to search.

If, for example, you have reviewed digital cameras for a long time, and the time has come to write a book about digital cameras, perhaps you need to be able to search your image library for images that were shot with certain cameras. If you set up your database effectively from the start and have been diligent about keeping it updated, finding and using what you need will be a breeze.

Asset managers are also becoming integral pieces of a variety of workflow puzzles, and the goal—at least on the part of manufacturers—has been to integrate the asset database with actual production tools, usually in a client/server environment. Quark, for example, recently announced its QuarkDMS, an asset management system that can be tied to a wide variety of programs, not just QuarkXPress. In this way, you can add Word files, Photoshop images, and more to a centralized database. The database then becomes a sort of file server.

It's a complex topic (the demo I got of it took more than an hour), but the point is that as our files proliferate and multiply, we need to be able to find them quickly and efficiently. This is more of an issue in larger organizations, but even at the lower level, archiving and retrieving is becoming a serious concern.

The upshot of asset management is that regardless of how powerful the software may be, it is up to the user and/or administrator to set it up correctly and efficiently at the outset.

Archiving

Archiving goes hand-in-hand with cataloguing, for a reason I'll explain in a minute—if it's not already obvious. Archiving brings up that original question: "Where do I put all these images?"

In the old days, we used to use our removable storage for archiving. I've still got several shelves of old 44-MB, 88-MB, and 270-MB SyQuest cartridges with old text, image, and multimedia files. The problem is: If I ever need any of those files, I'm in trouble, because my SyQuest drive died a long time ago, and the company is no longer in business. Some resellers still sell SyQuest drives, but for how much longer? And even when the drives were popular, it was a big pain getting one drive to read a disk (i.e., 44 MB) that was written on another drive (i.e., an 88 MB).

And heck, I've still got 740-KB floppies from the old Mac Classic days that I have been unable to read on newer Macs (and by "newer," I mean Macs that have appeared since 1992), never mind the fact that my current G3 doesn't even have a floppy drive.

Today, we have Zip and Jaz drives as removable storage—but we need to worry that we'll be able to read them in the future.

But the problem of being able to read our archives at some point in the future is only one issue we need to worry about with regard to archiving. There is also the space issue. Heck, we've found that a 100-MB Zip disk is often insufficient for basic, transient file transfer. And for some operations, even a 1-GB Jaz cartridge is insufficient!

One medium that we've had success with in archiving is the CD-ROM. It's ubiquitous enough that I probably don't need to even define it. And where once we would have had to spend thousands of dollars on a CD-R drive and mastering software, now it can all be had for less than $300. (In fact, as I write this, Airborne Express just delivered a QPS Que! USB CD-R drive that I bought from Mac-Warehouse for $299. It comes with Adaptec's Toast software that makes easy work of recording files to a CD-R. And if I wanted to, I could even record audio CDs with it that I can play on my audio CD player [which I have done]).

By the way, CD-R stands for CD-Recordable and simply indicates that a CD can be recorded on. As you probably know, once a CD is recorded, it cannot be recorded again. Well, that's not technically true. There are "multi-session" recorders that let you record batches of files on a single disc at different times. And there is also the CD-RW (CD-Rewritable), which lets you erase and re-record a CD. That's taking some time to catch on, but it's nice to know that this exists.

A CD-ROM can hold 650 MB of data, which is often sufficient for much archiving. And CD media is pretty cheap, so even if you need more than one, it's not going to break the bank.

But that raises the problem—or continues to raise the problem—of where to put the CDs. We've been backing up our monthly magazine issues on CDs since the early 1990s. We're gradually—well, quickly, actually—running out of space.

There are even-higher-capacity storage media available. The Digital Versatile Disc (DVD) holds more than 5 GB of data and is the same size as a CD. The recording hardware and software is not too expensive (I've seen it less than $300), and computers are now starting to ship with DVD players. That said, DVDs have yet to take off as a medium for anything besides movies, but that may change.

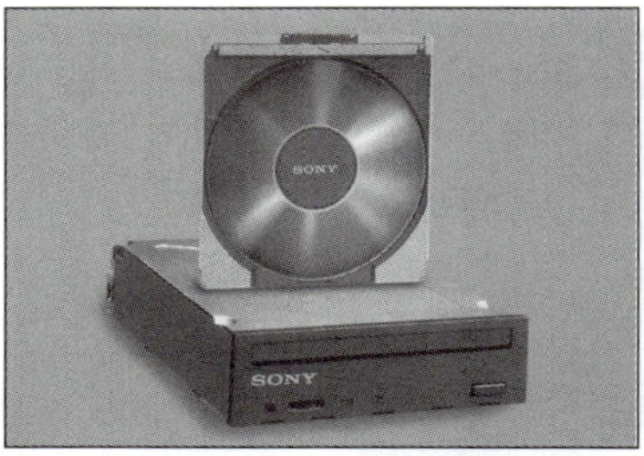

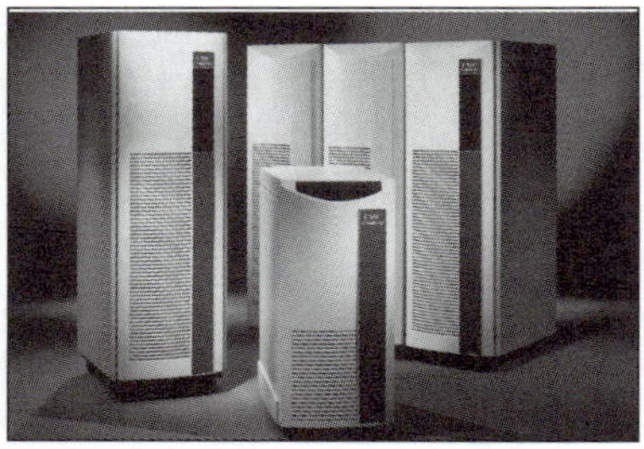

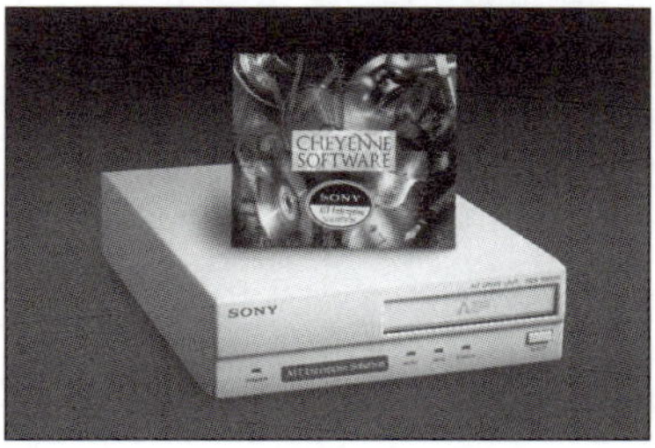

Mass storage options abound. Sony's rewritable DVD (top left) debuted some time ago, but nonrecordable DVD has yet to catch on. There are always RAIDs, such as EMC's Image Mover (top right), and there are tape backups, such as Sony's AIT drive (left).

There are also even more capacious media available, such as RAIDs. RAID stands for "redundant array of inexpensive disks" and is a set of linked hard disks that can store gigabytes and gigabytes of stuff. RAIDs are getting cheaper, and although most are designed for client/server environments, some new RAIDs—and USB- and FireWire-compatible RAIDs—are appearing for client systems. There are also multi-gigabyte tape drives that store data on magnetic tape. The drawback to tape drives is that they are slow to access.

You can see that there are a variety of options for archiving your data. So why does this go hand-in-hand with cataloguing? Well, unless you have an amazingly hyper-photographic memory, you probably don't remember what's on every disc. So being able to catalogue what's on a disc or bunch of discs will help immeasurably if and when you need to find something in the future. And if you don't need to find something in the future, why the heck are you keeping it?

We'll look at some of the newer options for storage in Chapter 9.

If you are a small shop, you can probably get by with a low-rent cataloguing and archiving system. Basically, what we do is store all our assets in a Canto Cumulus database, print out thumbnails and other limited but salient data, and keep the printouts with the disc on which the archive is kept. It's not the most searchable archive in the world, but as we tweak the system, we will get it to work the way we need it to.

Onward

In this chapter we've looked at some of the applications for digital photography—who's using it and how. We've looked at some bizarro applications that let you take digital images in whole new dimensions. We've also looked, albeit briefly, at what you can do with your images when you're done with them.

That's technically the end of the road as far as a digital camera workflow is concerned. In the next chapter, we'll take a look at what is happening at the high end of the digital camera continuum, namely, digital studio cameras: What are they? How do they differ from the cheapies we've been looking at? Should you buy one? What is a digital photo studio? How would I create one? Why would I want to be a client of one?

8

In the Studio

We've spent the bulk of this book talking about how to use low-end, point-and-shoot digital cameras, and we've seen that although they're not going to be producing any *National Geographic* covers, they have myriad uses if your needs are modest.

But very often your needs may not be modest. In the last chapter, we saw a few glimpses of the places where higher-end solutions are required.

So in this chapter we're going to spend a little time looking at the sorts of equipment you usually find in a photo studio—and by photo studio, I don't mean a cheesy little home office. Photo studios can be small or large, and can be commercial establishments—sometimes part of a service bureau, sometimes home-based concerns. The upshot is that there is more to a professional photo studio than simply cameras. There are several peripheral but crucial considerations, which we can divide into lighting, color management, and proofing. Oh, and the camera itself.

We'll touch on all these topics, but this is not meant as a complete and thorough look at how to set up a photo studio. It can be an expensive proposition, so if you're interested in going this route you'll want to do more research than this chapter will provide.

Cameras

Let's begin with the most obvious element of the photo studio—the camera. There can be some degree of confusion (which I will try not to compound) as to what the digital photography options are at the high end. These are most certainly not point-and-shoots, but there are some major differences among the various classifications at this level, although they often tend to get lumped into one category (and I'm as guilty of that as anyone). But here I shall try to set the record straight.

The devices in this category are often referred to as *digital camera backs*, or just "backs" for short. What this means is that they are not cameras per se; they are designed to be attached to what are called *view cameras*, or view camera fronts.

A view camera is essentially a traditional studio camera that could just as easily shoot with film. View cameras have high-quality optics, focusing, shutter, and aperture controls, etc. Many feature bellows focusing. Major manufacturers of view camera fronts include Bronica, Fuji, Hasselblad, Mamiya, Rollei, and Sinar. There are more, but those are the names that appear the most often. If you are in the market for a scanning back, be sure it is compatible with the size and make of your view camera. You often see the terms "medium-format" and "large-format" in conjunction with view cameras. As you would imagine, this refers to the size of the camera. Be sure that if you are buying a back, you pick the right size.

There are three basic categories of digital camera backs: multiple-shot backs, single-shot backs, and scanning backs. The type of back you select will usually be a function of what you are shooting. We'll see what that means shortly.

Multiple-Shot Backs

Sometimes called "three-poppers," these backs use rotating RGB filters that are superimposed on the area array CCD and, as the name implies, take three separate shots of the same scene—one that captures red data, one that captures green data, and one that captures blue data.

The advantage of the three-popper systems is that you get much better color fidelity; the camera takes its time to capture each separate color channel individually. (Some cameras take four exposures, but three is the most common.) The drawback, as you can imagine, is that by dint of the fact that three separate exposures are needed, such cameras are not suited to action photography—or photography in which there is any movement whatsoever, except perhaps on a geological scale. But for product or other still-life photography, assuming your subjects stand still, they are very well-suited.

Early models in this category were the Scitex Leaf DCB II and MegaVision's T2. The DCB II offers 2,048 × 2,048-pixel resolution, 14-bit-per-pixel color depth, and a file size of 24 MB. Ironically, photographers at the time liked the small file size, especially since it sped up a digital workflow. (As computing power and the baseline specs—in terms of CPU speed and RAM—have increased, though, the file-size issue is not as serious as it once was.)

A pioneer in this field is MegaVision, which has been selling its T2 multiple-shot camera back for years. Its most recent offering in this category is the T32, which has a 3,072 × 2,048-pixel CCD that can capture 18–36-MB files. The T32 is designed for large-format view cameras, such as those made by Cambo, Sinar, and Toyo.

MegaVision also has what is known as the BatPac, which, as its name may or may nor imply, is a sort of Batman-like utility belt—essentially a fanny pack that lets you tote around all your batteries, a RAM buffer, and a hard drive—that lets you take your MegaVision cameras out into the field.

Leaf also debuted a couple years ago the LeafVolare, a three-shot back that has a 2,048 × 3,072-pixel CCD, and the ability to produce

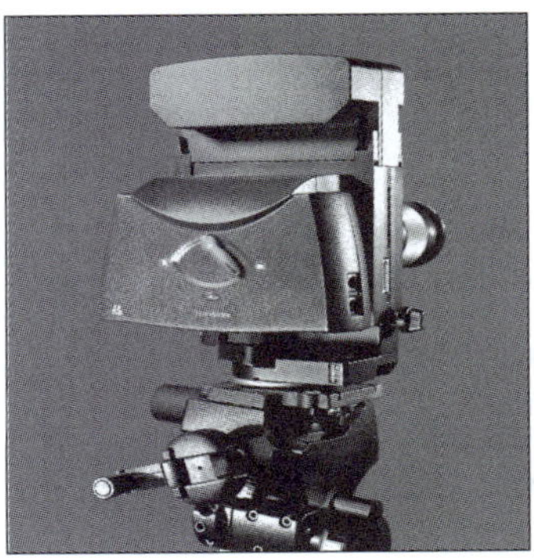

The Scitex LeafVolare, a three-shot camera back that has a 2,048 × 3,072-pixel CCD and is compatible with view cameras from Hasselblad, Mamiya, and Sinar.

18-MB files. The LeafVolare is compatible with view cameras from Hasselblad, Mamiya, and Sinar.

Single-Shot Backs

As you can guess, there is a category of digital camera back that takes only a single shot, capturing all its necessary color information in one fell swoop.

The advantage of the single-shot backs is naturally that they are faster than the three-shots, but there is a trade-off. They only capture red, green, or blue pixels, so the missing color data needs to be interpolated after the fact. That may or may or may not be bad. But every cloud has a silver lining, and new technologies and new chips and better software are making the single-shot backs a viable option in photo studios.

Some of the early models in this arena were the Kodak DCS 465, the Kodak DCS 400, and the Leaf Catchlight. Current models include MegaVision's S3, a successor to the S2. The S3 has a 3,072 × 2,048-pixel CCD, captures 36-bit RGB data, and offers a file size of 18 MB. The S3 is designed for medium-format view cameras from Bronica, Hasselblad, and Mamiya. There is also the BatPac option , if you want to go traipsing about on location with the S3.

Phase One, known for its high-quality camera backs, introduced the LightPhase in 1998, which has a 2,048 × 3,072-pixel CCD and can capture 18-MB files. The LightPhase is designed for the complete line of Hasselblad view cameras, as well as the Mamiya 645AF view camera.

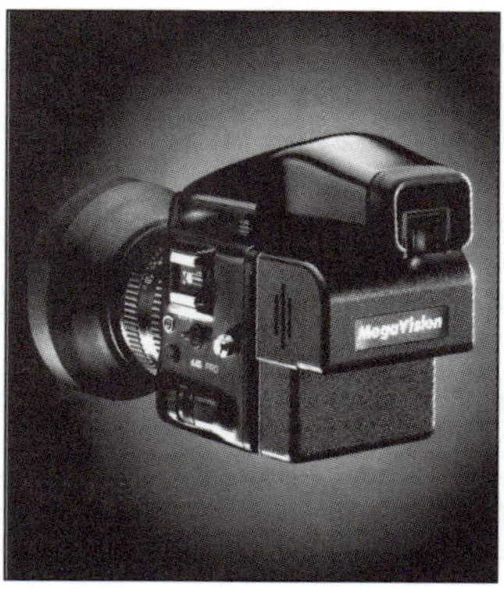

A pioneer in the realm of digital camera backs, MegaVision's original S2 single-shot camera back has a 2,048 × 2,048-pixel CCD and is compatible with view cameras from Bronica, Hasselblad, and Mamiya. It has been succeeded by the S3.

Sinar Bron's SinarBack Light has a 2,048 × 2,048-pixel CCD and is compatible with view cameras from Fuji, Hasselblad, Mamiya, and Rollei.

As we saw in Chapter 7, in 1999, Leaf introduced the Cantare, which has a 3,072 × 3,072-pixel CCD and is compatible with Fuji, Hasselblad, Mamiya, and Sinar view cameras.

Scanning Backs

At the extreme high end are the scanning backs. Scanning backs can be thought of as being like scanners that are pointed at three-dimensional subjects rather than reflective or transparent artwork. Scanning backs typically use linear arrays rather than the larger area arrays, and consequently sample only one line of data at a time. The advantages of scanning backs are that they yield the highest resolution, file size, and image quality, but the drawback is that they can be very slow. As a result, scanning backs are used primarily for still lifes and product photography, not for movement or action shots.

Despite the slowness, they do capture images with file sizes as high as 250 MB and are consequently the back of choice when doing extraordinarily high-quality or large-format photography.

Dicomed was a pioneer in this arena. The Dicomed FieldPro captured 6,000 × 7,520-pixel images at a file size of 129 MB. Dicomed also had a StudioPro system. The Dicomed product line is now being taken over by Better Light.

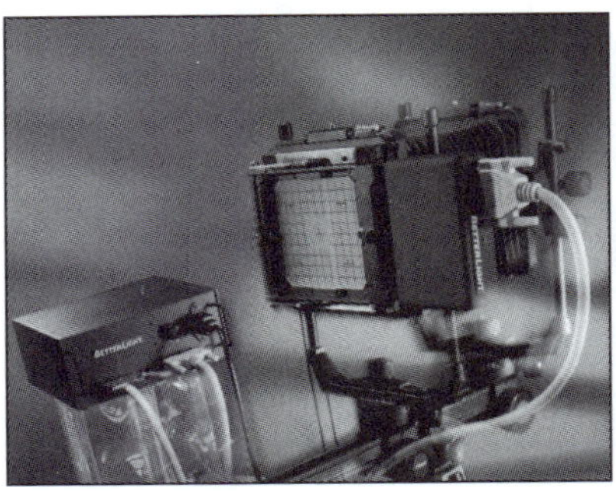

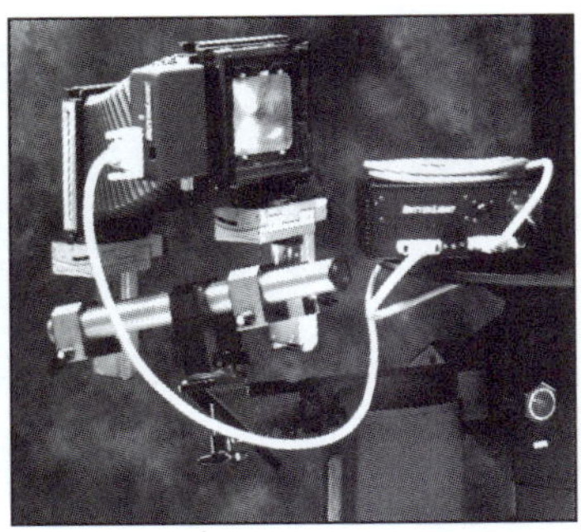

The Better Light Model 6000 (left) and Model 8000 (right) can capture 6,000 × 8,000-pixel and 8,000 × 10,660-pixel images, respectively, and are compatible with any standard 4 × 5-inch view camera.

Speaking of Better Light, they have several high-quality scanning backs. At the most fundamental level is the Model 4000, which produces 3,750 × 5,000-pixel, 53-MB files. The Model 6000 captures 6,000 × 8,000-pixel, 137-MB images, and the Model 8000 captures 6,000 × 10,000-pixel, 244-MB files. The Better Light models are compatible with any standard 4 × 5-inch view camera.

Better Light also has two new scanning backs, the Super 6K and the Super 8K, both of them designed for the economy-minded photographer.

Another major player in the scanning back market is Phase One, known for its earlier PowerPhase, later PhotoPhase, and recent PowerPhase FX backs.

The Phase One Studio Kit, which has been around for a while, can capture 2,500 × 3,600-pixel images. Phase One also has the 5,000 × 7,200-pixel PhotoPhase and the 7,000 × 7,000-pixel PowerPhase.

More recently, the very-high-resolution PowerPhase FX can capture images up to 10,500 x 12,600 pixels, and can provide file sizes of—are you ready? You may want to sit down—380 MB (24-bit RGB), 760 MB (48-bit RGB), and 1 GB (646.7-bit CMYK). Jeepers, that's a lotta do-re-mi. The PowerPhase FX is also said to be extremely fast, able to digitize at 240 MB per minute.

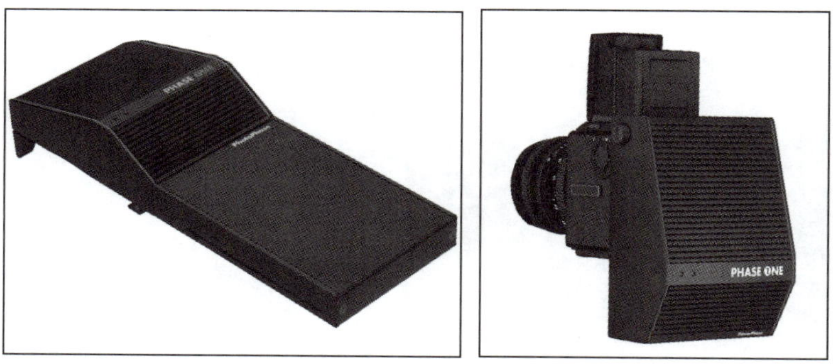

The Phase One PhotoPhase (left) and PowerPhase (right) can capture 5,000 × 7,200-pixel and 7,000 × 7,000-pixel images, respectively. The newer PowerPhase FX can capture images up to 10,500 × 12,600 pixels.

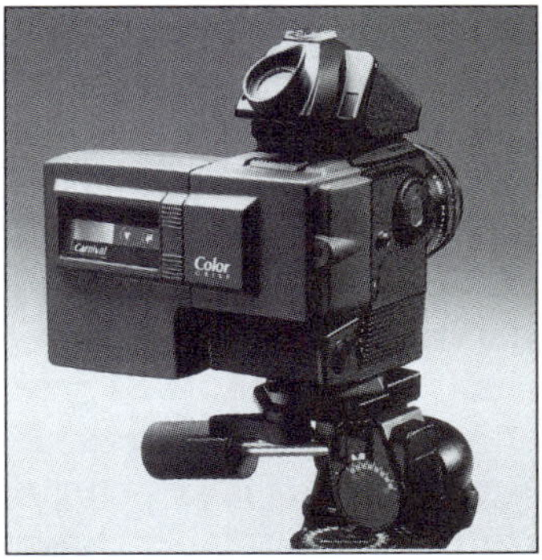

The ScanView Carnival 2000S was one of the early "three-popper" digital backs and was a popular camera in many digital photo studios. It has since been supplanted by the Carnival 2020, a hybrid camera back that can operate as both a single-shot and multiple-shot back.

Other Systems

As is to be expected, there are some other types of digital camera back systems that do not quite fit the categories we delineated above.

There is the Jenoptik Eyelike Digital Camera System, which can function as a single-shot or multi-shot (in this case four shots), or even scanning mode. The Eyelike captures 2,048 × 2,048-pixel images in either single- or multi-shot mode. The optional scanning module gives it the ability to function as a 6,144 × 6,144-pixel scanning back. The Eyelike can also be adapted to fit a variety of view cameras.

There is also the SinarBack from Sinar Bron, which is a sort of mutant, single-shot/multi-shot hybrid. The back has a 2,048 × 2,048-pixel microstepping CCD that captures full-color information for each pixel.

There is also a new system called the Foveon Studio System that uses three separate chips to capture RGB data simultaneously.

Most of these camera back systems can be tethered to a computer, and many offer on-screen live previewing, which is taking the place of the Polaroid preview shot in traditional photography. In this way, photographers and clients can see what they're going to get before the picture is actually taken. This helps determine things like lighting—and often, depending on the software, you can do image compositing, or swapping backgrounds with those that are digitally stored, before the picture is snapped.

The Leaf Cantare also boasts the ability to produce on-screen "contact sheets" once an image is shot, allowing for quick and easy review of captured images.

Additionally, in 1997, Phase One had introduced a QuickTime VR plug-in for the Image Capture software used by its scanning backs. We looked briefly at QuickTime VR and its role in immersive imaging in the last chapter, and here it is again. Essentially, the Phase One plug-in lets users place an object on a turntable. The turntable is rotated, and the Phase One camera back snaps an image at regular intervals—such as every 10-degree turn of the turntable. When the turntable (and object) has rotated 360 degrees, the software automatically converts the files from TIFFs to PICTs and stitches the images together to create a QuickTime VR "virtual object." Viewers accessing the QuickTime VR movie can then rotate it on screen with mouse clicks.

Phase One developed the turntable, and it can be controlled via the plug-in. The system was targeted at companies creating CD-based catalogues, as well as museums that want to give patrons access to "virtual art collections."

How Much Will This Cost Me?

Digital camera backs are not inexpensive, so there's little reason to think you're going to get scanning-back quality at a megapixel price. Prices are slowly decreasing, but nowhere near as dramatically as at the lower-end of the market. And there's no reason why they should; the low end of the market is targeted at completely different people than the high end.

So you're likely to be paying somewhere in the neighborhood of $10,000–$25,000. As I've said before, a lotta do-re-mi. But for those people investing in this equipment, this is their livelihood.

What we've started seeing over the past couple of years is the appearance of "entry-level" camera backs that have some sort of trade-off in quality and/or features. For less than $15,000 or even $10,000, you may be able to find a model that differs from its higher-cost brethren in that it is not portable; it may produce a lower—sometimes much lower—file size; and so forth.

Lights

As we said earlier, the camera is only part of the digital studio story. A second piece of the puzzle is lighting. Often, the type of camera you buy will determine the type of lighting you need to use. Different types of camera backs—as indeed, different types of cameras in general—have different lighting requirements.

For example, the multiple-shot "three-popper" cameras use strobe lighting, which a lot of photographers already have. As a result, some photographers found themselves going for those types of cameras in lieu of replacing their entire lighting system as well as buying a camera back.

In contrast, scanning backs require what are known as hydrargyrum medium arc-length iodide (HMI) "hot lights" or other continuous lighting systems like tungsten or high-frequency fluorescent lighting. Some studios report that their Dicomed and Phase One backs were extraordinarily difficult to light. Even with 1,200-watt HMI lights as well as 650-, 100-, and 200-watt tungsten lights, it was still hard to get enough light in the studio to do product shooting.

Two new solutions have appeared in recent years. The first is the Orbiculight from Astron Systems. Essentially a cove in which your products are placed, the Orbiculight is specifically designed for digital photography applications. The Orbiculight has three independent and fully dimmable daylight-balanced fluorescent lighting

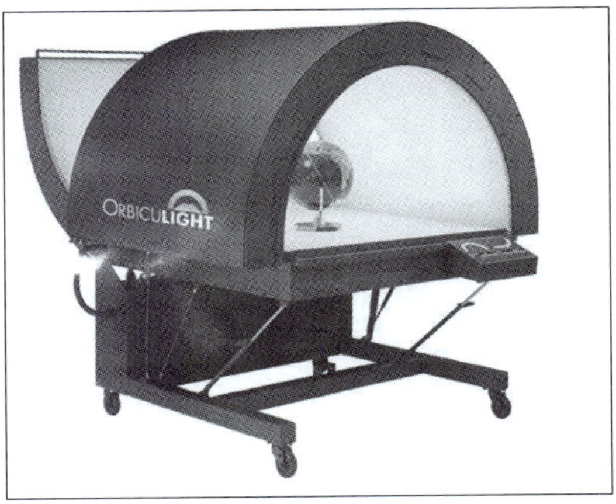

The Astron Systems Orbiculight.

components, comprising bed, dome, and cove, united as a single circuited system. All the independent components can be controlled by a single light-control module.

The Orbiculight also has features that facilitate simultaneous movements of the bed, dome, or cove, in many different combinations. Gas-filled springs and locking struts facilitate positioning and locking in any position. Gel tubes surround each light fixture, and the Orbiculight is designed to let users easily create millions of different lighting, color, scrim, or position combinations.

The Orbiculight is useful as a kind of small studio for product shooting. You're probably not going to be getting fashion models into the thing (however much you'd like to…), but for small to medium-size products—or elves—it is a useful lighting system. The Orbiculight lists for about $15,000, by the way.

A less expensive system, older than but similar to the Orbiculight, is designed for so-called "desktop studios." It is called the PictureMagic SL-3600, manufactured by Fairfield, New Jersey–based Tarsia Technical Industries. The PictureMagic is a 3-feet cubed system that uses quartz halogen lighting. It can get hot inside, so to keep perishables from perishing while they are being photographed, the PictureMagic vents heat away from the "set" using vibrationless fans. Not really designed for professional studios, it is a good option (for about $4,700) for the people doing the sorts of things we were doing in Chapter 4.

Another lighting system that professional digital photographers have found of great value is the LightComposer, manufactured by Denmark's based Martin Professional A/S. The LightComposer essentially consists of six light projectors mounted on a steel truss

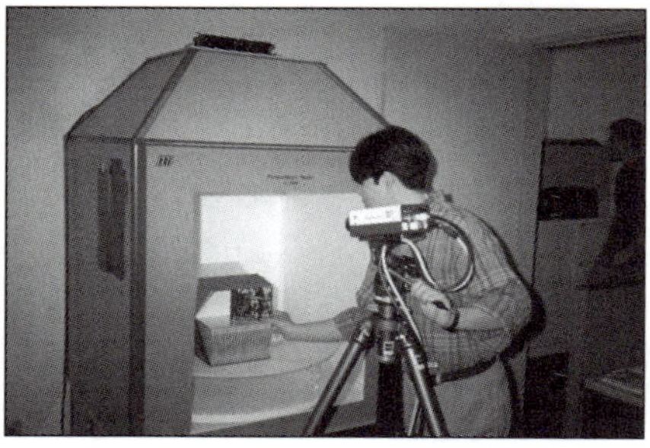

The PictureMagic SL-3600 "desktop studio."

framework, and is controlled by software running on a PC. Lighting adjustments are accomplished by moving mirrors inside each light fixture. From the computer and the LightComposer software, the intensity of each light can be controlled, and a framing feature allows the creation of pinpoint spotlights or wide flood effects. The LightComposer software interface also lets photographers change the color and patterns by using glass gobos within each light. The software can also save user-defined settings.

Although more expensive than the Orbiculight (around $50,000), the LightComposer is a full lighting rig that can be used to shoot a wide array of larger objects and even people.

Photographic lighting is a tough issue, especially at the high end. And remember, with low light, you need to increase your exposure time. And increasing exposure times on already slowly exposed scanning backs can easily throw an immense bottleneck into your workflow—especially if you aspire to be a photo studio working at full capacity.

Color Management

Color management is one of the most convoluted topics in the graphic arts field. It is complicated even further by the fact that its definition—or even the need for it—can vary according to whom you talk. The reason color management is so crucial is that when you are producing images for other people, they have certain expectations of what color they are going to get back.

For example, if you are shooting photos for a clothing catalog, and you shoot a blue shirt, the photo has to match the color of the fabric identically—and at each stage of the process—because ultimately, if someone buys that blue shirt, they're going to be mighty peeved if the fabric is nowhere near the color they saw in the catalog.

This means that your input equipment has to be able to capture color in the same way that the color is displayed on your monitor, which has to display color the same way that your proofing device prints color, which has to print color the same way that your service bureau's RIP will RIP color, which has to RIP color the same way that your printer's printing press will print color. That's a mouthful, but so is color management. The entire subject of color management is beyond the scope of this book, but here are some of the ways that studios are working to overcome color problems.

The problem, as many people see it, is that not only do you need to make sure your own house is in order, so to speak, or calibrate your own devices, you also need to make sure that you are calibrated with respect to the vendors to whom you send your work.

One place to start is with ColorSync, a system extension from Apple that essentially aims to create a level playing field with regard to color management. ColorSync creates a framework—at the system level—for managing color from peripheral to peripheral. Within this framework, color-management software can use captured image data to create your ICC profiles.

Essentially, you need to start by creating your color profiles, beginning with the digital camera. Shooting a standard IT8 color test target gives your profiling system the data it needs to create a profile. Usually, software that comes with the camera aids in the task of profiling the camera.

Monitors can be profiled using a variety of colorimetry devices, such as the X-Rite Colortron. Or a Gretag Spectrolino spectrophotometer can be used to measure the display of an IT8 test target, and the monitor can be profiled. And a test target can be printed on the color proofing device in-house, and profiles created for that.

Depending on your color-management software, all this info is fed into it and *voilà*! You have no color worries ever again!

Yeah, right.

Many experts are dubious, saying that all color management can only be color mismanagement, but if you are dealing with extraordinarily color-critical jobs, taking a crash course in color management may be a worthwhile investment of a day or so.

The real trick is getting your vendor's equipment calibrated with your own. After all, your color is only as accurate as the least-calibrated device in the chain, and if that device is your service bureau's RIP, does it mean you're S.O.L.?

Not really. It's actually pretty easy—at least in theory. You simply send a test file—the same IT8 or whatever test image you've using in house—out to your service bureau. You get back a color proof from the vendor, get out your trusty Colortron or Spectrolino, and measure it the same way you measured your own output test target. This lets you create one last output profile to feed into your color-management system.

Of course, this assumes that the vendor's output is going to remain consistent as time goes by, but it's a chance you'll have to take. If you notice any bizarre color stuff going on, be sure to send out another test file and profile again.

Proofing and Printing

The good news in this realm is that it is now cheaper than ever to do reasonable color proofing and printing. Part of that has to do with the rapid evolution of inkjet printing. If this book had been written as recently as two years ago, we would have been dwelling exclusively on dye-sublimation proofers.

Well, we will for a moment. Most photo studios are using desktop dye-sub printers, the most prevalent being the Imation Rainbow, the Kodak XLS 8650, and the Tektronix (now Xerox) 480X. Models from DuPont, Seiko, Shinko, and Tally are also popular.

Photographers also are fond of the Fuji Pictrography system. The Pictrography 3000 is a laser dye-transfer digital photoprinter that prints cyan, magenta, and yellow colors on photosensitive donor paper, which is then moistened with water to create a dye image that is then heat-transferred to a receptor sheet. The result is a 400-dpi continuous-tone print. (The newer Pictrography 4000 features faster speeds and larger paper sizes, but is the same basic technology.)

High-end proofing systems are not going away any time soon, and many high-end studios may need to avail themselves of them. But inkjet is proving to be a reliable, inexpensive, and accurate substitute for the lower end of the market.

Part of this is thanks to Epson. The introduction in 1998 of the Stylus Pro 5000, which came with an EFI Fiery RIP, proved to be a hot seller, and garnered praise across the graphic arts industry for its excellence as a proofing device, much of which was also thanks to DuPont's color-profiling technology that was part of the mix. The Stylus Pro 5000 and all it entailed listed for about $10,000—much cheaper than a comparable dye-sub setup. (The system is now about $8,000.)

Since then, Imation and Hewlett-Packard teamed up to produce the Matchprint Inkjet Proofing System, a combination of the HP DesignJet ColorPro GA inkjet printer and color-proofing software from Imation (based on their original Matchprint proofing system used by service bureaus). That is also an inexpensive system, and is a viable option in the proofing arena.

We do keep gravitating to the cheap end, don't we? But not every viable workflow solution has to cost tens of thousands of dollars. To wit: Adobe's PressReady, which we touched on briefly in an earlier chapter. It hasn't been out long enough for us to gauge its popularity in digital photo studios, but our experiments have shown it to be a viable, reasonably accurate means of gauging how color will output.

Photographers have also found less expensive "desktop" printers to be viable proofers.

I said at the outset of this chapter that I really didn't intend this to become a primer on how to set up a studio. This is merely a quick technological overview of the considerations that need to be taken into account before you get started. Remember: Setting up a professional photo studio is not cheap. It can easily cost in excess of $150,000 to create a good one. Sometimes more. Sometimes less.

Working with Photo Studios

Although many people reading this probably won't be inclined to run out and set up a photo studio, you may very well end up as the client of one. Although our little cheapo setup in Chapter 4 will do well for some things, often you may need quality photography that is far and above what you can accomplish with a megapixel point-and-shoot.

The modern digital photography studio is evolving in such a way that it is now easier than ever for photographers and clients to work together to ensure that both sides are happy with a job. Do I sound a bit too much like Little Merry Sunshine? Perhaps. But let's dwell on it a moment.

You are putting together a catalog. Let's say it is toys, just for fun. You have experimented with a cheapo setup, and you think I'm full of crap and there's no way your own inexpensive equipment is going to cut it. That's fine. So you find a local photo studio. They have scanning back cameras, an Orbiculight, and some other high-quality gear, and they can take on your job. You bring down your toys.

The photographer sets up his shots. The toy is put on the stage; the photographer is a pro, so it takes little time before it is lit properly; and as the client you are on hand to make sure it looks the way you want it. His camera setup is connected to a workstation, and he has a calibrated monitor. He previews for you the shot live on screen. Maybe you don't like the lighting. Maybe you want it a bit less harsh—or whatever; the point is that you can suggest changes before a single shot has been taken.

So he makes your changes, you okay the preview, and he takes a couple of shots. They are instantly available for review on screen, and you yea or nay them. If you okay them, it's off to the next shot. If not, they are deleted, and you try again.

And so on.

In a traditional photo environment, you would be able to see Polaroids of the composed shot and have to okay it from those, which can be hit-or-miss. Then you would have to wait until the film was developed before seeing the final shots. That could be a day later, and if you hated them, the photographer would have to restage and relight the products and do it all over again. The photographer would not be happy, and time would be lost. You'd be billed quite a bit for it.

In this case, you see everything right on screen as it is happening. And if you doubt the accuracy of the monitor, chances are the images could easily be printed to a color printer or proofer. If that has been calibrated properly, you'll be seeing a reasonably accurate proof of how they will look in print.

Alternatively, let's say you are thousands of miles from your photo studio. You can still benefit from the digital workflow; many photographers who have out-of-town clients will e-mail low-res images or even PDFs to the client. Studios are even posting images on password-protected Web sites for clients to review at their leisure. Through a combination of e-mail and the telephone, you as the client can convey exactly what your concerns are immediately, or within a reasonable response time. Your products can be kept on the stage with the lighting setup intact, so that if retakes need to be done, it is a simple process that doesn't involve having to set things up from scratch.

This whole process is changing the role of the client, even the role of the photographer. Clients are finding that they are assuming more responsibility than has been the case in the past. They have greater control over the imagery they are paying for—and they are paying less for it. And photographers are finding that they are taking over more of the strictly service bureau work—not just photography but also color correction, color conversion, retouching, compositing, proofing, and so forth.

There still are photographers and clients who don't see digital photography as viable or of high enough quality to work. Some are eager for it to reach a point where it is viable; some just wish it would go away.

Well, it's not going to go away, and although it's not for everyone nor for every application, many experts and photographers believe that the quality is there. And they must; they're investing in it, after all. But there is no doubt that as the technology evolves and new chips debut, the quality will only get better.

Low end or high end, and all the places in between—it's all pretty exciting.

Onward

Well, we've looked low, and we've looked high (end, that is), and now we've come close to the end of our whirlwind tour of the world of digital photography.

The next and final chapter is essentially our look at the future—or the future as it is developing in the present. I don't put much stock in the value of predictions, but what we will be looking at before we leave is some of the newer technologies that are emerging. We've seen some of them, albeit in passing, but now we can look at them full-bore, as it were. There are new CCDs coming out—and some folks even see the CCD as a dying breed. Is that true? CMOS chips are back in the news—are they likely to make headway?

In other words: Where do we go from here?

9

Where Do We Go from Here?

I said earlier that I don't put much stock in the value of predictions. Be they from industry pundits or from so-called professional psychics, they all tend to be rather self-serving and often dead wrong. Well, sometimes they're right, but there's always serendipity.

We've seen where we've been. Is there any way we can determine where we're going? In a way, yes. One of the big future issues we need to address is the very future of the imaging sensor itself, our old friend the CCD.

Imaging Sensors

Some have said that the CCD is a dying technology, that it is only so good, and that there are better technologies. That may or may not be true, and this verdict can vary according to whom you talk. Honestly, though, the CCDs that are currently used in the lower-end point-and-shoots probably have a few more megapixel milestones yet to go before it has maxed out. You can only cram so many pixels on a chip before you start to have problems. Numbers between 3 and 6 megapixels are usually cited as the upper limit for a conventional CCD. The reason for this is obvious: Unless you are making the CCD itself physically larger, and unless you want a camera the size of a shoebox—and manufacturers making point-

and-shoots do not—you need to shrink the size of the pixel to get more of them on the chip. On the surface of things, this doesn't sound bad—making the pixels smaller is what we want, right?

Well, not really. The smaller the pixel, the smaller its component photodiode (the actual light-sensitive bit of the pixel), and thus the less sensitive it is to light. So yes, you can keep boosting resolution, but you're trading off things like signal-to-noise ratio, dynamic range, and light sensitivity. Not so good.

So we've seen that the current crop of point-and-shoots has CCDs with more than 3 million pixels. Some say that will be the last megapixel milestone before we need a new technology; others say it may be 6 million pixels.

(The mid-range professional cameras and the high-end backs use more-expensive CCDs—that's one of the reasons why the cameras are so darn expensive.)

But there are also those who think that 3 Mp may be good enough at the lower end. After all, you can print your captures at 5 × 7 inches—or even 8 × 10 inches, if you're clever. Surely that's enough. Just because we *can* make higher-resolution CCDs, does that mean we *should*?

That's probably more a philosophical question than a technological one, but the point is that all it takes is for one manufacturer to come out with 4-Mp CCDs, and then everyone is going to have to do it. It's like airline ticket pricing. All you need is for one air carrier to lower fares, then everyone has to do it. *C'est la vie.*

Super CCD

But that all may be a moot point, since there are new CCD technologies in the works. The most conspicuous of these—or at least the one that has been announced first—is Fuji's new Super CCD.

Announced in late 1999, Fuji's Super CCD is a departure from the standard rectangular CCD. As we just saw, the problem with increasing "megapixellage" is that if you want to add pixels to a CCD, you need to make the pixels—and the photodiodes they contain—smaller so as to fit more in roughly the same size chip. But

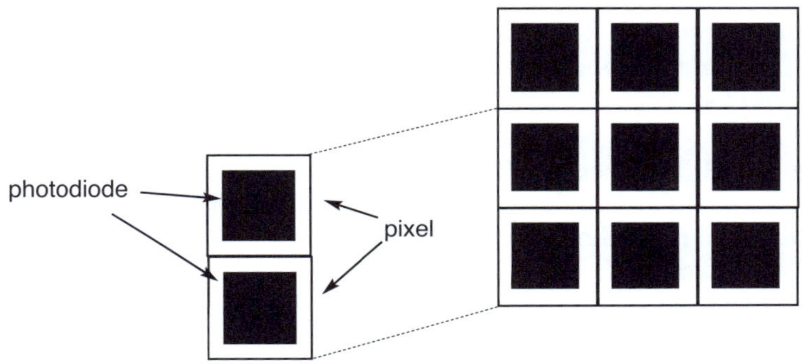

Conventional CCD array.

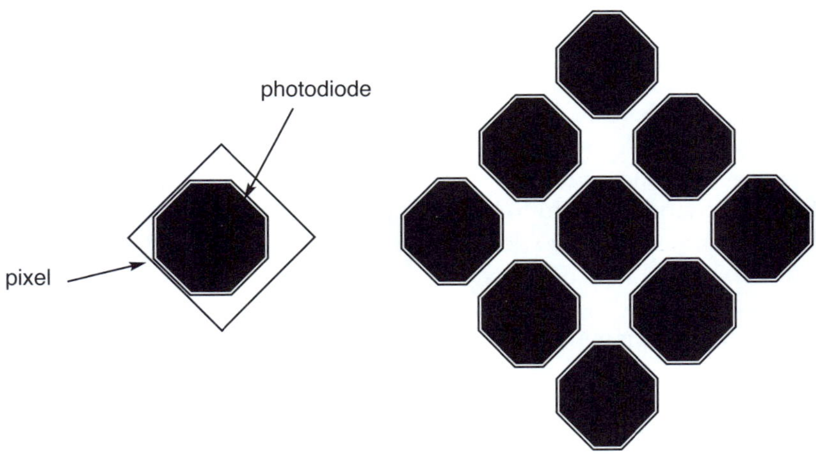

Super CCD array.

the trade-off is that when you reduce the size of a photodiode, you decrease its sensitivity to light. There's less surface area for the light to hit. So you get more pixels in your image, but you also get low efficiency of light capture.

What Fuji has done is design a new CCD to try to eliminate some of these problems. Their first step was to turn each pixel at a 45-degree angle. Without getting too technical here, this makes more efficient use of space on the chip.

The second step was to make each photodiode octagonal rather than rectangular. This has several benefits. First, the microlens that covers each photodiode is circular, regardless of the actual shape of the photodiode. In a conventional CCD with a rectangular photodiode, you've got a circular lens over it. In the Super CCD, you've got a circular lens over an octagonal photodiode—the shapes are more congruent, which aids efficiency of light capture. The photodiode can also be larger, and more can be packed together more efficiently. The octagonal pixels slot together in a honeycomb pattern, which is said to improve sensitivity, signal-to-noise ratio, and dynamic range.

The Super CCD also has a new signal processor that was designed specifically for the new honeycomb structure. Fuji says this improves the ability of the camera to upsample images. And ISO sensitivities are said to be enhanced as well, since the photodiode is larger (about 50 percent larger than a conventional photodiode).

Another problem conventional CCDs have—and that designers of the Super CCD has attempted to solve—is resolution that is greater on the diagonal than in either the vertical or horizontal, which causes unnatural-looking digital images, since human vision tends to prefer straight ups and downs. The reason for that problem was the square layout of the pixels on a conventional CCD. By putting the pixels at a 45-degree angle, the Super CCD shifts the resolution burden, as it were, to the horizontal and vertical.

That's the basic theory behind the new Super CCD. There are other technological benefits as well, but you get the idea. Fuji is touting

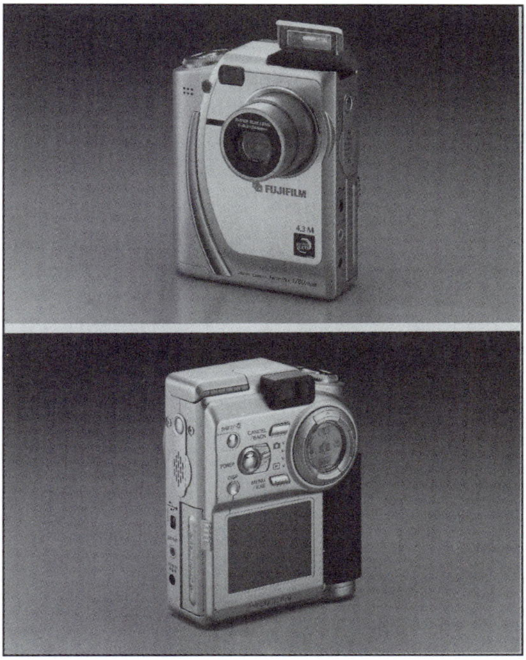

At the PMA show in February 2000, Fuji debuted the new line of FinePix cameras based on its new Super CCD technology — the FinePix 4700, targeted to the consumer.

as one of the benefits of the new CCD the ability to create a multifunction digital still camera and digital video camcorder—all using the same CCD.

The new CCD technology is nice, but is it being used in anything? Yes, it is. Fuji has introduced its debut Super CCD product line, which it is calling FinePix.

There are two initial models that have been announced, although they have not started shipping as of this book's press time. The consumer-level FinePix 4700 Zoom has a .58-inch Super CCD that can capture images as large as 2,400 × 1,800 pixels. The FinePix 4700 Zoom also can capture images at 1,280 × 960 pixels and 640 × 480 pixels. It does not capture uncompressed TIFFs, but has three JPEG compression levels—1:5, 1:11, and 1:27.

The camera has a 3× optical zoom (equivalent to 38–114 mm on a 35mm camera) and five exposure modes. Shutter speed can be as slow as 3 seconds or as fast as 1/2000 second. ISO equivalency can be

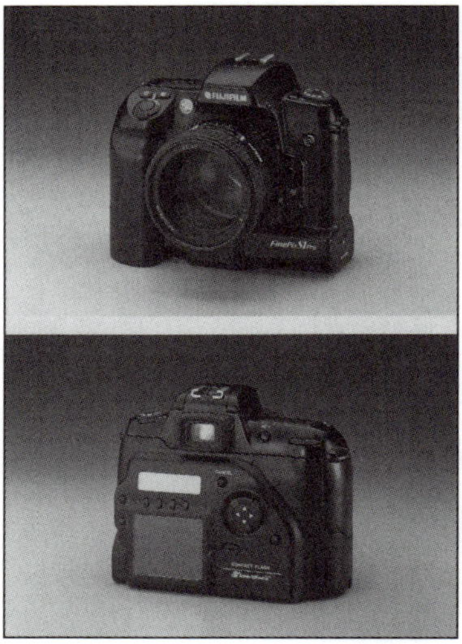

Fuji's Super CCD-based FinePix S1 (left), targeted at the prosumer.

toggled among 200, 400, and 800. It also has three metering modes—multi, spot, and center. The camera supports SmartMedia cards up to 64 MB. The camera can also capture up to 80 seconds of digital video with sound at 320 × 240 pixels at 10 frames per second.

The 4700 Zoom also has a built-in flash, as you would expect. When it appears, it will have a suggested retail price of $999.

At the professional level, Fuji also has debuted the FinePix S1 Pro, an SLR camera with having a 23.3 × 15.6 mm Super CCD that captures 6.1-Mp images—or 3,040 × 2016, for those playing along at home. Using a Nikon camera body, the S1 Pro also has a burst mode that enables continuous shooting at approximately 1.5 frames per second up to five frames. It has adjustable ISO equivalencies of 320, 400, 800, and 1,600, shutter speeds that range from 30 seconds to 1/2000 second, and a variety of exposure modes. It has slots for both SmartMedia (up to 64 MB) and CompactFlash, and also supports the IBM Microdrive.

The S1 Pro also supports three file formats—TIFF-RGB, TIFF-YC, and JPEG, and three JPEG compression settings. The S1 Pro also displays a histogram of captured images.

The FinePix S1 Pro is projected to be available sometime in the first half of 2000, with a suggested retail price of $4,000.

CMOS Redux

Many imaging experts are championing an alternative to the CCD in general, which we saw briefly in Chapter 2. That is the CMOS chip. The Soundvision camera we touched on was one of the first CMOS-based cameras to appear, and CMOS has occasionally turned up in point-and-shoots. Vivitar, for example, has a couple of low-resolution CMOS-based cameras.

And a company called Silicon Film Technology has a CMOS-based "film roll" called eFilm that can be used with conventional camera bodies. The eFilm "roll" can be inserted into any standard 35mm SLR camera and can take up to twenty-four 1.3-Mp images.

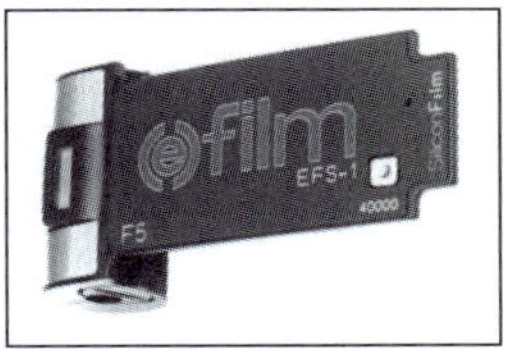

Silicon Film Technology's eFilm is a digital "film roll" that fits into any standard 35mm SLR. The film can be "developed" — i.e., transferred to a computer — by means of an ePort that connects to a USB port.

SFT also has an ePort, which is a download device that lets you transfer your eFilm images to a computer via USB connection.

But that's kind of an anomaly, although it's a cool idea.

At the low end, we may very well see some CMOS cameras for less than $500.

C-MOST

There is currently a flurry of CMOS activity at the high end. Scitex has recently released a white paper discussing its new technology, the Leaf C-MOST sensor. The first C-MOS-based sensor to be created specifically for high-quality, professional digital photography, it is designed to be integrated into 35mm, medium- and large-format photographic equipment.

The C-MOST sensor is a thin, 24 × 36 mm sensor that has 6.6 million pixels, being able to capture 3,150 × 2,100-pixel images. It is distinguished from other CMOS chips by an increased dynamic range, and thin packaging that allows it to be placed in the focal plane of a standard 35mm camera. Other advantages include on-chip processing (a staple of CMOS technology, since the CMOS technology itself was originally designed for computer processors) and an inexpensive manufacturing process.

The chip consists of two very thin layers of glass, between which the active layer of silicon is inserted. The glass plate that faces the direction the light is coming from (i.e., the lens of the camera) has been treated with a special coating to prevent ghosting, as well as color-correct spectral characteristics.

The C-MOST sensor boasts high signal-to-noise ratio and very good dynamic range. It is also designed to be scalable, and can be adopted to other sensor sizes.

We saw in Chapter 1 that one of the problems photographers were having with digital photography was that the chipsets needed to capture the images operated with different focal lengths than most photographers were used to. The C-MOST chip has been designed as an insert to 35mm cameras, and the imaging sensor is in the focal plane of the lens. (Kind of like a much higher-quality version of the eFilm from Silicon Film Technology that we just mentioned.) And the active area of the sensor is the same size as a 35mm frame, the goal here being to enable the sensor to be easily added to pre-existing 35mm equipment with no difference in magnification or effective focal length.

Other advantages of the C-MOST sensor include support for burst shooting (three frames per second), portability (it uses less power than a CCD, thus requiring fewer and/or smaller batteries), and support for live previews. A CCD sensor requires what is known as an external shutter to enable a live preview. A CCD cannot function under continuous lighting. The C-MOST chip has no such limitation and does not require an external shutter.

Scitex Leaf is certainly not seeking to switch over its entire product line to CMOS, at least not in the foreseeable future. Scitex says the C-MOST sensor has been developed to create imaging products that will complement its line of high-quality, CCD-based camera backs. Although no specific C-MOST-based products have yet been announced, I'm sure we'll be hearing about something by year's end.

New Features on Old Cameras

The new sensors are all well and good, but the current state of the technology—the CCD-based point-and-shoots—is still with us. In the current crop, the 3-Mp cameras, we're starting to see something of a shakedown in feature sets. As we've charted the evolution of the digital camera market, we can see how some features have come and gone.

We've seen that most cameras now have optical zooms. Initially that was a luxury; now it's pretty much par for the course. Epson, for example, whose first megapixel camera, the PhotoPC 700, was an excellent camera, has discontinued the model in favor of the version with an optical zoom. Their later models all feature optical zooms. Most cameras have this feature now.

The 3-Mp cameras also have digital video capabilities, which was kind of a rarity in the past. I suspect that now the cameras have the processing power, the internal memory, and the memory cards that enable video capture. The video capabilities are still not that robust, but they're getting there. (Most cameras have also been able to record sound for several years, although that become a somewhat less-than-bragged-about feature, for some reason.)

Some cameras still enable direct printing to a dye-sub or inkjet printer, although users don't seem to have been clamoring for it. It exists, but it's rarely touted anymore, perhaps because manufacturers have come to realize that digital cameras are bought because users want the ability to import and edit images on a computer.

Storage

Removable storage for digital cameras is also proliferating. At the moment, there are no real dominant players, except insofar as most cameras are using SmartMedia or CompactFlash—sometimes both. We've looked at these already, but there are some new devices coming out of which we should be aware.

The first of these is IBM's Microdrive, a very small (it's the size of a CompactFlash card) removable storage card. It's not a flash memory card like CompactFlash; it's basically a traditional Winchester hard drive, albeit a Lilliputian one. It weighs less than an ounce, yet holds 340 MB. IBM says that the data density will allow the Microdrive to be able to grow; capacities could easily exceed 1 GB.

The cool thing about the Microdrive—and IBM was very smart about this feature—is that it uses a standard CompactFlash Type II interface, which means that manufacturers can easily allow it to be read in CompactFlash slots and readers. In fact, the Microtech USB CameraMate that we love so much also reads Microdrive disks.

So basically, in the removable storage arena—at least as far as digital cameras are concerned—I suspect we will be seeing more of the same for a while anyway. CompactFlash and SmartMedia (and PC cards) are pretty well entrenched, so they'll be with us for a while. We'll continue seeing what we've been seeing—higher capacities ad cheaper prices. I've stopped indicating what the highest capacities are, primarily because I got tired of going back through older chapters and changing the numbers. This is how fast this is all changing.

My suspicion is that we'll probably start to see more cameras with slots for both cards. Depending on what other technologies work with these cards—PDAs, MP3 players, laptops, and so on—we can hope that eventually everyone will standardize on the same storage technology. Fortunately, this is starting to happen, so we may be in luck.

Printing

We looked at printers in close detail earlier, but look for the big developments in this arena to bring archival-quality printing to the desktop. Epson's new printers, inks, and media are making that a reality. Creating inexpensive, photo-quality inkjet desktop prints that are able to last as long as film-based prints is a milestone in the adoption of digital photography, at least as far as the consumer is concerned.

As for the graphic arts uses, well, it's nice but not thrilling, I suppose we could say. Inexpensive desktop proofing is what graphics users will be looking for.

Digita Operating Environment

One interesting wrinkle in the digital camera arena that is by no means new is the concept of a digital camera operating system. This has been pushed by a company called FlashPoint, which some time ago developed the Digita operating environment for digital cameras.

The basic point of Digita is this: Camera vendors build the Digita operating environment into the camera, which adds functionality beyond what the camera manufacturer has put in. Digita features the ability to upload third-party software to the camera and controls the behavior of that software, much like a desktop operating system. This software can allow you to use your camera in different ways, such as create presentations, edit and produce multimedia, and many other things.

FlashPoint also has a Digita Script programming language, as well as a Software Developers Kit, which lets software developers or enthusiasts create their own customized "applets" to suit their own nefarious purposes. These applets can be uploaded into the camera and will run in tandem with the Digita operating environment.

The Digita environment can also be used to automate camera features, automatically select camera settings, manage files, and so forth. The goal of Digita is to create a standardized operating environment for "digital appliances." (FlashPoint has also moved into the palm market, as well.)

Digita is far from prevalent, although camera makers like Epson, Hewlett-Packard, Kodak, and Minolta have signed on.

Some camera manufacturers, however, have bristled about engineering limitations placed on cameras that will be running a standard operating system, and camera makers like to be able to give their own customers features that other manufacturers do not provide.

I daresay there is not going to be any warfare over this issue, but is some degree of standardization likely to be a bad thing?

So Yet Even Still Once Again, Why Digital Photography?
We're winding down this book, and I'm sure you still have questions. Primary among them is probably the one I mentioned in the introduction. Namely: Is my investment going to go down the tubes?

And the answer is no. At this point in time, it has never been easier or cheaper to get involved in digital photography. As the new models come out, the older ones will come down in price. So if you don't mind being a generation behind the times, you can get into digital photography quite economically.

We've mentioned a lot of the issues involved over the course of the last 200 or so pages, but here is probably the most important question you should ask before trundling off to your camera store:

What am I going to do with the images?

Knowing the answer to that question will help you immeasurably.

Is it for print production, Web publishing, ersatz (or professional) photojournalism, high-end studio photography … or just for fun? Knowing your end use in advance will inform your buying decision. We saw in Chapter 6 how to determine reproduction size based on capture image size.

If you are going to print, but not extremely high-quality print, you can go the point-and-shoot route. At least 2.X Mp will do nicely. If you are publishing solely to the Web, you can easily go for a cut-rate, 1.X- or 2.X-Mp model. Not a real el cheapo camera, because you still need good image quality, but you don't need ridiculous resolutions. But if you think you're going to want more pixels in the future, wouldn't it be nice to know that you've got them?

If you are doing professional photojournalism, you may need to go with one of the mid-range professional cameras.

If you are looking to get into high-quality studio photography, you will probably need to investigate the digital camera backs.

If it's just for fun … well, pick whatever looks fun.

You also need to determine your priorities. Is price the most important consideration? If it is, you can get a decent camera for less than $800, but there will be a trade-off of features.

If features are more important—especially true photographic controls—be forewarned that you'll likely pay for them.

Is the highest possible image quality the most important consideration? In this case, you need to figure out how high "highest quality" is. Are we talking UXGA resolution? Are we talking 6-Mp professional camera? Or are we talking scanning-back resolution? If so, then we're taking money.

Onward

The digital camera and photography market is exploding. That may be needless hyperbole, and may be a bit more graphic than the situation really calls for, but the point is that there is now a confluence of technologies that is bringing digital into all our lives—whether we want it there or not.

Especially in the graphic arts field, the increasing digitization of everything is changing all of our roles, especially in small shops. Designers are becoming akin to service bureaus, in a way, as CTP shifts more of the responsibility to the content creation end. The line is blurring between where content creation ends and production begins.

All the way down the line, digital cameras are also starting to change our preconceived roles. We saw in Chapter 8 how the digital studio workflow has shifted more of the prepress tasks onto the photographer.

But even in smaller organizations—like *Micro Publishing News* and other companies that are using digital cameras for much of their imaging work—more and more people are becoming part of that prepress process. A reporter covering an event and shooting it with an Olympus digital camera—is that journalism, photojournalism, or prepress? If he downloads his own images and cleans them up in Photoshop, is that prepress? You bet it is.

But as we are seeing, prepress is going away.

Or is it going away? Or is prepress evolving—in some weird *Star Trek* kind of way—into something that no longer has need of a physical body, that is just pure thought? I think prepress is becoming sort of a ephemeral term that describes everything yet nothing. It's very Zen, in a way.

We're all doing prepress, even if no one wants to call it that anymore.

Glossary of Terms

Aliasing
An undesirable effect in digital images characterized by a visible jagged stairstep appearance along the edge of an image. Also called "jaggies."

Analog
Any continuous wave or signal, such as that produced by a sound wave or a varying electrical voltage. Analog is usually considered to be the "opposite" of digital. See also *Digital*.

Analog-to-Digital (A/D) Converter
Any device that converts an analog signal to discrete bits of digital data.

Anti-Aliasing
Any technique for removing or cloaking the effect of aliasing.

Aperture
The variable hole that allows light into a camera. The size of the aperture is called an *f-stop*. See *F-Stop*.

Archive
A presumably organized storage of files.

Area Array
A type of charge-coupled device comprising several rows and

columns of pixels that can capture a largish image in one shot. See also *Linear Array*.

Artifact
More or less perceptible "blemishes" or color shifts in a compressed image, caused by the lossiness of the compression algorithm. See *Compression*.

Auto Focus
In a camera, an automatic mode in which the camera determines what it thinks the subject is and focuses on it.

Bit
One unit of digital data, either 0 or 1. Eight bits equal 1 byte.

Bit Depth
A number that refers to how many bits of data are required to describe each color pixel comprising a digital image. A bit depth of 24 bits per pixel means that each red pixel is described by 8 bits of data, each green pixel is described by 8 bits of data, and each blue pixel is described by 8 bits of data. Ergo, $8 \times 3 = 24$.

Bitmap
A digital image that comprises a series of dots or pixels, such as a photographic image. In contrast is a vector image.

Blooming
Defect of a digital image caused by one CCD pixel becoming saturated and "leaking" into neighboring pixels.

BMP
A file format for bitmap images on the Windows platform.

Brightness
The quality of lightness or darkness an image exhibits.

Byte

A unit of data equal to 8 bits. A kilobyte (KB) is roughly 1,000 (or actually, 1,024) bytes. A megabyte (MB) is roughly 1,000 (actually 1,024) kilobytes, or roughly 1 million (actually 1,048,576) bytes. A gigabyte (GB) is roughly 1,000 (actually 1,024) megabytes, or roughly 1 billion (actually 1,073,741,824) bytes. There are also terabytes, petabytes, and exabytes, but let's not go there.

Calibration

The means of adjusting a device so that its input and output values will closely—if not identically—match those of another device or devices. In imaging and prepress, calibration usually refers to the process of getting each device in a workflow—camera, scanner, monitor, printer—to identically represent color.

CCD

See *Charge-Coupled Device.*

Center Metering

In a camera, a light meter that evaluates a region around the center of a frame to determine proper exposure. See also *Spot Metering*.

Charge-Coupled Device (CCD)

A light-sensitive sensor or photocell used to capture images in a scanner or digital camera. A charge-coupled device detects light hitting it and converts that light to electrical voltages. These voltages are then converted to digital data. Special dyes on the CCD capture red, green, and blue info. All of this is collated, once the data is in the camera, scanner, or computer, to display a captured color image.

CMOS

Abbreviation for complementary metal-oxide semiconductor, a type of imaging sensor that occasionally turns up in digital cameras.

CMYK

Short for cyan, magenta, yellow, and black (K actually stands for "key," referring to the black plate), the color space required for process color printing. Cyan, magenta, and yellow are the three primary colors of colorants from which all the printed (and printable) colors are derived. Black is added for enhancement. See also *RGB* and *Spot Color*.

Color Separation

A prepress process—once done photographically, now done digitally—in which a color image is converted into four separate images or plates (cyan, magenta, yellow, and black) for color printing.

Color Space

The specific system used to represent the colors in an image, such as RGB, CMYK, or grayscale.

CompactFlash

A physically small, somewhat high-capacity (128 MB and counting) flash memory storage card used as "digital film" in many consumer- and prosumer-level digital cameras.

Compositing

Merging one image or elements of one image with one or more other images.

Compression

In digital imaging, a reduction of the file size of a digital image by means of algorithms that describe the image in less space than the "raw" image. Compression can either be lossy—the algorithmic "shorthand" throws some data away irretrievably—or lossless.

Continuous Tone

A type of image comprising an unbroken gradation of tones, as opposed to discrete dots.

Contrast

The degree of difference between two regions or pixels in an image. Contrast also refers to the degree of difference between light and dark.

Cropping

Cutting out a portion of an image and discarding the rest.

Digital

Data that exists as discrete units of (usually) numeric code, such as some pattern of 0s and 1s. Digital is usually considered to be the "opposite" of analog. See also *Analog*. Digital is used to refer to any technology, skill, or activity that involves digitizing data, i.e., digital photography.

Digital Camera

A type of camera—which can range from very low-end "point-and-shoots" to very high-end studio cameras and scanning backs—that eschews traditional silver halide film and instead captures images by means of an electronic sensor, either a CCD or CMOS chip.

Digital Film

Somewhat colloquial term for flash memory cards used to record digitally captured images. See *Flash Memory*.

Digital Photography

Photography in which images are captured in digital form in the camera itself, as opposed to traditional photography that records images on silver halide film.

Digital Zoom

A feature found on many digital cameras that slices a chunk out of (usually) the center of an image, leaving you with a low-resolution "closeup." Also referred to as "digital telephoto."

Digitizing

The act of converting analog data to digital form. In the case of images, digitizing can be done either with a scanner or a digital camera.

Dot Gain

A phenomenon of offset printing that causes halftone dots to become slightly enlarged during platemaking and/or printing, resulting in continuous-tone images that end up printing darker than expected.

Dots per Inch (DPI)

A measure of resolution referring to how many pixels a device can either capture, display, or print in a linear inch. A Macintosh computer monitor can display 72 dots per inch (DPI). A laser printer can often output at least 300 DPI, and so forth.

Downsampling

Reducing the file size and/or resolution of a digital image. See also *Upsampling*.

DPI

Abbreviation for dots per inch. See *Dots per Inch*.

Dye Sublimation

A type of imaging system used in a variety of low-end and high-end printers that uses thermal dyes to transfer an image to special substrates. Although dye-sublimation produces excellent, long-lasting images, it can be an expensive process. Also referred to as *dye-sub*.

Exposure Bracketing

A photographic technique in which a photographer takes a number of pictures with varying degrees of exposure compensation, in the hope that at least one will have the proper exposure.

Exposure Compensation

In a camera, a control that under- or overexposes an image to correct for inadequate (or too adequate) lighting conditions.

F-Stop

The size of a camera's aperture—the hole that allows light into the camera and to strike the CCD or film. An f-stop, or f-number, is the ratio of the focal length of the lens to the diameter of the aperture. Standard f-stops are f/1.4, f/2, f/2.8, f/4, f/5.6, f/8, f/11, f/16, f/22, f/32, and f/64. Each f-stop differs by a factor of 2 in the amount of light that is allowed to pass into the camera.

Flash

A light source, either built-in and/or available as an accessory, for a camera. Most flashes can either be turned on or off, and many can be set as auto flashes, meaning that the camera will decide if the light is low enough to warrant the use of a flash.

Flash Memory

A type of RAM/ROM hybrid storage used for various types of removable storage cards, be they SmartMedia or CompactFlash.

Floppy Disk

A low-capacity (up to 1.44 MB), once-ubiquitous magnetic storage medium for computers. Early floppy disks—which were actually floppy—were 5.25 inches in diameter, but these evolved into 3.5-inch hard-shell diskettes (though the disk inside was still "floppy"). Floppy disks still have their uses, but some newer personal computers lack floppy drives. Early digital cameras such as the Sony Mavica used floppy disks as a type of digital film, but the file sizes of captured images have rendered this an increasingly insufficient storage solution. Imation has introduced the SuperDisk, a 120-MB floppy disk.

Focal Length

In a camera and camera lens, the distance between the center of the lens and the focal point when the camera is focused at infinity.

Focal Point

A spot in a camera where all the light rays entering the lens converge and the image is the sharpest.

Gamma

A measure of the contrast of an image.

Gamut

The complete range of displayable or reproducible colors in a particular color space. The CMYK space has a much narrower gamut than does the RGB color space, for example.

GB

Abbreviation for gigabyte. See *Gigabyte*.

GIF

A file format for Web-based images.

Gigabyte (GB)

A unit of data equal to roughly 1,000 (actually 1,024) megabytes, or roughly 1 billion (actually 1,073,741,824) bytes.

Grayscale

An image or color mode in which an image is represented as various shades of gray on a scale from pure white to pure black.

Hard Disk

A (typically) high-capacity, magnetic storage medium found in nearly all personal computers. At one time, a 50-MB hard disk was high-end; now, if you have less than 10 GB, there's something wrong with you. The hard disk is where the computer's operating system is stored, as well as all locally saved files and applications. Many computer users need more than one hard disk, whether external or internal. Hard disks are faster working than floppies, Zips, and other types of removable storage.

Histogram
A chart showing the distribution of image densities from lightest to darkest.

Inkjet
A technology used in printers that forms images by means of carefully placed ink droplets.

Interpolation
See *Upsampling*.

ISO
Abbreviation for International Standards Organization. The ISO does lots of things, but in digital photography, ISO refers to CCD sensitivity, or how receptive to light the CCD is. The numeric ISO values are derived from "film speed" in traditional photography.

JPEG
Short for Joint Photographic Experts Group, JPEG is a file format and compression algorithm used for digital images. Although lossy, the degree of JPEG compression can usually be controlled.

KB
Abbreviation for kilobyte. See *Kilobyte*.

Kilobyte (KB)
A unit of data equal to roughly 1,000 (actually 1,024) bytes.

Landscape
A picture oriented so that it is wider than it is tall. See also *Portrait*.

LCD
Abbreviation for liquid crystal display, a small color screen on the back of a digital camera that lets you review captured images, compose shots, or access menu options.

Linear Array
A type of charge-coupled device that has a single row of pixels that captures an image by advancing one row at a time. See also *Area Array*.

Line Screen
In offset printing, the number of halftone dots per linear inch.

Lossless
File compression that results in no degradation whatsoever to the compressed file. See *Compression*. See also *Lossy*.

Lossy
File compression that causes more or less visible degradation to the compressed file. See *Compression*. See also *Lossless*.

Macro Mode
On cameras, a shooting mode that lets you get very close (usually within 1 or 2 feet, sometimes less than 1 foot) to a subject.

MB
Abbreviation for megabyte. See *Megabyte*.

Megabyte (MB)
A unit of data equal to roughly 1,000 (actually 1,024) *kilobytes*, or roughly 1 million (actually 1,048,576) bytes.

Megapixel (Mp)
An area array charge-coupled device (CCD) having greater than 1 million pixels.

Megapixel Digital Camera
A digital camera having a *CCD* of 1 megapixel or more.

Mp
Abbreviation for megapixel. See *Megapixel.*

Noise
Term for the graininess of a digital camera image, caused by inadequate exposure.

NTSC
Abbreviation for National Television Standards Committee, a term that is used to refer to the standard for television broadcasting in North America and Japan. The standard specifies a frame rate of 29.97 frames per second, a screen frequency of 59.94 Hertz (Hz), and a screen consisting of 525 video lines. For our purposes, all this means is that when a digital camera is NTSC-compatible, it can be connected to a television.

OPI
Abbreviation for Open Prepress Interface, essentially a prepress workflow system whereby high-resolution images are stored on a central file server and low-resolution "proxy" images are placed in a page layout. When the layouts are collected and/or RIPed, the system automatically swaps out the proxies and puts in the high-res versions. In this way, individual workstation resources are conserved, since you do not need as much processing power and RAM for the low-res images as for the high-res ones.

Optical Zoom
A camera feature that allows you to focus—or zoom—more closely on distant objects. Be careful of so-called "digital zooms."

Parallax
In cameras that use a dual lens system (one "proper" lens through

which the picture is actually taken, and one alternate lens that functions with the viewfinder), parallax is the slight change in perspective between what you see in the viewfinder and what the camera will actually capture. Using a TTL (through-the-lens) viewfinder eliminates the problem of parallax.

Parallel

A means of connecting a peripheral device to a PC. Faster than serial.

PC Card

Short for PCMCIA (Personal Computer Memory Card International Association), a PC card is a somewhat small, somewhat high-capacity removable flash storage card used for notebook computers and digital cameras.

PDF

Abbreviation for Portable Document Format, a type of file format created by Adobe Systems. A PDF, these days, can be exported from just about any application, or created easily enough by means of Adobe Acrobat. A PDF preserves all your fonts, images, graphics, text, etc., allowing you to transfer documents to others, and these documents can be read by anyone, regardless of what fonts they have installed, or even what operating system they're using. PDFs are good ways of transmitting booklets and other documentation, and are even used in proofing.

PICT

A file format for bitmap images on the Macintosh platform.

Pixel

The smallest unit that can make up an image, whether displayed on a monitor, output from a printer, or captured by a digital camera.

Pixellation

An image that has been enlarged beyond the amount of data it contains is said to have pixellated. In other words, you can clearly see all the individual pixels. In still other words, it is blecchy.

Pixels per Inch (PPI)
An alternate term for dots per inch (DPI). See *Dots per Inch (DPI).*

Plug-in
A small program that runs through another program, or as an accessory to that program, typically Photoshop.

Point-and-Shoot
A camera—which can be a film camera, but for our purposes is digital—that is designed so that it can simply be aimed at a subject and shot, rather than having to futz around with lens, aperture, exposure, and other settings.

Portrait
A picture oriented so that it is taller than it is wide. See also *Landscape.*

PostScript
A page-description language created in the 1980s by Adobe Systems, used to consistently and predictably output text and graphics (on any PostScript-compatible printer, that is).

PPI
Abbreviation for pixels per inch, which is synonymous with dots per inch. See *Dots per Inch (DPI).*

Process Color
Printing with four colors of ink—cyan, magenta, yellow, and black—combinations of which produce the range of printed and printable colors. See also *Spot Color.*

Proofing
Essentially, looking over or reviewing a document or page and

flagging/fixing errors, often in spelling, typing, etc. Color proofing is a bit thornier and involves printing a color version of a page or document to a color printer or proofer, which has been calibrated in such a way that it will accurately represent the color output of the printing press to which the document will ultimately be sent. (This is a lot more complicated than it sounds, but you get the idea.)

RAM

Abbreviation for random access memory. See *Random Access Memory (RAM)*.

Random-Access Memory (RAM)

Volatile computer storage—often referred to simply as "memory"—used to store the operating system, system extensions, open application programs, and open files. Essentially, it is the computer's workspace. RAM is described as "volatile" because it is erased when the power is shut off. On the plus side, it is a fast means of data storage, and can be written to and read from very rapidly.

Raster

A *bitmap* image.

Raster Image Processor (RIP)

Hardware or software that interprets PostScript language code from a computer or application and converts it into the series of dots that can be output by a printer, imagesetter, or other output device.

Read-Only Memory (ROM)

Nonvolatile computer storage used to, among other things, store a computer's start-up instructions. It is the data stored in ROM that instructs the computer how to start the operating system. ROM is described as nonvolatile because data remains stored in it even when the power is shut off.

Resolution

A measure of how many pixels in a linear inch an image comprises. Resolution is a prime determinant of how well an image will reproduce. Images with greater resolution will have less of a pixellated appearance than images with low resolution.

Removable Storage

Collective term for the bewildering array of media available for storing, backing up, or transporting files. At one time, 44-MB and 88-MB SyQuest cartridges did the job; now, SyQuest is out of business and Iomega's 100-MB Zip and 1-GB or 2-GB Jaz cartridges are the de facto standards for file transfer. In digital cameras, SmartMedia, CompactFlash, and PC cards are commonly used removable storage media.

RGB

Short for red, green, and blue, RGB is the default color space for computer monitors and digital cameras, especially since they are the three primary colors of light from which all the colors of the spectrum are derived. See also *CMYK*.

RIP

Abbreviation for raster image processor. See *Raster Image Processor*.

RIPing

Neologism used to refer to the process of converting PostScript code to the series of dots that can be output by a specific device. See *Raster Image Processor*.

ROM

Abbreviation for read-only memory. See *Read-Only Memory (ROM)*.

Scanner

A device, either a flatbed or drum type, that uses optics and a charge-coupled device to digitize still images. Scanners range in price and quality from low-end flatbeds costing less than $200 to high-quality, high-resolution drum scanners costing in excess of $10,000.

Scanning Back

A high-quality digitizing device that attaches to a view camera. Used to take high-quality, high-resolution images, often in a studio setting.

SCSI

Short for small computer systems interface, SCSI (pronounced "scuzzy") is an old and popular option for connecting peripherals to personal computers.

Serial

A somewhat slow means of connecting a peripheral device to a computer, be it Macintosh or PC.

Shutter

The thingy in a camera that opens or closes to let light in.

Shutter Speed

In a camera, the measure of how long the shutter remains open, exposing the film or CCD. Shutter speeds can be measured in seconds or thousandths of a second.

SLR

Short for single-lens reflex, a type of camera that has a TTL viewfinder; i.e., the shot is composed using the same lens that will actually capture the image.

SmartMedia

A physically small, somewhat high-capacity (32 MB and counting) flash memory storage card used as "digital film" in many consumer- and prosumer-level digital cameras.

Spot Color

In color printing, a color that is not reproducible as a combination of the CMYK primaries. Spot colors are printed with special ink formulations. See also *Process Color*.

Spot Metering

A camera function that lets the user select a specific area of the composed frame that will be used by the camera to determine proper exposure. See also *Center Metering*.

Still Camera

A camera that takes still (i.e., non-moving) images, as opposed to a video camera.

Terabyte

A ridiculously large unit of data equal to roughly 1,000 gigabytes, or about 1 trillion bytes.

Thumbnail

A small version or preview of an image, used for quick review.

TIFF

Short for Tagged Image File Format, TIFF is a standard, cross-platform file format for bitmap images.

TTL

Abbreviation for through-the-lens, a type of optical viewfinder that allows you to compose shots through the same lens the camera uses to actually take the picture, rather than a secondary lens offset from the primary lens. Using TTL viewfinders, you tend to get a more accurate preview of what the camera will actually capture. Non-TTL viewfinders (and some TTL viewfinders) exhibit the problem of parallax.

TWAIN

A standard computer interface often used to facilitate direct access of a connected imaging peripheral—such as a scanner or digital camera—by an application.

Universal Serial Bus (USB)

A newish, cross-platform technology for connecting peripheral devices—scanners, digital cameras, printers, storage devices, and so on—to personal computers. USB is fast, and USB devices can be connected and disconnected on-the-fly, without needing to restart the computer.

Unsharp Mask

A software technique—descended from an earlier photographic technique—that sharpens an image by analyzing sets of adjacent pixels.

Upsampling

Increasing the file size and/or resolution of a digital image. Also referred to as "interpolation." See also *Downsampling*.

USB

Abbreviation for Universal Serial Bus. See *Universal Serial Bus*.

UXGA

Having a resolution of 1,600 × 1,200 pixels, as a monitor or CCD.

Vector

In contrast to a bitmap, a vector image is described mathematically as curves and shapes. As a result, vector images can be enlarged without noticeable pixellation.

VGA

Having a resolution of 640 × 480 pixels, as a monitor or *CCD*.

View Camera

In high-end studio photography, a camera with high-quality optics to which a scanning back or insert can be attached to capture images with very high resolutions.

Viewfinder

On a camera, the small lens that you look through to frame a picture. Some digital cameras eschew optical viewfinders in favor of using the back-panel LCD to compose shots. Some cameras also have TTL (through-the-lens) viewfinders rather than dual-lens systems, the latter of which can cause the problem of parallax.

White Balance

A camera control that corrects for variations in the color of light, which can vary by light source.

XGA

Having a resolution of 1024 x 768 pixels, as a *CCD*.

Zoom

A camera lens that supports multiple focal lengths, usually ranging from telephoto to wide angle. "Zoom" can also be used to refer to wide-angle to telephoto range that is accomplished digitally rather than optically.

Resources

What follows is a listing of manufacturer information for many, if not most, of the products we have mentioned in this book. Models listed below each entry are not meant to represent a manufacturer's entire offering, merely to give a representative sample.

Digital Cameras

Agfa
www.agfaphoto.com
Megapixel digital cameras: ePhoto 1280, ePhoto 1680, CL30, CL50.

Better Light
www.betterlight.com
High-end scanning inserts: Model 4000, Model 6000, Super 6K, Super 8K.

Canon USA
www.usa.canon.com
Megapixel digital cameras: PowerShot S20, PowerShot S10, PowerShot A50, PowerShot Pro70. Mid-range professional digital camera: EOS D2000.

Casio
www.casio.com
Megapixel digital cameras: QV2000 UX/Plus, QV7000SX, QV5500 SX, and more.

Eastman Kodak Company
www.kodak.com
Megapixel digital cameras, mid-range professional digital cameras, and digital scanning backs: DC 200, DC 210, DC 215, DC 240, DC 265, DC 280, DC 290, DCS 315, DCS 330, DCS 520, DCS 560, DCS 620, DCS 660, DCS 420, DCS 460, DCS 465 Back, and others.

Epson America
www.epson.com

Megapixel digital cameras: PhotoPC 750Z, PhotoPC 850Z, and others.

Fuji Photo Film
www.fujifilm.com
Megapixel digital cameras and mid-range professional digital cameras: MX-1200, MX-1700, MX-2700, MX-2900, DS-260, DS-560, DS-565, FinePix 1400 Zoom, FinePix 4700 Zoom, FinePix S1 Pro.

Hewlett-Packard Company
www.hp.com
Megapixel digital cameras: PhotoSmart C500, PhotoSmart C500 xi.

Konica Photo Imaging
www.konica.com
Megapixel digital cameras: Q-M200.

Leica Camera
www.leica-camera.com
Megapixel digital cameras and mid-range professional digital cameras: Digilux Zoom, S1 Pro, and others.

MegaVision
www.mega-vision.com
High-end scanning backs: S2 and S3 single-shot backs, T2, T32 three-shot backs.

Minolta Corporation
www.minoltausa.com
Megapixel digital cameras: RD-3000, 3D 1500, Dimâge EX 1500.

Nikon Inc.
www.nikonusa.com
Megapixel digital cameras and mid-range professional digital cameras: Coolpix 800, Coolpix 950, Coolpix 990, D1.

Olympus America
www.olympus.com
Megapixel digital cameras: D-360L, D-450Z, D-460Z, D-620L, C-2020, C-2500L, C-3030Z, and others.

Panasonic Company
www.panasonic.com
Megapixel digital cameras: PalmCam PV DC2590, PalmCam PV-SD4090 SuperDisk, PalmCam PV-DC2090.

Phase One
www.phaseone.com
High-end scanning backs: LightPhase, PowerPhase FX, PhotoPhase vII, StudioKit vII.

Polaroid Corporation
www.polaroid.com
Megapixel digital cameras: PhotoMax PDC-700, PDC-640, PDC-300.

Ricoh
www.ricoh-usa.com
Megapixel digital cameras: RDC-4200, RDC-4300, RDC-5000B, RDC-5300.

Sony Electronics
www.sony.com
Megapixel digital cameras and mid-range professional digital cameras: Mavica MVC-FD91, MVC-FD88, and MVC-FD83; Cybershot DSC-D700, DSC-D770, DSC-F505, DSC-F55, and others.

Toshiba America
www.dsc.toshiba.com
Megapixel digital cameras: PDR-M3, PDR-M4, PDR-M5.

Vivitar Corporation
www.vivitar.com
Sub-megapixel digital cameras: ViviCam 2700, 2750, 2800, 3000, 3100 (CMOS).

Removable Storage

Delkin Devices
www.delkin.com
Produces the eFilm line of PC Card, CompactFlash, and SmartMedia cards and readers.

Iomega
www.iomega.com
Zip, Jaz, Clik! drives and media.

Lexar Media
www.digitalfilm.com
Produces CompactFlash and SmartMedia cards and readers.

Microtech International
www.microtechint.com
Produces SmartMedia and CompactFlash readers, as well as the USB CameraMate.

SanDisk Corporation
www.sandisk.com
Produces flash memory cards, invented CompactFlash, sells card readers.

Simple Technology
Toshiba America
www.dsc.toshiba.com
SmartMedia storage cards, removable storage readers and options.

Printers

Alps Electric
www.alps.com
MD-1300 and 5000 printers.

Canon USA
www.usa.canon.com
BubbleJet series of inkjet printers.

Epson America
www.epson.com
Stylus Color, Stylus Photo, and Stylus Pro series of inkjet printers.

Hewlett-Packard Company
www.hp.com
DeskJet and DesignJet series of color inkjet printers.

Tektronix (now Xerox)
www.tek.com
Phaser series of color laser, dye-sublimation, and thermal wax transfer printers.

Image-Editing Software

Adobe Systems
www.adobe.com
Photoshop, Acrobat, ImageReady, InDesign, PressReady, PhotoDeluxe.

Corel
www.corel.com
PhotoPaint, CorelDraw.

Equilibrium
www.equilibrium.com
DeBabelizer batch image-processing program.

MetaCreations
www.metacreations.com
Painter, Kai's Power Tools, Canoma.

Microsoft
www.microsoft.com
PhotoDraw 2000 image-editing program.

Right Hemisphere
www.righthemisphere.com
Deep Paint painting and illustration tool.

Synthetik Software
www.synthetik.com
Studio Artist drawing and painting program.

Ulead
www.ulead.com
PhotoImpact and other image-editing programs.

Plug-Ins

Alien Skin Software
Eye Candy and other plug-in software.

AltaMira Group
www.altamira.com
Genuine Fractals compression program.

Andromeda Software
www.andromeda.com
Shadow Filter, Series 1 Filters, and other plug-ins.

Chroma Graphics
www.chromagraphics.com
Magic Mask and other plug-ins.

Enroute Imaging
www.enroute.com
QuickStitch, QuickStitch 360, and PowerStitch panorama creation programs.

Extensis
www.extensis.com
A ton of plug-ins including PhotoFrame.

Inklination
www.inklination.com
XHatch pen-and-ink effects.

LizardTech
www.lizardtech.com
MrSID compression program.

Main Event Software
www.mainevent.com
PhotoScripter tool for automating Photoshop functions via AppleScript.

SoftEdge Distributors
www.sedistributors.com
A distributor of Photoshop plug-ins from overseas, including various Neal's titles, such as Neal's Radioactive Backgrounds.

Color Management

Aurelon
www.aurelon.com
ScreenCheck and DeskCheck Calibrator color-proofing tools.

Gretag
www.gretag.com
Spectrolino spectrophotometer, color-management software.

Imaging Technologies
www.color.com
ColorBlind color-management software.

Imation
www.imation.com
Matchprint and Matchprint Inkjet proofing systems, color-management software.

Monaco Systems
www.monacosys.com
EZ Color, MonacoProof, MonacoProfiler, MonacoMatch, and other desktop color-management tools.

X-Rite
www.xrite.com
Colortron colorimeter, Digital Swatchbook, ColorShop software.

Sources of Information

Digital Imaging Group
www.digitalimaging.org
Industry consortium that developed Flashpix and is working with the ISO JPEG committee of JPEG 2000.

Imaging Resource
www.imaging-resource.com
An on-line collection of reviews of digital cameras, as well as news about related peripherals. Has numerous sample images, and a detailed digital camera buying guide.

Micro Publishing News
www.micropubnews.com
News, product info, and reviews relevant to content creators and designers.

About the Author

Richard Romano is the managing editor of *Micro Publishing News*, a newsmonthly in the Cygnus Graphics Network that provides industry news, product information, and hardware and software reviews for content creators, electronic designers, and print buyers. Romano writes news items and features on new technologies and coordinates and writes hardware and software reviews. He has been using digital cameras since 1994, when he borrowed an Apple QuickTake for a multimedia production he was working on. From 1997 to 1999, Romano was also a product reviewer and coordinator for *Digital Imaging*, a then–sister publication of *Micro Publishing News*.

Romano is also the editor-in-chief of *The GATF Encyclopedia of Graphic Communications*, published in 1998 by The Graphic Arts Technical Foundation, as well as its Yearbook 2000 supplement. He is also author of a forthcoming book on Adobe InDesign, to be published in summer 2000 by Macmillan Computer Publishing.

Romano is a graduate of Syracuse University's Newhouse School of Public Communications and has a certificate in multimedia technology from New York University. Originally from New York City, for some reason he now lives in Los Angeles.

Index

D

E

F

H

I

J

K

L

T

U

V

W